ALFA ROMEO
G·I·U·L·I·A
HISTORY & RESTORATION

Pat Braden with Jim Weber

Motorbooks International
Publishers & Wholesalers ®

First published in 1991 by Motorbooks International
Publishers & Wholesalers, P O Box 2, 729 Prospect
Avenue, Osceola, WI 54020 USA

Motorbooks International is a certified trademark,
registered with the United States Patent Office

The information in this book is true and complete to
the best of our knowledge. All recommendations are
made without any guarantee on the part of the author
or publisher, who also disclaim any liability incurred in
connection with the use of this data or specific details

We recognize that some words, model names and
designations, for example, mentioned herein are the
property of the trademark holder. We use them for
identification purposes only. This is not an official
publication

Motorbooks International books are also available at
discounts in bulk quantity for industrial or sales-
promotional use. For details write to Special Sales
Manager at the Publisher's address

Library of Congress Cataloging-in-Publication Data
Braden, Pat.
    Alfa Romeo Giulia : history and restoration /
Pat Braden
        p.   cm.
    Includes index.
    ISBN 0-87938-529-4
    1. Alfa Romeo automobile—History.   2. Alfa
Romeo automobile—Conservation and restoration.
I. Title.
TL215.A35B73 1991
629.222′2—dc20   91-10059

On the front cover: The 1974 GTV 2000 owned by
Brad Fried of Woodland Hills, California, and the 1966
Duetto owned by Phil Guiral of Long Beach, California.
Ron Avery

Printed and bound in the United States of America

Contents

Acknowledgments

This book is more personal than may be immediately apparent. I was a young adult when the Giulia was new, and a large part of the fabric of my life has a thread of Alfa Romeo woven through it. Alfa Romeos have been a hobby since 1959, and I have owned more than fifty of them. That is the kind of intensity that causes in-laws to rage, spouses to despair and psychiatrists to lean forward with a faint smile of anticipation.

Over the years, many enthusiasts have contributed to the tapestry of knowledge this work represents. Many, but not all, have recognition here: Joe Benson, Don Black, Ed Bond, Don Bruno, Antonio Cerlenizza, Ron Crawford, Fred diMatteo, Pat and Glenna Garrett, Ed Geller, Enzo Giobbe, Ed Hancock, Malcolm Harris, Keith Hellon, John Hoard, Nick Holt, Peter Hull, Bill Knauz, Phil Lampman, Doug Langevin, Fred Lynch, Vojta Mashek, Norm Miller, Craig Morningstar, Franco Perugia, Paul Pfanner, Bill Pringle, Stu and Carole Sandeman, John Shankle, Roy Slater, Chuck Stoddard, Martin Swig, Paul Tenney, Roby and Rob Thalmann, Dave Trindler, Dick van der Feen, Neil Verweij, Henry Wessells, and Tom and Dale Zat. Every Alfa Romeo writer owes a debt to Luigi Fusi, which I joyfully acknowledge here. To Tim Parker and Michael Dregni, special gratitude for enduring this book's very long gestation.

Jim Weber has provided encouragement and counsel, but most of all, friendship over the years. Jim came up through the Alfa Romeo organization when it was ARI and has contributed his vast knowledge to keep this book as accurate—and as insightful—as possible.

Over such a protracted period there come sorrows as well as joys. I want to memorialize here my wife of twenty-two years, Marie, whose vivid memory is so intertwined with the era this book recalls.

There is a final item to confess: the automotive obsession was inherited. My father was a young man when the Model T Ford began to replace the horse across rural America. The Depression forced him to leave the boot-heel of Missouri and look for work in the industrial North. That is how a gregarious young traveling salesman and his farmer's-daughter wife came to spend the rest of their lives depending on the AFL-CIO and Plant 4, Chevrolet Motor Division, Flint, Michigan. He had the Masons, fishing and cars. Given his milieu, one could not hope for more.

Progeny frequently prove inscrutable. Just as his itinerant-farmer parents would never have understood what it meant to work in a factory, my father never quite understood what his only child did to earn a living as a writer. Nor would he ever have dreamed his child would dedicate a book to his memory. But he would have been so proud. This one's for my dad, Verlon Lee Braden.

Pat Braden

Introduction

Ever since its beginnings in 1910, Alfa Romeo has been a small automobile manufacturer with a disproportionately large influence in the market. This is because, for most of its history, Alfa Romeo has been at the cutting edge of automotive engineering and style. Alfa Romeo remains one of the few touchstone marques that define the term sports car.

It was not until after its fortieth year, however, that Alfa Romeo entered into serial production. And it is my premise that Alfa Romeo's decision to turn away from making exclusive, hand-built cars of impeccable technical merit and become a mass-producer has proved almost fatal. The mistake was that Alfa Romeo management failed to develop a mass-marketing capability commensurate with its mass-manufacturing capability. Instead, it continued to act as if it were still a producer of made-to-order cars. Several decades have had to pass before this premise could become defensible; Alfa Romeo's absorption into Fiat makes it now credible.

The short-term result of the decision to become a mass-producer certainly augured well as the first Alfa Romeo designed for mass-production was remarkably successful, the 1900 sedan introduced in 1950. With a total production of 21,304 units, the 1900 retained Alfa Romeo's sporting heritage while making ownership much more affordable. The next mass-produced Alfa Romeo model, the Giulietta, represented still another successful step down-scale, since it cost approximately half the price of a 1900. In all, 177,690 Giuliettas were produced between 1954 and 1965. Alfa Romeo was clearly on a roll.

The Giulia exceeded the success of the 1900 and Giulietta combined. In the ten years from 1962 to 1972, a total of 265,877 Giulias were produced. Essentially, customers were still flocking to Alfa Romeo on the basis of its prestigious image.

And the Giulia owner was indeed lucky. The Giulia is an exceedingly rare combination of limited-production engineering at a mass-production price—the best of both worlds. That is the Giulia's charm.

The Giulia experienced staggering model proliferation. During that ten-year model run, those quarter-million Giulias were fragmented into eight major model lines. Why so many Giulia models?

With perfect hindsight, we can now appreciate how blindly Alfa Romeo tried with the Giulia to compete as a mass-producer. Conventional wisdom requires the successful mass-producer to have a marketing organization that determines market needs and specifies a product that meets the needs of the target market. Instead, Alfa Romeo did not even have a marketing department until near the end of the Giulia's life.

In the absence of marketing intelligence, Alfa Romeo offered virtual prototypes as trial balloons. Would the market support a Zagato-bodied, tubular-chassis Giulia? Go ahead and make 124 to find out. A GTC cabriolet version of the coupe? Make up a batch of ninety-nine. What about a Quattroruote Zagato replicar? Make ninety-two.

Now, based on Alfa Romeo's history prior to 1950, these numbers seem reasonable, and they must have seemed reasonable to Alfa Romeo's management in the 1960s as well. To gain the perspective Alfa Romeo's management did not have, consider that Honda's American plant manufactured approximately the same quantity of cars as the entire Giulia production history, but only two models—and in only nine months.

Alfa Romeo's make-a-batch approach ensured that the majority of its models were doomed to economic failure even before they rolled onto the showroom floor. Most Giulia models fall well below the break-even point of manufacturing economy:

Alfa Romeo's 1964 production line-up included, in the first row, from left, the Giulia Sprint GT, Giulia Sprint Speciale and Giulia Spider. Behind this trio, in profile, is a Giulia Tubolare Zagato. In the last row from left, the 2600 Berlina, 2600 Spider, 2600 Coupe, Giulia Berlina 1300, Giulia Berlina Super, Giulia 1600 Sprint and Giulietta Berlina.

eight Giulia models had production runs of less than 1,000 cars! A boon to the enthusiast, certainly, but Alfa Romeo survived such insanity only because it was state-owned and too mired in bureaucracy to go bankrupt.

There is other evidence of Alfa Romeo's marketing incompetence. By 1967, Alfa Romeo owned the sport sedan category, a niche it created with the 1900 sedan in 1950 and perfected with the Giulia Super, the quintessential sport sedan. Nevertheless, Alfa Romeo virtually abdicated leadership of the sport sedan category in the 1970s to concentrate on economy cars for the Italian market.

Finally, Alfa Romeo let the model proliferation diminish its honored image as a manufacturer of exclusive sports cars. At the same time, the change to mass-production techniques damaged its reputation for impeccable quality. Toward the end of the Giulia's production, Alfa Romeo began to lose money. The long slide into debt finally culminated in its purchase by Fiat in 1987.

We are now on the threshold of benefiting from Alfa Romeo's largesse in producing so many rare cars. Beginning in about 1988 or so, the prices of Giulietta-derived, series-produced Alfa Romeos began to rise as they became the object of specula-

tion by collectors. The first car to go through the roof was the 750 Series Giulietta Veloce, primarily as the result of an article in *Road & Track* magazine that estimated the value of the car in the year 2000 to be $20,000. Sure enough, about four months later, ads began appearing for $20,000 Giulietta Spider Veloces; up to that time they were bringing under $10,000!

The sudden rise in the value of the Giuliettas has also inflated the values of the more-reliable and more-powerful Giulias. The most desirable Giulia, the Zagato-bodied TZ, has always commanded the highest prices of the family. By the mid 1990s, we will probably witness the sale of a TZ for $500,000 and the much rarer TZ 2 for $1 million. Giulia Sprint Speciales, bodied by Bertone, bring about $30,000 and any Giulia capable of rolling on its own tires is probably worth at least $5,000.

The phenomenon of appreciation is a wave that trails the new introduction of a car by about thirty to forty years, and when it hits, a number of predictable things happen. The older enthusiasts, who still regard the cars as inexpensive pleasures, are thrust aside by those who buy them for purely speculative purposes. What follows is a period of hard feeling during which the owners feel betrayed and the speculators go into a feeding frenzy, further driving up the values of the cars. Slowly, the number of owners who really appreciate the cars as motor vehicles dwindles to a few wealthy enthusiast owners who cannot be seduced to sell by the constantly rising values of the cars. Acrimonious accusations are made by the enthusiasts against the speculators, and there is a gnawing envy of the wealthy owners. During this period, most cars are traded as commodities from speculator to speculator and never really find a home. The restorable cars are lavishly saved and the poorer cars are sacrificed for parts. Slowly, in this futures market, the cars settle at a price related to their true value as automotive designs and the speculators rush off to catch the next wave. The net result of the entire sequence is to establish a car's place compared to all the other classics that exist.

We are currently at the beginning of an active futures market for the Giulia. I think this book contains ample evidence that the Giulia is a superior automotive design that will stand the test of speculation. Ultimately, I predict that any model Giulia will be more desirable than any Giulietta and will have settled at a higher value—simply because the Giulia is a better car. Much the same argument applies when the Giulia is compared against other marques: I think the Giulia will prove more valuable than most sports cars of its era simply because it is a better automobile.

1

Origin of the Giulia

The cars that form the roots of the Alfa Romeo Giulia are pure legend. These cars range from the glorious P2 that Enzo Ferrari raced for Alfa Romeo and Scuderia Ferrari to the Tipo 158 Alfetta that dominated the Formula 1 Grand Prix scene for years before and after World War II. The Giulia continued this lineage in spirit, beginning with its debut at the Monza racetrack near Alfa Romeo's factory in Milan on June 27, 1962.

The company that became Alfa Romeo was created in 1908 in Milan to construct an Italian taxicab under license from the French Darracq firm. The enterprise failed, and in 1910 the remains of that company became the Anonima Lombarda Fabbrica Automobili, or Lombardy Automobile Manufacturing Company, better known by the initials ALFA. The new, all-Italian firm began building automobiles of its own design, alongside production of tractors and plows.

Whatever the aspirations of the founders, or the hopes of Nicola Romeo, who added his name to the firm in 1920, Alfa Romeo has survived where

The 1910 ALFA car shown in a retouched photograph from the Alfa Romeo archives. The side-valve four-cylinder engine created 24 hp. All extant pre-World War

II Alfa Romeos are in the corporate museum at the firm's headquarters in Arese, and some of those have been reconstructed from bits and pieces.

A 1923 Alfa Romeo with a torpedo-style body on an RL chassis. The base-model RL had a straight six-cylinder engine of 2916 cc that produced 56 hp. Publicity photographs such as this, with its painted-in background, were about as far as Alfa Romeo ventured in trying to sell its products, since it had no marketing department at the time.

many other firms—such as Darracq and Bugatti—have failed. Alfa Romeo has endured two world wars, a great worldwide depression, absorption into the Italian government's bureaucracy, the Institute for Industrial Reconstruction in 1933, and the recent purchase by Fiat.

The history of Alfa Romeo is one of technical excellence, created by an amazing succession of engineers. Giuseppe Merosi developed the early Alfa Romeos up to and including the RL Series. Vittorio Jano was the architect of the great racers of Alfa Romeo's halcyon years of the 1920s and 1930s, before he left to work at Lancia. The designers of the modern era—Gioachino Colombo, Bruno Trevisan, Wifredo Ricart and Orazio Satta—took over a legendary heritage and carried it intact all the way to the Giulia. These engineers wreathed the badge of Alfa Romeo, and have given its enthu-

An RL Super Sport Targa Florio racer with an early quadrifoglio badge on the hood. By 1925, the straight six engine of 3620 cc was pumping out 125 hp in race trim, enough to propel the car to 112 mph or 180 km/h. Note the plate to protect the driver's elbow from burns on the hot exhaust pipe.

siasts a history equaled by few other modern manufacturers.

Alfa Romeo 1910-1925: The Pioneer Years

Alfa Romeo produced three basic models between its origin and the introduction of the great RL Series in 1923. The first Alfa Romeo powerplant was a four-cylinder, 4.0 liter monobloc engine with a cylinder head cast in unit with the engine block. Spark plugs were located above the side-mounted valves. The chassis that carried this engine was based on a conventional ladder-type frame with solid front and rear axles. The vehicle was originally designated the 24 hp model, but later became the 20-30 hp and then the ES model as its details were improved. The 4.0 liter series was designated by the letters A through E.

A smaller engine of 2.5 liters was introduced soon after the original 4.0 liter, with designations ranging from A through C during the same time span. The 2.5 liter relied on the same basic cross section as the larger engine, and the cars used a similar chassis.

In 1913, Alfa Romeo introduced the 6.0 liter 40-60 hp model that continued in production as a racing car until 1922. The maximum output of this engine in race tune was originally 82 hp at 2400 rpm, or almost 14 hp per liter of engine displacement. To understand this power rating in contemporary terms, compare it to the 18 hp per liter or 130 hp at 2200 rpm estimated for the 7.6 liter Grand Prix Peugeot of only one year earlier. The 1912 Peugeot achieved its superior efficiency due to its double-overhead-camshaft (dohc) engine designed by pioneer Ernest Henry.

In 1914, Alfa Romeo constructed a single Grand Prix racer based on Henry's design of the 1912 Peugeot. The Alfa Romeo dohc powerplant had a 4.5 liter displacement, and like most engines of its day, was built up of an assembly of castings, including the oil sump, crankcase, engine block and cylinder head. Also typical of the era was the

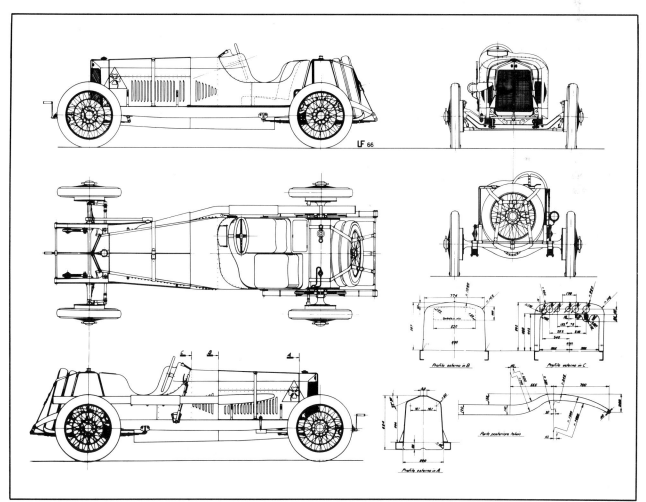

Factory drawings for the RLSS Targa Florio revealed the staggered seating arrangement that permitted the aggressive driver to flail his elbows while turning the huge steering wheel without endangering the riding mechanic's ribs. The belly pan beneath the car was also shown.

The car that destroyed designer Giuseppe Merosi, his 1923 GPR. The initials stood for Grand Prix Romeo, after Nicola Romeo, the engineer that took over ALFA in 1915, and soon brought about the corporate name change to Alfa Romeo. The name of the GPR race car was also later changed to the P1. The P1 was an early attempt to better the contemporary and all-dominating Fiat racer, but a test of the car only succeeded in killing driver Ugo Sivocci, seen here at the wheel before he met his fate.

exposed valve mechanism, with the camshafts supported in a cast-up assembly that also carried the adjustable valve tappets.

By its own standards, Alfa Romeo had achieved a remarkable increase in engine efficiency with the new dohc 4.5 liter. Its 1913 engine had produced 73 hp from 6.0 liters; its 1914 dohc Grand Prix engine created 88 hp from 4.5 liters, putting it at the same level of horsepower per liter as the 1912 Peugeot. Top speed of the 1914 Grand Prix racer was 145 km/h (90 mph).

By 1921, Alfa Romeo was challenging the likes of Rolls-Royce in the luxury-car arena. Alfa Romeo's G1 of 1921 was not a success but did signal the firm's high level of ambition. The G1 was based on a six-cylinder, 6.3 liter flathead engine with seven main bearings for engine longevity. It rode on a 134 in. wheelbase that must have provided a magnificent ride for its day. The oldest Alfa Romeo currently in private hands is a racing G1 owned by Ross Flewell-Smith in Australia.

In 1923, Giuseppe Merosi developed his masterpiece, the six-cylinder, 3.0 and 3.2 liter engine that powered the RL Series of Alfa Romeo sports and race models. The 3.0 liter RL engine produced 56 hp at 3200 rpm when introduced. The RL Targa Florio model also made its debut with a seven-main-bearing crankshaft that helped create 125 hp at 3800 rpm. The RL Series were large, imposing cars with sturdy and reliable engines and plenty of passenger room. In their three years of manufacture, the RL and Targo Florio racers swept the Italian competition from hillclimbs to the namesake Targa Florio races of 1923 and 1924 to the Italian Touring Car Grands Prix of 1923 and 1924.

In 1923, Alfa Romeo built the first of its 2.0 liter, six-cylinder P1 Grand Prix race cars, to be followed in 1924 by the 2.0 liter, eight-cylinder, dohc P2 racer. In the hands of Alberto Ascari, Giuseppe Campari, Enzo Ferrari and others, the P2 established Alfa Romeo as a force to be reckoned with in the racing world. At the 1924 Italian Grand Prix at Monza, P2s swept the first three places, and their race record continued

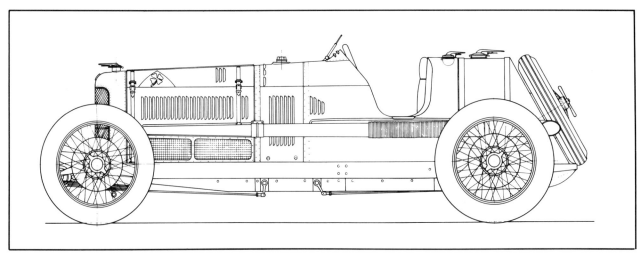

This later drawing for the Alfa Romeo P2 was a study in verticals—note how upright the driver had to sit! Drivers who filled that seat and brought the P2 to some of its greatest wins included Alberto Ascari, Giuseppe Campari, Achille Varzi and Tazio Nuvolari. With a

straight eight-cylinder engine of 1987 cc and 156 hp beneath the hood, the car was still winning races as late as 1930—some seven years after production officially ended.

The car that made designer Vittorio Jano, his 1925 P2, which also earned Alfa Romeo a wreath around its emblem. This 2.0 liter supercharged car absolutely dominated the race courses for years. Top speeds were quoted as high as 140 mph or 225 km/h.

A 1926 6C1500 Gran Sport fitted with a third headlamp for night races, probably the Mille Miglia. A supercharger had been fitted to the 1487 cc straight six-cylinder engine, as denoted by the sloped radiator. A spotlight was also fitted next to the driver's window for assistance in spotting turns in the dark.

unabated until 1930, run by Scuderia Ferrari, Alfa Romeo's official racing team based in Modena.

In 1925, construction of the RL exceeded 1,100 cars, the first Alfa Romeo model to reach such production levels, marking it as a great success. And in the same year, the P2 brought Alfa Romeo its first world championship in Grand Prix racing.

Alfa Romeo 1926–1951: The Glory Years

Beginning in 1927 and continuing until 1951, Alfa Romeo embarked on a series of cars that would win over the world both on the racetrack and on the growing network of streets and roads. Designed by Vittorio Jano, the six-cylinder 6C1500 gave way to the 6C1750 in 1929; larger-displacement engines with increased power output would continue with the 6C1900, 6C2300 and 6C2500.

Jano's engines situated the six cylinders inline with initially three stages of tune for the 6C1500 and 6C1750: single-overhead-camshaft and dohc versions, and a supercharged dohc. The supercharged engine carried the blower at the front of the crankshaft and the cams were driven by a geartrain and a tower shaft from the rear of the engine. The cylinder head and engine block were cast of iron.

The 6Cs were offered in two different wheelbases and a number of series comprising different details, such as the supercharger plumbing and gearboxes. Bodystyles ranged from out-and-out racers to proper sedans fitted to the long-wheelbase bodies.

The race record of the 6Cs was illustrious. Wins were marked in races throughout Italy, international Grands Prix, the Mille Miglia in 1928, 1929, 1930, 1932 and 1933, and the twenty-four-hour endurance race at Le Mans in 1931.

Alongside the 6Cs, Alfa Romeo began development of a series of eight-cylinder engines. Under the spur of fascist dictator Benito Mussolini, Alfa Romeo and Maserati were locked in a technical battle with Germany to produce the more successful race car in order to retain Italy's Grand Prix dominance against the might of the newly arrived German factory teams of Mercedes-Benz and Auto-Union.

The first of the eight-cylinder racers was the 8C2300 Monza based on an inline engine with double overhead camshafts, detachable cylinder heads, dry-sump lubrication and a single supercharger mounted on the right side of the block. The chassis

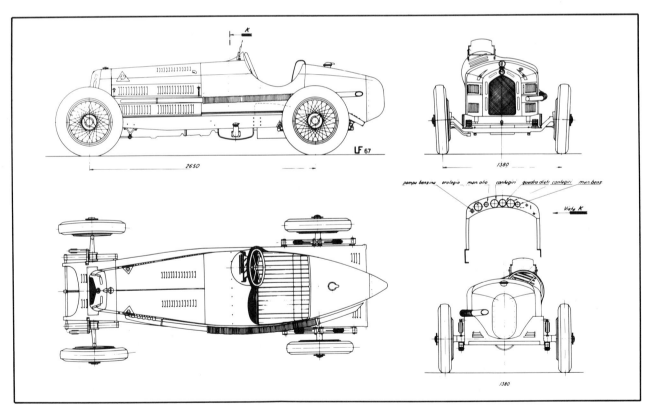

The 8C2300 Monza represented a half-step between sports car and Grand Prix racer. Its two-seater bodywork would be narrowed for the P3, the first true monoposto Grand Prix car. The 8C2300 engine was a slight modification on the regular production engine, fitted with a racing magneto instead of coil ignition. The slot-ted shroud around the radiator also appeared on production cars and was even occasionally retrofitted to the 1750 series cars. Two 2.6 liter versions of the engine were produced, one by Alfa Romeo and the other by Enzo Ferrari's Scuderia Ferrari.

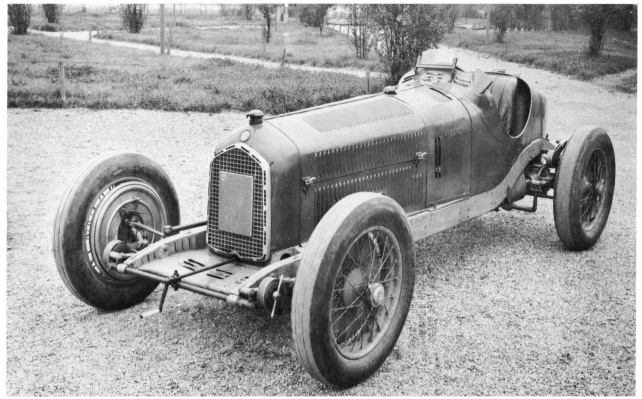

Unbeatable in the early 1930s, the Type B P3 was based on a straight eight-cylinder engine of 2653 cc that created 215 hp with twin superchargers and the unique rear-drive system that equalized torque reaction on acceleration between the two driving wheels. The engine from this car would make its way into the sporting 8C2900 A and 8C2900 B cars, as well as the Type C Grand Prix racer.

rode on solid front and rear axles, and the car was capable of a top speed of 210 km/h (130 mph).

The 8C2300 was a fabulous car in specification, though somewhat less successful to drive. Its chassis was virtually the same as the six-cylinder car that preceded it, and the increased power of the eight stressed the frame rails something beyond their limits. To cope with the power of the engine, Alfa Romeo fitted large brakes, which, when applied, were sufficiently powerful to bend

The four-wheel independent suspension of the Type C was combined with the 2.9 liter engine of the Type B to create the 8C2900 A, a two-seat sports car intended originally as a factory racer. In the end, however, only six were produced. The car evolved into the 8C2900 B, an Alfa Romeo "regular production" car of some thirty-five examples, constructed in 1937.

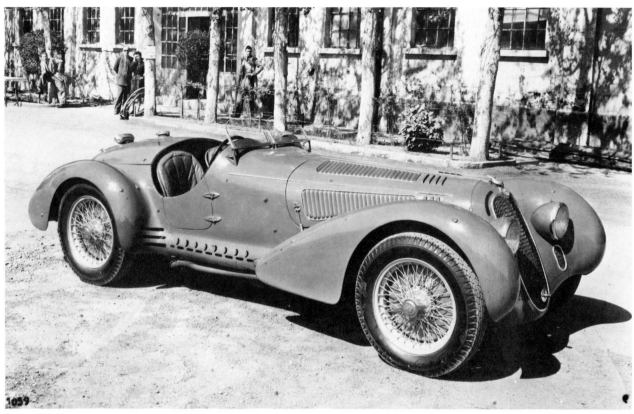

One of the most beautiful Alfa Romeos ever, a Touring-bodied 8C2900B. With the 2905 cc engine producing 180 hp at 5000 rpm from a supercharger, these cars could top 115 mph or 185 km/h.

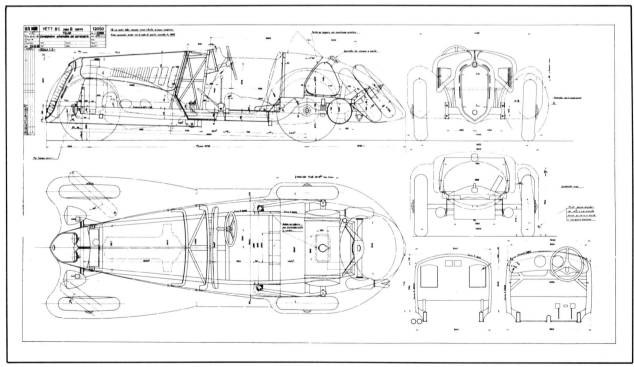

This engineering drawing of the 8C2900 B sports car displayed numerous interesting details, including the dual spare wheels and the separate oil and gas tanks at the rear. From above, it was clear that the front section of the body was streamlined for good aerodynamics.

the front of the frame rails slightly. Since the brakes were mechanically operated, the bending of the frame rails tended to release the brakes, relieving torque and straightening the frame rails, which, in turn, reapplied the brakes. The resulting chassis oscillation could be stopped only by releasing the brakes entirely.

The 8C2300 chassis was available in both long and short versions and three series, identified by the second digit of the serial number. The short chassis usually carried lightweight bodywork by Zagato or Touring and was used extensively—and successfully—for racing. Some four-place convertibles were offered by bodybuilders such as Castagna, Figoni and Graber.

Prior to the entrance of the German teams in 1934, Alfa Romeo was virtually unbeatable on the racetrack. After the P2, it had developed its racing engines from its regular passenger-car engines. In 1935, this development had led to a dohc straight-eight racing engine displacing 2.9 liters and pro-

In the late 1930s, Alfa Romeo tried to remain competitive with a twelve-cylinder engine, which appeared in high- and low-chassis cars, both with four-wheel independent suspension. This 1936 high-chassis car carried a 4.0 liter engine developing 370 hp, not nearly enough to stay up with the Germans.

This photograph from the Alfa Romeo archives was identified as a 1935/36 12C engine. It was most certainly not the 60 deg. V-12 that powered the Grand Prix car of those years. Instead, it appeared to be a prototype of the 1.5 liter 1940 Type 512 engine that would be placed mid-ships, in the style of the GP Auto Unions. The down-draft Dell'Orto carburetors were clearly prototypes, as the 512 used two-stage supercharging through a gigantic triple-throat Weber carburetor.

An early Type 158 dohc straight eight-cylinder engine from 1938 with the front accessory drive for the water pump and two oil pumps for pressure and scavenge. The 1.5 liter engine gave 195 hp using a single-stage supercharger.

ducing 255 hp at 5400 rpm with the aid of two superchargers, one for each set of four cylinders.

With the entrance of the German teams in Grand Prix racing, Alfa Romeo found itself with some thirty-five racing engines that were suddenly

obsolete. According to one account, the mechanics simply detuned these engines slightly and put them in passenger cars, offered to the public as the 8C2900 B.

The technical specifications of the 8C2900 B are dazzling even today. In addition to twin superchargers, the engine featured monobloc construction in aluminum alloy; the cylinder head was cast integral with the block so there was no head gasket. A train of gears running up the middle of the engine was responsible for driving the camshafts and all accessories, including the two superchargers and two oil pumps as the engine used dry-sump lubrication. The four-speed transmission of the 8C2900 B was carried at the rear in unit with a differential that drove halfshafts located by trailing arms.

The rear suspension was by transverse leaf, while the front suspension used canted A-arms and a shock and coil-spring assembly. Short- and long-chassis models were offered in both coupe and convertible designs. A few spiders constructed by Carrozzeria Touring were produced, and these cars are perhaps the most desirable Alfa Romeos of all.

The 8C2900 B was at once the most exotic passenger car ever offered to the public and the pinnacle of Alfa Romeo production. Moreover, it was the prewar car that carried the seeds from which the highest-performance postwar designs would grow.

Meanwhile, the ongoing war with the German factory teams sparked Alfa Romeo to develop the 12C-36 in 1936 and the 12C-37 in 1937. Both race

The Type 158 Alfetta was developing only 275 hp from its 1479 cc eight-cylinder engine when it posed for this 1947 photograph. By 1950, the 158 would come into its own with 360 hp, and beat the world. The large radiator grille and single exhaust pipe were the Alfetta's trademarks.

By 1951, the Type 158 had been superseded by the Type 159 Alfetta, the ultimate development of Alfa Romeo's 1.5 liter straight eight-cylinder voiturette racer. A new twin-stage supercharger gave the engine an output of more than 400 hp. A youthful world champion Juan Manuel Fangio sits at the wheel.

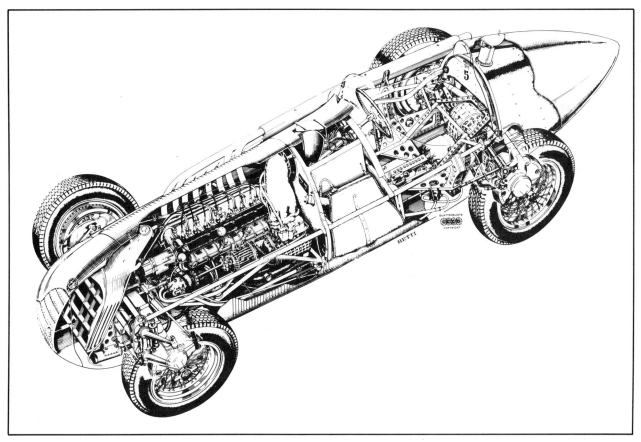

A Betti drawing of the Type 159 mechanicals.

The 6C2500 was built in small quantities before World War II and revived postwar, as shown by this beautiful short-wheelbase Touring-bodied coupe. Chassis were also bodied by such famed Italian carrozzerie as Stabilimenti Farina and Ghia.

cars used V-12 engines with superchargers, the former displacing 4.1 liters and the latter 4.6 liters.

In 1938, Alfa Romeo brought its racing team back within the factory fold from Scuderia Ferrari and renamed the team Alfa Corse, or Alfa Racing. Work had begun on a series of 3.0 liter Grand Prix cars in inline eight, V-12 and V-16 form. The 1938 season began on a high note with the V-16 16C 316 winning the opening Italian Grand Prix.

Also in 1938, Alfa Romeo started work on one of the milestone race cars that would go on to earn the works its laurels, the Tipo 158, more affectionately known as the Alfetta. The car was built around its inline eight-cylinder engine of 1.5 liters, run with a two-stage supercharger. The cars were constructed through 1950, giving way to the Tipo 159 Alfetta in 1951. The Alfetta initiated its career by winning the 1938 Milan Grand Prix and ended it by winning the 1951 Italian Grand Prix at Monza—a life span of fourteen years, nevermind the war.

Alfa Romeo's transition to low-priced, mass-produced cars following World War II actually had its roots in the late 6C models built in the mid 1930s. In 1933, the 6C1900 sedan was produced in a small run of 197 cars, but the model was much more pivotal than its production figures suggest as it represented Alfa Romeo's early attempt to broaden its market range by introducing a low-priced car.

The engine of the 6C1900 was a stopgap design, being mechanically similar to the line of twin-cam 6C engines that had been introduced in 1926. The 6C2300, which replaced it in 1934, was significantly different in design and was much more modern in that it permitted certain manufacturing economies that the earlier cars eschewed.

One of these economies was the use of a chain at the front of the engine versus a geartrain to drive the overhead camshafts. The 6C2300 cars were the first Alfa Romeos with a design that reflected any sense that cost was an object.

In 1935, the 6C2300 B was introduced and continued in construction through 1937. The 6C2300 B was the first mass-produced car to offer independent rear suspension. In 1939, the 6C2500 made its debut as a replacement for the 6C2300 B.

In the immediate postwar years, the 6C2500 remained the standard Alfa Romeo. A large, comfortable vehicle, it was powered by a six-cylinder 2.5 liter twin-cam engine. These cars were fitted with bodies of every conceivable description, from seven-passenger limousines to two-seat convertibles and competition coupes.

Because of excellent suspension design and lightweight bodywork, the 6C2500 behaved in a much more controlled manner than its gross size would suggest. The 118 in. wheelbase and supple suspension combined with exceptionally light and precise steering to make the 6C2500 probably the most comfortable touring car Alfa Romeo had ever produced.

A short-wheelbase, 106 in. version of the car 6C2500 was offered, and there were several different stages of tune over the years the model was produced. The most potent of the stages was the Super Sport engine. With three carburetors, it developed 110 hp at 4800 rpm compared to the 95 hp at 4600 rpm of the Sport model. Several competition versions of the 6C2500 were developed. These attractive spiders and aerodynamic coupes distinguished themselves enough to keep Alfa Romeo's sporting tradition alive.

Alfa Romeo also constructed several six-cylinder derivations. The first, the 6C3000 CM, was a development of Alfa Romeo's interest in competing with the likes of Ferrari. The development work was undertaken by Orazio Satta at about the same time the world was absorbed in flying saucers, so the cars became known as Disco Volantes. An original four-cylinder C52 design was replaced by the six-cylinder 6C3000 CM of 3495 cc that developed 275 hp and took second overall in the 1953 Mille Miglia.

The second derivation was introduced in 1950 as the 6C3000 C50. It displaced 2955 cc and developed 168 hp at 6000 rpm. This was a design by Giaochino Colombo, but was scrapped in favor of Satta's design.

Predecessors to the Giulietta

The four-cylinder predecessors of the Giulietta were quite different in character if not design. The original twin-cam 1900 cc four that was first introduced in 1950. Like the Giulietta, this first twin-cam was produced in two series: the original 1950s version of just under 1900 cc, and the much more sporting 1900C which had been introduced in 1952. The 1900C Alfa Romeo TI sedan was fast and comfortable and, like the Giulia Super, certainly one of the most sporting and desirable sedans ever produced.

Several beautiful coupes were created around the 1900 mechanicals as well, the most notable being the Zagato, a favorite of weekend racers. Only one 1900 Zagato spider was produced.

The 1955 Touring-bodied 1900 was certainly one of the most beautiful Alfa Romeos of all time. Not surprisingly, the same basic bodystyle was also found on the Lancia Flaminia, Maserati 3500GT and 250 Ferrari.

A large Alfa Romeo, the 2000 was produced alongside the Giulietta. The 2000 was totally eclipsed by the Giulietta, which offered nearly the same performance and twice the charm. The specifications of the 2000 had it a faster car than the Giulietta, but in the real world one could grow old waiting for the 2000 to see any speed greater than what was available in the Giulietta.

The 2000 was available in the usual trio of sedan, coupe and spider, and was intended to be an upscale companion to the Giulietta. In fact, the 2000 belonged to a line of Alfa Romeos quite different from the bulk of the small and popular four-cylinder twin-cam cars. It was a vestigal car of the great days when Alfa Romeos were the preferred sporting vehi-

The Giulietta Spider we all know, designed by Pinin Farina. This car, shown at the 1984 Alfa Romeo Owners Club national meet, was the earliest Giulietta Spider in private hands. The 1956 model is serial number 00007. Externally, it is identical to later-production Giuliettas although internally, many mechanical advances were later made.

cle for the rich. The 2000 suffered in comparison even to its immediate predecessor.

The Giulietta 1954-1961

In 1968, Luigi Fusi showed me a prototype Giulietta engine that displaced 750 cc. Since the earliest Giuliettas have been given a 750 Series designation, it seems clear that the Giulietta was

Alfa Romeo's designers were busy in the early 1950s creating a new line of four-cylinder, mass-produced cars that would signal a dramatic change in philosophy at the firm. In the past, Alfa Romeo had concentrated on limited-production luxury tourers and spiders and its race cars. Now, following World War II, the company was looking to build cars in the middle of the price range. The result was the great Giulietta line that would eventually include berlinas, coupes and spiders; it would also give birth to several series of lightweight racers as, after all, that was where Alfa Romeo began. This car was Bertone's proposal for the new Giulietta spider, which Alfa Romeo did not choose. It is a considerably chunky-looking car, and a hint of the aerodynamic-exercise BAT 9 can be seen in the rear fender line.

The dashboard and controls of the Giulietta Spider 00007 were significantly different from the production models but was identical to the dash on the prototype Giuliettea in the Alfa Romeo museum. The pods anticipated the styling of the later 2.0 liter Spiders. The 101 Series transmission in this car was non-standard.

A prototype Giulietta engine with the inline four-cylinder double-overhead-camshaft design that would be the basis for the Giulias as well. This prototype was notable in that it did not have a chain tensioner and appeared to be fitted with a spin-on oil filter versus the production cartridge filter. Factory archives indicate that this was an 1100 cc version of the engine; the author believes that this was the first prototype engine, having a 750 cc displacement.

originally intended to have a displacement of 750 cc.

This 750 cc engine has become something of a mystery, for when I revisited the factory in 1985, no one was able to remember it—even to the point of assuring me that no such engine ever existed. The factory archives contain a photograph of the engine. My premise is that this photograph of the 750 cc prototype engine, which was distinguished by its lack of a cast-in chain tensioner, has been inadvertently mislabeled as an 1100 cc prototype. The latter, larger prototype engine surely existed also, but I think a clerical error has virtually legislated the earlier engine out of existence. The only individual I have found to reassure me of the existence of the 750 cc prototype engine served as the chief engineer at Alfa Romeo's US facility when it was located in New Jersey.

The significance of the small displacement is that there was a 750 cc supercharged Italian formula class in the early 1950s, so the small prototype engine suggested that there was an Alfa Romeo racing endeavor that never quite made it beyond the planning stage. Alfa Romeo's plans for a 750 cc supercharged car have never been documented, and no mention of it occurred in the literature, with the possible exception of the 750 Competition Prototype car of 1955. This car was originally designed along the same lines as the Abarth 207 A with Boano body (including external Abarth exhaust) but was fitted with a 1488 cc engine with a bore and stroke of 77x82 mm, presumably Giulietta-based, but with the same stroke as the Giulia.

Alfa Romeo could have planned to market a normally aspirated version of the racing 750 cc engine, with slightly larger displacement, in a passenger car. Thus, the real source of the Giulietta Series may have been to create a normally aspirated road-going version of a supercharged formula car.

The final Giulietta engine had a 74 mm bore and 75 mm stroke, giving a displacement of 1295 cc. It continued the tradition of twin overhead camshafts and hemispherical combustion chambers that had been established in 1927 with the 6C1500 Super Sport.

But unlike any preceding Alfa Romeo production engine, the Giulietta had replaceable wet-sleeve liners. This design differs from those designs that use steel liners that are press-fit in an aluminum cylinder cast into the block. The steel pressed-in liners are not washed directly by coolant, and are thus dry in the aluminum block.

In contrast, the Giulietta block was essentially a hollow box with no aluminum bores into which liners were to be pressed. At the bottom of the Giulietta block there were machined holes into which the freestanding cylinders were inserted. At the bottom, the cylinders seated against the block; at the top, against the head. Thus, coolant bathed every part of the cylinder, and the sleeves were wet. The advantage of the Alfa Romeo wet-sleeve design is that it gives superior cylinder cooling and easy cylinder replacement when a rebuild is necessary. Because of its wet-sleeve design, the Alfa Romeo block is infinitely rebuildable and the wearing surfaces, including the cylinders and bearings, are easily replaceable. Cast-in cylinders may be resurfaced only once or twice before the block is scrap.

The reason manufacturers do not flock to the wet-sleeve engine is that the design requires superb engineering to maintain the seals at both the top and bottom of the freestanding cylinder. There are inherent dangers in the design when the block and head are aluminum and the cylinders steel, because the expansion rates of the two metals differ. As things heat up and cool off, the dimensions of the major components change significantly and at different rates. During expansion and contraction, only a slight amount of movement of the cylinder against the head gasket will cause the gasket seal to fail. Finally, there is a tendency for the dissimilar

A 750 Series 1300 cc Veloce engine with its dual 40 DCO Webers and distinctive airbox. The Veloces were streetable but required a definite effort to get underway from a stop sign. They were literally factory hot rods.

metals to cause electrolysis, which corrodes the softer aluminum.

It is a measure of Alfa Romeo's engineering excellence that all the potential problems asso-

An early 1956 750 Series Giulietta Sprint Veloce with its sliding plexiglass side windows and small headlamps. The car with its 1300 cc engine was very competitive: in Sprint Veloce form, the engine put out 90 hp at 6500 rpm versus 80 hp at 6300 rpm for the Sprint. Most of the difference was in the dual sidedraft Weber carburetors

mounted on the Veloce instead of the single downdraft Solex on the standard engine. The car pictured here was the class winner and 11th overall finisher in the 1956 Mille Miglia, driven by Sgorbati and Zanelli. The car actually finished ahead of the 2.0 liter class winner, a Maserati.

ciated with the wet-sleeve design are unknown to Giulietta and Giulia owners. The engines are remarkably reliable and able to absorb punishment that would destroy less-sophisticated designs.

Another reason the four-cylinder Giulietta and later Giulia engines can take so much punishment is that they have five main bearings supporting the crankshaft many engines have only three. Another contributor to long engine life is the large, finned oil sump that helps reduce heat and maintain proper oil viscosity. Many small details also contribute to the engine's robustness. For example, the metal around the exhaust valve seats is cooled first by the water exiting the water pump, so the coolest water available is applied to the hottest part of the engine.

The early Giuliettas with a single downdraft Solex carburetor had a fuel pump located at the front of the head, driven off a narrow cam on the camshaft. The crankshaft pulley was aluminum, and given to rapid wear. The generator was originally bolted to a single boss on the cam-chain cover. This proved to be a weak design, for when the generator mounting bolt loosened, as it always did, the aluminum mounting boss wore quickly. The typical repair was to press in a steel sleeve for the

mounting bolt. Initially, oil pressure was measured mechanically from a gallery toward the rear of the engine on the exhaust side. The early Giuliettas had stamped-steel sumps, and the later Veloce had a cast-aluminum one. In addition, the Veloce had a back mount for the generator that helped keep it in place. All Giulietta Spiders and Coupes were equipped with oil-temperature gauges.

The higher-output Giulietta Veloce engines were equipped with dual sidedraft Weber carburetors. These engines were fed by an electric fuel pump located near the rear axle. To permit the sidedraft Webers to clear the inner fender panel, the Veloce engine was canted slightly to the driver's side by fitting a longer motor mount on the passenger's side. The Veloce engine had significant detail differences from the normal Giulietta engine, including forged Borgo pistons, special connecting rods, higher-lift camshafts and a cast-aluminum two-piece finned sump. The earliest Sprint Veloce cars had aluminum panels and sliding-plexiglass door windows. The earliest Giuliettas came with a solid tubular transmission housing into which the gear sets were assembled with a large puller.

Over the years, there have been significant refinements to the basic engine. Giuliettas built

Alfa Romeo Model Designations

Each Alfa Romeo model carries its own series designation of three digits. For early Giuliettas, a letter following the numbers indicates the model of the series. For later Giuliettas and Giulias, the model designation is a two-digit number separated from the series number by a period.

The numbering scheme is most helpful in the parts manual, for the first five numbers of a part indicate series and model (generally), with subsequent numbers for parts group and specific part number. The following numbers give the series and model of the Giulias.

Giulia Chassis Number Series

Chassis codes	Model	Years
101 Series		
10112	Sprint	1962–1964
10118	Spider Veloce	1964–1965
10121	Sprint Speciale	1963–1965
10123	Spider	1962–1965
10123	Quattroruote Zagato	1965
105 Series		
10502	Sprint GT	1963–1966
10503	Duetto	1966–1967
10508	Quattroruote Zagato	1966–1967
10511	TZ	1963–1967

Chassis codes	Model	Years
10511	TZ 2	1965–1967
10512	Berlina 2000	1971–1978
10514	TI Berlina	1962–1967
10516	TI Super	1963–1964
10521	GTV 2000	1971–1977
10524	Spider 2000	1971–
10525	GTC	1964–1966
10526	Super Berlina	1965
10530	GT Junior 1300	1966–1972
10532	GTA	1965–1967
10536	GTV 1600	1965–1968
10539	TI 1300 Berlina	1966–1972
10544	GTV 1750	1967–1972
10548	Berlina 1750	1967–1972
10551	GTV 1750 US	1968–1972
10557	Spider 1750	1967–1971
10559	GTA 1300 Junior	1968–1972
10562	Spider 1750 US	1968–1972
10564	Montreal	1971–1977
10571	Berlina 1750 US	1968–1972
10591	Spider 1300 Junior	1968–1972
10593	Junior Z 1300	1970–1972
115 Series		
11500	Berlina 2000 US	1971–1974
11501	GTV 2000 US	1971–1974
11502	Spider 2000 US	1971–1974
11524	Junior Z 1600	1972–1975

between 1956 and 1959 all had the same configuration. However, in 1959, Alfa Romeos began appearing—unannounced—with new gearboxes and engines that were slightly different.

The most noticeable change was that the shift lever of the gearbox was made to telescope slightly when you pressed down on it to overcome the reverse-gear lock-out. Moreover, on closer inspection under the car, it was clear that the transmission case was completely new, since it split longitudinally into two halves. The new four-speed Giulietta case was almost identical to the five-speed unit fitted to the 2000 model introduced in 1958. It differed only in that the tail casting on the 2000 was longer to accommodate a fifth gear. It was not long before five-speed Giuliettas were running around with transmission parts pirated from the larger cars. Not a cheap conversion, but it was an exceedingly satisfactory one, especially on the Veloce.

The significant differences in the new Giulietta engine were almost all dimensional. While the bore and stroke remained the same, the newer engines had larger main bearings, camshaft bearings and valve-stem diameters. The camshaft lobe width was also increased to improve load-bearing capacity. A steel crankshaft pulley was fitted and the generator mount strengthened. In addition, the fuel pump was relocated low on the engine where it could be driven off a cam on the shaft that drove both the distributor and the oil pump.

These new parts carried numbers beginning with 101, and the cars that used them are referred to as 101 Series Alfa Romeos. According to factory records, the 101 designation had been introduced with the Giulietta Sprint Speciale in 1957. Practically, it became the standard designation of all Giuliettas in 1960.

At the time, the purpose of these increases was not fully appreciated. In fact, Alfa Romeo had created the basis for the Giulia engine, and was field-testing a small-displacement version of it in the 101 Series Giuliettas made from 1959 to the introduction of the Giulia in 1962.

The earliest surviving Giulietta, on display at the Arese museum, had side curtains, a curved windshield reminiscent of the Lancia America convertible, and a three-pod instrument cluster located immediately in front of the driver. The oldest Giulietta in the United States, serial number 007, carries an obviously handmade windshield assembly that matches the later production models in configuration, has roll-up windows, but retains the three-pod design of the instrument panel. For the production version a unified instrument cluster was adopted. Very early production cars featured a gearshift lever that curved upward to give the final several inches of the lever an almost vertical position; later versions of the lever were straight.

As mentioned above, Alfa Romeo lengthened the wheelbase of the Giulietta Spider in 1959. The

The 101 Series Giulietta Sprint had larger grillework than the 750 Series cars. With the exception of the Giulietta script on the front fender and the reflector under the taillamp, this car could just as well be an early Giulia.

The Type 103 prototype was a front-wheel-drive car styled along the same lines as the Renault R8 sedan. Its development was shelved in favor of the Giulia, which still managed to share many of its styling features, most especially the greenhouse.

101 Series long-wheelbase Giuliettas are easily identified by the fixed vent window in the door, while the Sprint Coupe has a larger grille and larger taillights. The changeover, unannounced and unexplained, caused total confusion among enthusiasts because some short-wheelbase 750 Series bodies were delivered with the newer 101 Series engines and transmissions, while some 101 cars used 750 transmissions with 101 engines.

No accounting has ever been given of exactly which cars, by serial number, carried what mixture of engines and transmissions. Part of this lack is no doubt due to the fact that Alfa Romeo did not keep meticulous records of its production: many Alfa Romeos show serial numbers that cannot be accounted for using Luigi Fusi's quintessential book, *Tutti le Vetture Alfa Romeo dal 1910.* It is clear that the variation stemmed from the happenstance of parts availability at the factory: as the supply of the 750 engines and transmissions was greater than the supply of bodies, the older running gear was fitted to the newer body. Similarly, there appear to have been more engines than

The engine compartment of the Type 103 showed the engine mounted transversely.

transmissions, for a 750 Series engine mated to a 101 Series transmission was not uncommon.

The situation has become hopelessly confused over the years, for people have generally discarded the earlier engines and replaced them with the more robust later models. This is, in fact, not an easy retrofit. The transmissions differ in their length, their mountings, the location of the shift lever, the bolt pattern on the bellhousings and the flywheel diameters.

The model confusion was finally ended by the appearance of a new Giulietta parts catalog for 1960 that showed all the new parts numbers beginning with 101, although the Giulietta TI body was still number 753 in 1960. By 1961, all new Alfa Romeos were in the 101 Series.

Type 103

Alfa Romeo was moving rapidly in the early 1960s. It had a hot seller in the Giulietta and it is clear the management wanted to keep the momentum going. In 1959, the factory began the design of an 896 cc front-wheel-drive car with a 103 Series designation (cars with the cast-iron 2.0 liter engine were Series 102).

During this time, Alfa Romeo had an agreement with the French firm, Renault, to assemble Dauphines in Italy. Renault's advertising made much of the Dauphine's rear-engine configuration, and the company claimed that the front-wheel-drive design of cars such as Saab and DKW was less stable. The Corvair (and later, Ralph Nader) also became part of the which-end-drive discussion, contributing further to the heat but not the light of the argument. How Renault would have blushed had the public learned its Italian connection was developing a front-drive car!

Alfa Romeo's 103 Series transverse twin-cam engine was unusual in several respects that deserve notice here. First, it had no intermediate sprocket to halve the speed of the cam chain. Instead, double-size pulleys were fitted to the ends of the twin overhead camshafts. A single-throat downdraft carburetor sat behind the engine while the exhaust manifold sat up front, next to the radiator. The engine had an extremely deep block that also served as a sturdy mount for the transaxle unit. Driveshafts to the front wheels were located behind the engine-transaxle assembly. In layout, the 103 was not far from the new 164.

An entirely new body was designed for the 103. It was much more squared-off than the Giulietta sedan, and the front hood line featured a shallow V to improve forward visibility. Strikingly similar lines can be seen in the production Renault 8, a further reflection of the close working relationship between the Italian and French firms. (Fiat and Simca had a similar arrangement, which allowed for, among other things, the Simca-based Abarth coupe.)

The prototype front-wheel-drive Alfa Romeo was ready for testing in 1960, but plans for its production were set aside to permit engineers to concentrate on the new Giulia engine. The 103 was later re-evaluated for production, but rejected in favor of the design that eventually became the Alfasud.

The Type 103 powerplant was an experimental unit with features that would probably not have gone into production under any circumstance. The serpentine drive-belt to the generator was remarkable. So was the heavily-ribbed block and double-size camshaft-drive sprockets.

2

Giulia Sedan

The new Giulia sedan was introduced at the Monza racetrack on June 27, 1962. The production sedan featured a slight scallop running along the side of the car just under the window line and another, smaller scallop running along the top of the car just above the rain gutter. The hood depression of the prototype 103 was eliminated, and the front grille-work of the current 2600 sedan was adapted to the

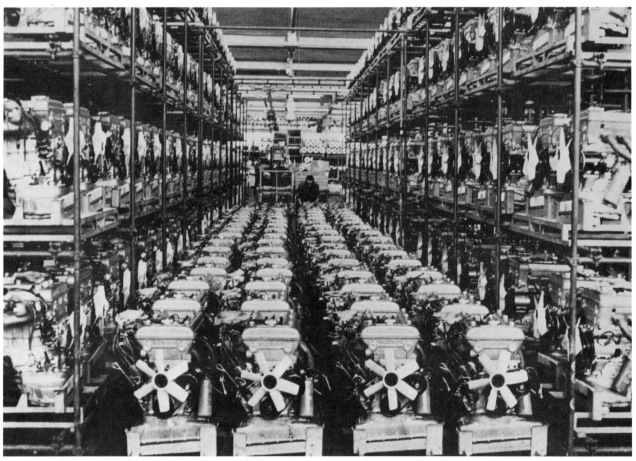

The production lines roll—an inventory of Giulia engines fills the factory storage bays.

smaller car. The gearbox was identical to the 101 Series Giulietta, but now carried a fifth gear, as the 2000 model cars had since 1958.

Mechanical Specifications

The engine, which took most of the press' attention, was essentially a 101 Series Giulietta with its bore and stroke changed to 78x82 mm for a displacement of 1570 cc. To accommodate the longer stroke, the height of the block was increased, but the bore centers were unchanged. Sodium-cooled exhaust valves were standard. The engine offered 92 hp with the single downdraft Solex carburetor and a compression ratio of 9.0:1, compared to the Giulietta's 53 hp and 7.5:1 compression ratio. The larger engine of the Giulia TI sedan gave it almost the same performance as the Giulietta Veloce Spiders and Coupes and, at the same time, made it much more tractable. While the Veloce was notorious for its lack of low-end torque, the Giulia engine provided ample torque for less-than-full-throttle getaways from a stoplight. Moreover, the Giulia engine proved more reliable than the Giulietta.

The engine, however, was not the significant story of the Monza introduction in 1962—the sedan body was. The Giulia sedan would go on to become the highest-production body in Alfa Romeo history, appearing in its final form as the Giulia

What's in a Name?

When it was originally introduced, the Giulietta name recalled the star-crossed lovers of Verona who had been immortalized by Shakespeare's *Romeo and Juilet*. That was an official factory intent, and at its introduction in 1954, the Giulietta was accompanied by two actors dressed as Romeo and Giulietta, to give them their proper Italian names.

Giulietta is the Italian diminutive of Giulia, and therefore a larger Giulietta deserved to be christened the Giulia. The new name carried a subtlety that further enhanced the mystique of the Giulietta: not only was that earlier car a jewel, it suddenly became a small jewel, and by implication, its new, larger sister was now somewhat more imposing.

Diesel in 1976. In addition, it has become one of the most-loved Alfa Romeos because of its superior strength, comfort, excellent accommodations and driving position. It was a favored car for the Italian freeway police in both its sedan and station-wagon form. In its later Super tune (with dual Weber carburetors—but less race-prepared than the TI Super) it was able to catch all but the most exotic speeders. While enthusiasts were most interested

A phantom view of the Giulia sedan showed its state-of-the-art suspension in detail. Features such as the four-wheel disc brakes and an aluminum twin-cam engine made it one of the most sophisticated sedans available in 1962.

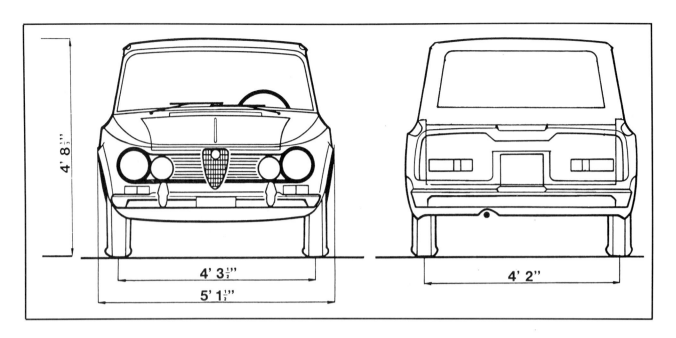

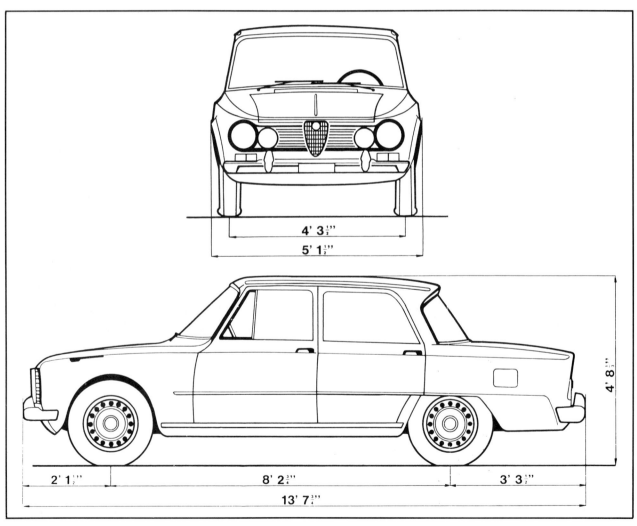

Exterior dimensions of the Giulia sedan. The car made excellent use of its interior space and provided much more living room than the compact interior suggested. The TI stood for Turismo Internationale.

in the sporting coupes and spiders, the Giulia sedan was in many ways their equal in performance and undoubtedly their superior in comfort and accommodation. It was easy for enthusiasts to overlook a sedan when voluptuous coupes and spiders abound, but the charm of the Giulia sedan, once tasted, was not easily forgotten.

The first news American enthusiasts had of the Monza introduction centered on the engine and ignored the new sedan body entirely. From the American Alfa Romeo newsletter of July 1962: "On June 28 [sic], a new 1570 cc Alfa Romeo called the Giulia was introduced at Monza. According to *Motoring News, Competition Press* and Commandante Morrone of Alfa Romeo (South Africa), the Giulia appears to be identical in outward appearance to the Giulietta—except for a false air intake on the hood. Berlina T.I., Spider, and Sprint ver-

sions will be produced." The oversight was corrected in the August issue of the newsletter, when a small photograph of the new Giulia sedan was reproduced.

Additional details of the car were also listed: "In addition to information carried in the July issue of the *Owner*, we can now add the following, applicable to the TI only: triple-shoe front drum brakes; ball-jointed A-arm front suspension; rubber bumpers inside the front coil springs and shock absorbers now between the springs and wheels at the apex of the A; at the rear, rigid axle and radius rods are retained; rear coils are lower mounted not on the axle but on the trailing radius rods; radius arms are fabricated angle pieces; [the] base on the torque reaction triangle is almost the width of the car; all grease nipples except two at universals on the drive shaft have been eliminated."

The engine compartment of the Giulia TI shown in a 1962 press photo. The location of the fuse block just behind the battery in this photo caused major corrosion—and therefore, electrical—problems. The TI engine was slightly canted toward the left or the driver's side. Carburetion came from the single downdraft Solex and power was 104 hp at 6200 rpm.

The triple-shoe front drum brakes were fitted only to the first 2,000 cars produced. Otherwise, the American summary nicely characterized the significant mechanical changes between the Giulietta and Giulia sedans. Enthusiasts will be interested to know that this early description noted a change in the Giulia's suspension that was, indeed, revolutionary for Alfa Romeo. This suspension, identified as the Type 105, became the pattern for all subsequent Alfa Romeos in the Giulia line-up, including the spider and coupe.

In its review of the Giulia TI, *Road & Track* magazine reconfirmed its well-known Alfa Romeo enthusiasm. The review began: "If there's another car that offers more for the same price, we can't think what it is." The review concluded, "We could get hooked on the Alfa TI. In fact we are."

In spite of their enthusiasm, the reviewers at *Road & Track* had some misgivings about the car's appearance: "the TI won't win any beauty prizes. It is boxy, square at all corners and it has more of the looks of one of the workaday medium-size Fiats

The grille of the 1962 Giulia TI was certainly busy. Later models would simplify all the bars. The early cars had four headlamps.

than the sleek sexiness we ordinarily expect attached to the Alfa emblem."

The squareness of the new car—the Giulietta sedan was definitely round in comparison—had utility, however, for it provided interior room and seating that was hard to match. According to *Road & Track:* "The seating position is high, the steering wheel is located at just the right angle and in just the right place, and the vision is excellent in all directions. It is a car that encourages vigorous driving and everything conspires to it being conducted allegro con brio."

While its engine had only a single Solex carburetor, the TI offered a drivetrain that was remarkably sophisticated for a sedan in 1962, and *Road & Track* gave it due mention: "Underneath that unprepossessing exterior, however, there is as

fine a set of 1600 internals as you'll find anywhere. This engine . . . is attached to that fine all-synchro 5-speed gearbox . . . and a better combination can hardly be imagined."

Giulia Suspension

Early reviews in the enthusiast press missed a significant point of the new Giulia sedan—the new front suspension. In fact, the *Road & Track* review incorrectly called it "the same as the Giulietta . . . with unequal A-arms. . . ." The Giuliettas—and the first Giulia spiders and coupes—had unequal-length A-arm front suspension with concentric spring-shock absorber assemblies, a common configuration. The Alfa Romeo's A-arm geometry was adequately refined to give superb road handling while maintaining a supple suspension, which

Alfa Romeo introduced its sports version of the TI as the TI Super in 1963. The TI's single downdraft Solex was replaced by two sidedraft Weber carburetors, pushing power to 112 hp at 5500 rpm. This is a TI Super at Monza *in 1966 with a group of journalists at the wheel. Note the four headlamps fitted to this car, perhaps from a standard TI.*

meant lots of body roll. In fact, the Giulietta front suspension carried limit-straps to prohibit body roll beyond an acceptable limit.

On the Giulia TI, and all later 105 Series cars, a single transverse stamped member replaced the upper A-arm of the Giulietta design, and the shocks were positioned outside the coil springs. To locate the upper member, an adjustable trailing arm was used. Geometrically, this was still an upper A-arm, but the base of its triangle was much broader, and displayed at a significant angle to the axis of the car—and also to the triangle formed by the lower A-arm. The new front suspension reduced camber change as the suspension moved, and thus improved front-end stability. Other suspension detail changes included the use of stamped trailing members and a revised transverse member for the solid rear-axle suspension.

On a more practical note, the Giulia suspension also introduced no-maintenance suspension joints. The greased bearing surfaces of the Giulietta suspension gave way to large rubber bushes. The initial idea of never having to lubricate the suspension was appealing, but Giulia owners soon learned that rubber was not a perfect material for a suspension. It was attacked by ozone and became brittle, causing the joint to seize. Neglected, frozen joints tore the suspension from the Giulia body; fortunately, the suspension gave ample warning before catastrophic failure occurred by squeaking loudly when things began to deteriorate. The hapless owner who ignored the squeaks, however, may have found his front suspension missing after negotiating a deep pothole.

Repairs to the rubber bushes, short of replacement, included injecting brake fluid or automatic transmission fluid into the rubber with a hypodermic syringe to soften the rubber. Since brake fluid is hydroscopic, its use is actually self-destructive. The only sure fix, of course, was to fit new parts.

On really rough roads, the new suspension design stressed the top trailing link's foremost joint excessively. Owners who drove on rough roads found that they had to replace the joint frequently. Trouble with the joint was indicated by a solid clunk when the suspension was working over a rough road. No repair to the joint is possible; it must be replaced when worn.

Giulia TI Super

In March 1963, Alfa Romeo upgraded the Giulietta Sprint Speciale to 101 Series Giulia status by giving it the larger engine with dual Weber carburetors and a compression ratio of 9.7:1. The changes were good for 112 hp, compared to the 100 hp of the Giulietta Sprint Speciale version. One month later, on April 24, 1963, Alfa Romeo invited the press to Monza for a tour in the TI Super, a race and rally version of the TI Berlina fitted with the same

The usual configuration of the Giulia TI Super replaced the two inner headlamps with air intakes for the engine. The bodywork used slightly thinner-gauge sheet metal, all sound-deadening material was deleted and non-operating plexiglass windows were put in the rear *doors. Total weight savings was some 200 lb. Campagnolo 6x15 in. lightweight aluminum alloy wheels were also standard, ideal for racing, as shown here on the Grecua/Meimaris TI Super that swept the three-hour Tatoi race in 1968.*

Giulia TI Super at speed during the July 19, 1966, 500 kilometer endurance race of Buenos Aires. The 1600 cc car won its class.

In 1969, the Giulia 1300 TI featured a much more simple grille and only two headlamps.

dual-Weber 112 hp engine as used in the Giulia Sprint Speciale.

On the TI, the gear change was on the steering column, while the TI Super carried it on the floor. The TI Super also had front bucket seats, round gauges and a three-spoke steering wheel (as would appear later in the Super Berlina).

Since all the Giulia sedan bodies carried identical sheet metal, grillework would be used to set apart the various models. The grille of the TI had eight horizontal chrome strips and four headlamps. The external identifying feature of the TI Super was a pair of wire-mesh-covered air intake grilles that replaced the inboard pair of headlights.

As suggested by this press photo, the 1300 TI was a fine car for touring—spacious, economical and reliable. This is a 1969 model.

While the bodywork differed little in looks, it was made of a slightly thinner gauge of sheet metal. In addition, all sound-deadening material was deleted from the car, and nonworking plexiglass windows were used in the rear doors. Lightweight fixed-back competition bucket seats were mounted up front, and Campagnolo aluminum-alloy wheels sized at 6x15 in. were available. Overall, 200 lb. had been lightened from the car compared with the base TI.

The TI Super was homologated in the Fédération Internationale de l'Automobile (FIA) Group 2 Touring Car race class, as was the later GTA. In the hands of factory racers and privateers, the TI Super had a long, successful life as a competition version of the TI, but it was never an easy car to drive on the street due to its high state of tune.

The TI Super was built for only two years. It was introduced in mid–1963 and was discontinued in 1964. Only 501 cars were built.

TI Supers that have survived today are all likely to have been extensively raced, so it is impossible to generalize on what kind of equipment or modifications a buyer is likely to find. The cars are highly collectible, and a TI Super with documented history is a blue-chip investment even though it may look tatty.

The Long Sedan Lineage: TI to Nuova

In 1964, a 1300 cc version of the Giulia TI, the Giulia 1300 Berlina, was introduced. It was distinguished by its three, widely spaced chrome strips in the grille and minimal external trim. The 1300 Berlina had the two-spoke steering wheel, bar-type speedometer and round tachometer instrumentation of the TI, but featured a four-speed floorshift and developed 78 hp from its Solex carburetor.

The 1300 TI appeared in 1966, and carried three horizontal chrome bars on the grille like the 1300 Berlina, but it had a five-speed gearbox. The 1300 TI developed 82 hp with a single twin-throat Solex carburetor.

The Giulia Super made its debut at the 1965 Geneva auto show. It had five chrome bars on the

This photo of the Giulia 1300 TI showed the two parallel scallops that distinguished the Giulia sedans. One large scallop ran just under the greenhouse, tying together the front and rear fenders. The second scallop, located over the door sill, echoed the larger one. Shades of the Type 103 were also evident.

grille and a chrome strip running under the door sills. Inside, it had a three-spoke steering wheel, styled along the lines of the famous Nardi wheel. Bucket seats replaced the standard seats of the TI.

Under the hood, dual sidedraft Weber carburetors replaced the TI's single downdraft Solex. With the new carburetion and a higher state of tune, the engine produced some 98 hp.

Road & Track tested the new Super and loved the details but not the basic sedan body. The review's headline read: "A sporting sedan with almost everything but beauty."

Lest the casual reader miss the aesthetic verdict, the editors underlined their coolness for the sedan's styling in the opening paragraph: "It's nothing much in the way of pretty, what with slab sides and boxy lines, but it sure is everything else a car of this type ought to be." Neither did they like some of the interior details, most noticeably the heater: "One of the standard Alfa jokes concerns their use of a heater indicator light—a very practical accessory because otherwise you'd probably never be able to tell whether the heater was on or not."

Such are the judgments of what was to become the single most popular sedan in Alfa Romeo his-

tory and, arguably, one of the greatest sedans of all time. True, it was slab sided and vertical in a tradition one usually associated with certain British Triumph Mayflower sedans. The virtue of the slab-sidedness was that it provided ample interior room, although the Super was found to be short in driver legroom by *Road & Track*, perhaps because they had not yet discovered the typical Alfa Romeo arms-extended driving position. There were other advantages to the Giulia body. The sedan was surprisingly aerodynamic, although its drag coefficient (Cd) of 0.34 was probably only a coincidence of its design. In comparison, the Cd of a Maserati Ghibli was 0.35 and the Porsche 911 was 0.34. As a result of the low turbulence, at speed the Giulia sedan was remarkably quiet and stable.

The seating position in the sedan was certainly upright and, as a result, provided superb comfort and visibility. The seats in the Super were adjustable for rake, allowing the American driver to have the steering wheel a bit closer to his chest than the typical Italian driving position permitted. The TI dashboard had a round tachometer integrated into a bar-type speedometer, bench seats and either floor or column shift, although the column shift was more common. A plastic, two-spoke steer-

A 1966 Giulia 1300 with its typical steering wheel and dash with horizontal bar-type speedometer. The same

dash arrangement was also available for the 1.6 liter Giulia TI.

The 1969 1300 TI interior was finished in a heavy-grade plastic that has proved most durable over the years. The somewhat plain, three-spoke steering wheel was used in a number of Giulia models.

Alfa Romeo's models tended to decorate the landscape somewhat suggestively. This was the 1300 TI with the standard stamped-steel wheels and the chrome Alfa Romeo wheel covers.

ing wheel was standard. The Super's dash had two large instruments positioned in front of the driver: a speedometer on the right with a fuel gauge in its lower segment, and a tachometer with water-temperature and oil-pressure gauges around the bottom.

In spite of the joke about the heater light, ventilation and heating on the Giulia was light-years ahead of the Giulietta unit, which also had a light to tell you it was on. However, since the Giulietta's heater motor had a tendency to seize, the Giulietta owner could always tell that his heater was on by the piercing howls made as the heater motor bearings tried to free themselves to turn the fan. My original Super was quite competent to keep me warm in high-speed subzero dashes to the upper reaches of Michigan for an entire winter. The secret was to block off completely the front of the radiator with cardboard.

A cheapened version of the Giulia Super, the 1600S, was introduced at the 1970 Turin auto show. It was advertised as the "long-distance Giulia," and developed 95 hp from an engine that was virtually identical to the TI. Like the TI, it had three chrome strips on the grille. The car was not successful and was withdrawn after about a year with a total production of 2,212.

The Giulia 1300 Super appeared at the Turin show in 1970. It featured some of the refinements of the 1750 Series sedans that had been introduced in 1967. The 1300 Super, like the Giulia Super, offered dual Weber carburetors, but produced only 89 hp because of its smaller displacement.

The Giulia TI was discontinued in 1967, the 1300 Berlina was discontinued in 1971 and the Giulia Super ceased production after 1972, as did the 1300 TI and 1300 Super. In 1976, a Giulia Diesel was produced with a Perkins 4.108 engine that gave 55 hp.

The Giulia sedan was modified by Colli of Italy into a stylish station wagon, which I am sorry to say, Alfa Romeo did not import to the United

Not to be confused with the sport TI Super, the Giulia 1300 Super was introduced in 1965. It differed from earlier models only in subtle details, such as the new front bumper and wheel covers.

States, for it would have offered all the Giulia advantages of performance, comfort and reliability with additional cargo capacity. The wagons were extensively used by the highway police in Italy and some ambulances were also fashioned from them.

Only a few Colli wagons found their way to the United States. One of the wagons that did make it was imported by an officer of the American distributorship, and then sold when the owner returned to Italy. A California Alfa Romeo dealer has a Giulia panel wagon with no rear side windows. And, while it hardly counts, it's noteworthy that a member of the San Diego chapter of the national Alfa Romeo club has a Super sedan that was converted in Mexico to an El Camino-like pickup truck.

I believe that Colli modified stock sedans, rather than fabricating the entire body from scratch. The one Colli I have examined seemed to have been entirely stock Alfa Romeo except for the rear bodywork. Indeed, it would be easy for any panel-beater to fabricate a wagon from the sedan, but I've never read anything about exactly how the conversions were accomplished. Because of the basic strength of the body and the fact that the new construction would probably add strength, no additional reinforcing should be required to create a sturdy and serviceable wagon.

The last of the line, the Giulia Nuova Super, appeared in 1974 and was in production until about 1978. It was offered in both 1300 and 1600 versions: the 1290 cc version developed 103 hp while the 1570 cc model turned out 116 hp. Both had a single chrome spear on the grille, four headlights and a rounded Alfa Romeo "heart," similar to that on the Alfettas. Like many of the later Giulias, it shared many components with the 1750, 2000 and Alfetta sedans.

As significant as the Giulia sedan was to Alfa Romeo history, most enthusiasts paid scant attention to it, preferring instead to concentrate on the spider and coupe. It was their loss. If I may quote one owner, "Real Alfa enthusiasts drive sedans." And I can assure you, the happiest were in Giulia Supers.

The interior of the 1300 Super was awash in durable plastic. The fuel gauge was located between the tachometer and speedometer. Toggle switches between the seats were part of a central console.

This 1966 Giulia 1300 had an unique grille and no bumper overriders. The slots on the air inlet beneath the windshield were horizontal rather than vertical.

Giulia Production

Our sole source of Giulia production figures comes from Luigi Fusi's book, *All the Cars Since 1910.* Data for the early models were kept by Fusi personally, and few exceptions to his personal listings have been found.

The postwar figures in his book, which are official Alfa Romeo data, have proved much less gospel-like. It is not unusual to find a modern Alfa Romeo with a serial number not covered in Fusi. Indeed, there is some anecdotal evidence that Alfa Romeo used creative license in numbering its vehicles, especially those of limited production. Given the unaccountable bureaucracy of which Alfa Romeo was a part, some confusion was inevitable—if not actually desirable.

It is important to distinguish between the data in Fusi and the availability of models in the United States. There were no 1970 model cars sold in the United States because of emissions legislation, and exceedingly few in 1975 because of the model changeover. Alfa Romeo remained in full production during these years, as the figures show.

Since Fusi does not distinguish between model and calendar years, there is additional confusion in trying to understand just exactly how many cars were produced over a specific period of time. Typically, a model year begins in the fall of the preceeding year. While there is no evidence that the prewar models made any distinction between calendar and model years, Alfa Romeo certainly makes the distinction now: the 1991 model 164 sedan was first sold in the United States in June 1990.

On the other hand, the production data frequently anticipated real model availability. For instance, the 1750 model was introduced in 1967, yet was only available in the United States beginning in 1969. Some of this delay may be attributed to fine-tuning for the United States market: the much-delayed Milano introduction to the United States is recent enough to be memorable to everyone. From a United States standpoint the data make models appear to have a longer life than was actually the case.

While we have had this information for twenty-five years, no one has really stopped to do much with it. Even a most cursory look can prove instructive, however. I do not feel that the data are accurate enough for specific quantitative comparisons, however I think the general trends they indicate are both accurate and enlightening.

Americans tend to think of Alfa Romeo as a producer of interesting convertibles and coupes, with occasional sedans thrown in for practicality. Nothing could be further from the truth. Alfa Romeo sedans are the mainstay of its production. And, several of its highest-production sedans have never been imported to the United States.

Giulia Production Numbers

Model	Years	Production
Sedans		
Giulia TI	1962–1967	71,148
Giulia TI Super	1963–1964	501
Giulia 1300, 1300 TI	1964–1972	172,571
Giulia Super	1965–1972	124,590
Giulia 1300 Super	1972–1975	85,200
Giulia Super 1.3, 1.6	1972–1974	NA
Giulia Nuova Super, 1300, 1600, Diesel	1974–1978	104,337
1750 Berlina	1967–1972	11,880
2000 Berlina	1971–1977	89,840
Coupes		
Giulia 1600 Sprint	1962–1964	7,107
Giulia Sprint GT	1963–1966	21,850
Giulia Sprint GTV	1965–1968	12,499
Giulia 1300 Sprint	1964–1965	1,900
GTA 1600	1965–1969	493
GTA-SA	1967–1968	10
GT 1300 Junior, Jr. 1.3, 1.6	1966–1977	91,964
GTA 1300 Junior	1968–1972	492
1750 GT Veloce	1967–1972	44,276
2000 GTV	1971–1977	37,921
GTAm 1750, 2000	1970–1971	40
Spiders		
Giulia 1600 Spider, Spider Veloce	1962–1965	10,341
Duetto	1966–1967	6,325
Spider 1300 Junior, Jr. 1.3	1968–1974	NA
1750 Spider Veloce	1967–1971	8,722
2000 Spider Veloce	1971–1977	21,993
Spider	1978–Current	NA
Zagato-bodied cars		
Giulia TZ, TZ 2	1963–1967	124
Quattroruote Zagato	1966–1968	92
GT 1300 Junior Zagato	1969–1972	1,108
GT 1600 Junior Zagato	1972–1975	402
Special-bodied cars		
Giulia Sprint Speciale	1963–1965	1,400
Giulia GTC	1965–1966	1,000
Montreal	1970–1977	3,925

The Giulia Super was a fast, comfortable sedan. It was identified by its five-bar grille with four headlamps. This press photo showed other identifying trim items: the chrome strip running under the doors and the chrome trim piece on the hood.

Colli built a station wagon conversion on the Giulia which proved a most practical vehicle. Reliable and commodious, the Giardinetta was used by the highway police in Italy, as well as numerous other firms.

The relatively short wheelbase made the Colli conversion somewhat cramped for ambulance work, but you could be sure it would get you there as fast as possible. This was a racetrack ambulance.

Evolution. This late Super carried cap-style wheel covers but no chrome under the doors or on the hood. The five bars remained on the grille but the background was blacked out. The exterior was identical for 1300 and 1600 versions. The last of the Supers carried a grille which copied the fat, heart-shaped grille of the 2000 Berlina.

The Giulia 1600S was a plain-Jane car billed as a perfect long-distance tourer. That was, in fact, exactly what all Giulia sedans were.

The Giulia Diesel was produced for a single year, 1976. Though it carried the fourteen-year-old Giulia Berlina body, most of the trim for the Diesel was borrowed from contemporary Alfa Romeos.

A curious combination of old and new, the dash of the Giulia Diesel combined the original Giulia Super instrumentation with a 2.0 liter Berlina console and steering wheel.

The 1974 Nuova Super 1300 featured a blacked-out grille, flat hood and no chrome trim strips on the body.

The 2000 Berlina was built from 1971 to 1974 in the 105 Series in Italy and as the 115 Series in the United States. While the European version used dual sidedraft Weber carburetors, the US import was fed through the Spica mechanical fuel-injection system.

3

Giulia Spider and Duetto

The Giulia 1600 Spider was introduced—with the TI and Sprint—at Monza on June 27, 1962. The car was virtually a reengined Giulietta, with the false hood scoop, larger taillights and revised instrument faces being the easiest identifiers. The Giulia spider engine featured a unique air intake for the Solex carburetor.

One of the earliest road tests of the new Spider in the United States was written by Bob Taylor for the May 19, 1963 issue of the *Newark* (NJ) *Sunday News*. It's worth noting that Alfa Romeo's US headquarters were in Newark at the time.

Taylor got to the increased performance early in his review: "Rated by the manufacturer as capable of 107 miles an hour, it turned in a speed of 112 miles an hour. It also got 27 miles to the gallon of gas during four turns of the track, although Alfa Romeo says only that it will get 25.2 in average usage."

The review continued in almost requisite praise by the reviewer of Alfa Romeo road handling: "The car . . . turned out to be one of the most capable sports cars tested in this long series. It was magnificently efficient on curves, rounding them as if they were straight. There was little lean of the body nor any heavy wheel-jumping apparent to the driver, and the steering was neutral from 30 miles an hour up to that 112." Similarly, reviewers seemed obliged to praise the Alfa Romeo gearbox: "The five-speed shift on the Alfa, synchronized on every gear, is a marvel. Operation is smooth and the synchro mechanisms always efficient. Fifth gear is an overdrive and fourth is direct," Taylor wrote.

Mechanical Specifications

The Spider body was remarkably comfortable for a convertible, especially to enthusiasts who thought that sports cars had to have side curtains and tops that flapped like sails. "The Maryland run showed the Giulia to be a comfortable cruiser," Taylor reported. "It has the longest seat adjustment of any sports car. . . . The top on the test car was completely waterproof in a rain storm if the car's occupants took pains to make sure a cloth drip panel was outside the top of each side window." Taylor concluded his report: "This road tester rates it as one of the world's really fine automobiles."

Car and Driver magazine summed up the differences between the Giulietta and new Giulia in its road test: "The differences amount to various subtle changes that have proved most effective. The new model is about two inches longer, both in wheelbase and over-all length, and its front track is slightly wider. . . . The Giulia has a new ball-bearing worm and roller steering box. . . ." Unfortunately, all those differences did not exist, since the Giulia used the Giulietta body and most mechanicals.

Nevertheless, *Car and Driver* was appreciative of the car's handling: "The Giulia's unhesitant steering response surpasses what is ordinarily described as quick and precise—it has these qualities to a degree that calls for new adjectives. There is absolutely no trace of the Giulietta understeer, the car remaining perfectly controllable up to the point of breakaway.

"The suspension seems taut and works noiselessly even when observation tells you that considerable wheel travel is occurring. The rear suspension . . . remains one of today's best arguments against accepting the additional cost of independent rear suspension."

There was some feeling, when the Giulia was introduced, that Alfa Romeo should have adopted independent rear suspension (IRS) to compete with Porsche. After all, the reasoning went, Alfa Romeo had produced a very successful IRS with its 2.5 liter cars, and to be competitive in the current market, should have provided the enthusiast with a fully independent suspension. Most road tests touched on the controversy obliquely, as did the *Car and Driver* test. In a *Cars Illustrated* test of June 1964, the same subject was approached: "The Alfa Romeo Giulia does not feature independent all-round suspension, and if all rigid axle systems were as good as this, there would have been no need for independence to have been invented in the first place."

Thus, two basic arguments in favor of Alfa Romeo's traditional solid-axle rear suspension emerged: it was less expensive (*Car and Driver*) and worked as well as the more exotic IRS (*Cars Illustrated*). The point has been proved; in 1987, no one lamented the lack of IRS on the modern spider, which still carried the Giulia (indeed, Giulietta) unit.

The Giulia's market position was evaluated in *Cars Illustrated*'s road test, providing the modern reader with a reminder of Alfa Romeo's competition in 1964: "Why did Alfa Romeo decide on 1600 cc for the upgraded version of its best-selling open two-seater? Why not 1800 cc as MG has done (and Sunbeam can be expected to do)? The question is easily answered . . . its 1.6 liters give performance comparable with that of the 2.2-liter Triumph TR-4 and the fuel economy of some 1000-cc cars."

The road test concluded: "Few cars can rival the 1600 Alfa for sheer driving enjoyment . . . the car does everything so effortlessly, with proper use of the five-speed gearbox, that one gets the feeling of commanding much more power than it actually puts out. And as for fatigue, it just seems never to set in—this car's all fun."

At $3,400 for the Spider and $3,700 for the Veloce, the Alfa Romeo filled a marketing niche almost by itself, being more expensive than the MGB or Fiat and significantly less than the Jaguar or Mercedes. Yet, so far as quality of ride and level

The first of the Giulia Spiders arrived in 1962 and bore close resemblance to the Giulietta's bodywork. The major difference was the addition of a decorative hood scoop on *the Giulia Spiders, a feature that was not included on the new Giulia Sprint Coupes. This is John Kremer's immaculately restored Spider. Michael Gyson*

The last of the Giuliettas were christened as the 101 Series by the factory and the 101 distinction was carried over to the new Giulias as well. The new Spiders differed from the old Giuliettas by the upgraded Giulia engine and the five-speed standard transmission. The standard Spider version used a single downdraft Solex carburetor; in 1965, a Veloce version was made available with dual sidedraft Webers.

of trim, the Alfa Romeo was closer to the higher-priced cars.

In 1964, the standard sports car was still the MG. If one had limited resources, then the Midget or Healey Sprite was the only choice. Slight affluence qualified one to consider the Triumph Spitfire, or for just a bit more, the MGB. All these British cars were traditional in concept (the IRS of the Spitfire being a notable exception), and gave the generally harsh ride, Spartan interior and good road-holding features the enthusiast had learned of in British cars and equated with a "real" sports car. British tops leaked much more than was necessary, and contributed to the image that the true enthusiast drove top-down, even in the rain.

The Sunbeam Alpine was a more refined car in ride, but it was not taken seriously by the enthusiast because of its more supple suspension and refined character. The Jaguar, always its own standard, cost significantly more than the Alfa Romeo, but the eager Alfa Romeo enthusiast imagined his car almost as fast as the Jaguar—or the Corvette—though both those cars were really in another league. The only competitor in this group was the Datsun roadster, which had only limited distribution and even fewer fans.

The front end of the new Giulia with its distinctive hood scoop, needed to clear the air cleaner on the 1600 cc Giulia engine. While it certainly added to the styling, the scoop was in fact only decorative, being blocked off inside.

Fiat had always been careful to provide serious domestic competition for Alfa Romeo, and was large enough to bracket whatever market its competitor chose. The inexpensive 850 was introduced in 1966, and was rear-engined and sporty. It was more of a competitor to the Spitfire and Midget than the Alfa Romeo. The 1100 TV roadster was cheaper than the Alfa Romeo, slightly less luxurious and less powerful. Its replacement, the 1200 roadster, continued to undercut the price of the Alfa Romeo convertibles and offer a more modern bodystyle to boot. The 124 Spider was direct competition for Alfa Romeo, with a twin-cam engine, fine appointments and almost equivalent performance. The 124—and Fiat in general—was derided by most enthusiasts as inferior. In fact, it was a fine car but its factory support in the United States was abysmal. It might have survived its rust-proneness had the US Fiat organization been more committed to customer service.

Alfa Romeo enthusiasts considered Porsche the only true competition, even though it was significantly more expensive. The 356 Series was a benchmark car, and the rivalry between Alfa Romeo and Porsche was as much social as mechan-

Underneath the new Giulia's hood sat the new Giulia engine and the reason for the hood scoop—the unique air-intake system for the single downdraft Solex carburetor with its large airbox and dual air tubes. The airbox was fed through the front grille.

ical. The Porsche fan would quickly explain that, being better engineered, the cars required less tinkering than the Alfa Romeo.

The new dashboard layout for the Giulia Spider was substantially updated from that of the Giulietta Spider. The fascia was a metal piece painted body color, and the gauges were set into the face. Padded leatherette covered the top of the dash. The steering wheel was designed after the popular Nardi wheels of the day. Note the Pininfarina plaque mounted in the center to cover the hole for the optional radio.

A Giulia Spider dashboard with the optional radio in place above the gearshift. The rearview mirror was mounted on top of the dash.

Both cars had civilized interiors, protection from the elements and superior road-holding ability. Porsche was the reason Alfa Romeo had to live with the frequent criticism that its solid rear axle was antique. Alfa Romeo owners could only respond that the solid rear axle was much more forgiving as one approached the limits of adhesion. The arrival of the 912 and 911 Porsches left the rivalry unchanged.

No one took the 190 Mercedes roadster seriously as a sports car, although a few 190 SL cars did race. In fact, the Alfa Romeo approached the 190 SL in comfort and quiet more closely than enthusiasts cared to admit. In retrospect, the Alfa Romeo was much closer in character to the 190 SL than the other sports cars it competed against at the time. Which explains the fact that, stock, the Alfa Romeo wasn't that competitive a sports car on a twisty course. A bit too soft and heavy, it could be turned a winner only with some significant modifications. In fact, the spider is not a true racing car; Alfa Romeo assigned that duty to its line of coupes from Zagato and Autodelta.

Giulia Spider Veloce

Alfa Romeo has always been sensitive to maintaining its performance image, and everyone knew that it would only be a matter of time before a Weber-carbureted version of the Giulia spider would appear, paralleling the standard and Veloce tunes of the Giulietta.

The Veloce engine appeared in 1963—in the Bertone-bodied Sprint Speciale—and it showed up the following year in the spider, which became the Giulia Spider Veloce. Note that the term *normale*, used to distinguish the lesser-tuned version of both the Giulietta and Giulia, was never used by the factory or contemporary enthusiasts to describe the car. The descriptor has been added rather

recently to give the lesser stage of tune a proper name.

Veloce means fast, and the Giulia Spider Veloce was truly fast. Indeed, its top speed was 5 km/h (3 mph) greater than the legendary 8C2900 B. Though Alfa Romeo has since applied the term Veloce to many of its models, the Giulia Spider Veloce remains, for the enthusiast, the last true Veloce.

In its test of September 1965, *Road & Track* compared the new Giulia Spider Veloce to both the Giulia Spider and the Giulietta Super Spider, the Weber-carbureted version. The test concentrated on the changes that produced the Veloce version: "The most obvious of these differences is additional power: the 1300 Super Spider's 103 bhp (risen to 108 in the 1570-cc 1600) has reached 129 in the 1600 Veloce, bestowing a comparable and thoroughly welcome rise in torque from 86.8 at 4500 rpm to an estimated 105 at 4000.

"Owners of 1300s have all experienced stop-light-despair syndrome as they delicately fiddled their little jewels off the line, trying to maintain sporting aplomb as the hulks roared by. The 1600 Veloce has no such problem: its Weber-fed engine leaps eagerly up into the meaty high-revolution range, and even pulls well farther down the tachometer." While the Giulietta Veloce certainly had no torque, the Giulia Veloce had both torque and excellent top speed. *Road & Track* found 109 mph on tap, very close to the 110 mph claimed by the factory.

The seats of the Spider received mixed reviews. The *Cars Illustrated* test reported that the Spider "features two of the best bucket seats for driver and passenger we have ever encountered. More than adequate support for the thighs and shoulders is provided, and despite some fairly hard driving at no time did passengers feel the need to hang on to a grab handle to prevent themselves from sliding about." *Car and Driver* called them "relatively inexpensive. Both offer backrest adjustments which give such good support in any position that non-stop all-day drives are quite pleasant." However, Bob Taylor found that "There was a little ache induced at the base of the driver's spine for the first 100 miles...." *Road & Track* observed that "the side pads were fundamentally deadening over a long trip, and definitely were not designed for the broad of beam."

It appeared that, while Alfa Romeo never changed the basic configuration of the spider seat, there were at least two different degrees of padding used. My own Giulia Veloce seats definitely matched the *Road & Track* description, being two of the deepest buckets I've ever experienced. On the other hand, the typical Spider had a very shallow bucket that was much more comfortable for enthusiasts. There is no documentation that Alfa

In 1957, Alfa Romeo worked with Pinin Farina in creating the Superflow 6C 3000 CM, pictured here at the Portello works. When work began on an update of the Giulia Spider in 1965–1966, Alfa Romeo and Pininfarina looked back to the Superflow design for inspiration. The two-tone paint job worked well on the original car to highlight the dramatic styling. The light front bumpers tended to make a wraparound beltline with the side trough, but the stripe down the hood only detracted from the basic lines of the car.

Rear view of the Superflow 6C 3000 CM. The Duetto's boattail shape was there already in 1957, and thankfully the production car would forget the tailfins.

The Superflow in spider form appeared at the Geneva show in 1959. The fins were gone and the trough ran through the rear wheel skirt. The nose of this car was interesting in that it provided a look at an alternate headlamp treatment. Only a slight scallop was required to clear the base of the headlamps, and the entire nose section dropped more rapidly than on the Duetto.

Romeo changed the contour of the seats for the Veloce, but personal experience suggests that they did.

While reviews of the Giulia Spider were uniformly positive, there was still a growing sense that the basic body had been around too long. In its review of the Giulia Spider Veloce, *Road & Track* observed of the Giulietta, Giulia and Giulia Veloce Spiders: "These three models are markedly similar to the eye. In fact, one observer asked, 'When are they going to change that design? I thought it was a '59 with a new paint job.' This canard will be instantly rejected by Alfisti as both irrelevant and irreverent, but it is nevertheless true that Bertone's

The production Duetto of 1966–1967 had a less severe side trough than its Superflow prototype and the front headlamps were much more integrated into the body-work, especially with the plexiglass headlamp covers. The nose of this car was especially tidy. Translated, Duetto meant "duet," indicating the two-seater.

original Sprint lines modified by Pininfarina into the svelte Spider version, have been with us without significant change for nearly a decade. And, just as true, the lines are as clean, honest and pleasing to the eye today as they were in the prototype."

For all its aesthetic qualities, the Giulia Spider was nevertheless dated by 1965, and even the appearance of the Veloce version could not hide the fact. Alfa Romeo had not been idle, however, and had been preparing for a new body to grace the Giulia mechanicals.

The Duetto

It is typical that Alfa Romeo would leave the development work for a new body to the bodybuilders. Both Pininfarina and Bertone had worked closely with Alfa Romeo over the years, and both names were carried on current production cars in the Bertone coupes and Pininfarina Spiders. A number of concept cars were produced in the

1950s that, in retrospect, had much to do with the appearance of the new Spider. Several idea cars built on the Giulietta chassis were notable, for elements of those cars appeared on the new Spider, introduced at the Geneva auto show in March 1966.

Probably the earliest one-off of any significance to the Duetto was the Giulietta Sportiva prototype, which introduced the flowing lines that would finally distinguish the new Giulia Spider. Few details of this Sportiva are relevant, except for the slightly sloping nose with a bulge for the grille, covered headlamps and generally smooth execution.

A much more significant development was Alfa Romeo's 1957 Disco Volante with Superflow bodywork by Pinin Farina. This car continued the development of smooth, flowing lines and covered headlights, but also introduced a striking—and large—"blood trough" along the side of the car. This motif was carried on many subsequent cars, in-

The 1750 Spider Veloce was a Duetto with a slightly larger engine, different hubcaps and, in the United States, Spica fuel-injection.

The Spider 1300 Junior was introduced in 1968 and was identical to the Duetto except for its smaller 1300 cc engine.

In 1970, the rounded tail of the early Duettos and Spiders had been chopped off leaving a square tail. Structural changes were also made to the floor pan at the same time and as a result, there was a bit less legroom in the square-tail Spiders than in the earlier cars. Covered headlamps were available in most countries, but in the United States they were not legal, although many Spider owners added them later. This was an early 2.0 liter Spider with the cap-type wheel covers.

54

cluding the Daytona Ferrari, designed by Pininfarina in 1966, and the Rover 3500 sedan.

At the 1959 Geneva auto show, Pinin Farina introduced another Alfa Romeo prototype on the Giulietta chassis that was almost a dead ringer for the Giulia Spider that would appear in 1966. This car had a symmetry unmatched by any other modern car: the pointed lines of the nose were almost duplicated at the tail. The resulting appearance was aerodynamic and caused a long overhang at the rear.

Road & Track summed up the development of the new Duetto spider in its July 1966 announcement story: "The new body is also by Pininfarina, and it is as different from the old as ravioli from antipasto. It is fresh and bullet-like, not like anything else on the road but not exactly radical either. Like many new models, it is essentially a version of an earlier show car theme—in this case a Pininfarina design from the 1961 Turin salon. Unlike most production adaptations of show designs, this one is almost a literal translation, save for the headlights and the top."

No one really liked the Duetto, as it was called, translated as "duet," signifying a two-seater. Of course, the reviewers could wax eloquent about the Alfa Romeo mechanicals and revel in the fact that the new Duetto sported dual Weber carburetors as standard equipment (the term Veloce became a marketing, not technical designation) and four-wheel disc brakes. But even *Road & Track* had to admit: "We found almost no disagreement among members of our staff about the appearance of the new model—no one liked it as well as the Giulietta or the Giulia. One condemned it as a contrived design with meaningless styling gimmicks. Another said, 'I think Pininfarina missed the ball this time.' Somebody else commented, 'They did this shape five years ago on a show car and it isn't any better now.'"

Other critical comments made by *Road & Track* regarded the seating position: "It was difficult to find a position where the lower rim of the steering wheel did not interfere with the legs...." *Motor Sport* criticized the painted fascia, and *Car and Driver*, in its May 1967 review, faulted the Duetto's motor noise: "A prospective owner starting the Duetto for the first time might well be severely disappointed. Due, perhaps, to the extensive use of light alloy in the engine, there is a good

In 1974, Alfa Romeo re-introduced the Spider Junior, but made it available with either the 1300 or 1600 engine. Note the small European-style headlamp rims.

deal of clatter. . . ." In addition, the staff found a slipping clutch, disappointing fuel economy ("possibly because of a body shape that is more stylish than aerodynamic"), visibility ("all-round vision of the Duetto was in some respects a little disappointing") and wind noise ("The car's most serious fault was excessive wind noise: at speeds above about 70 m.p.h. in top, wind roar began to drown the engine until at high speeds the engine was barely audible at all"). For counterpoint, *Road Test* magazine in August 1967 observed: "With the windows up, wind noise is quite moderate for a car of this type."

Alfa Romeo had taken care to build excitement before the introduction of the new Giulia Spider. It created a contest to name the car (the winning name was submitted by Guidobaldo Trionfi of Brescia, Italy), and, for the US market, held a shipside party on the SS *Raffaello*. For that event, the May 1966 review in *The Alfa Owner*, the American club publication, served as a general introduction to what was new: "A gala party aboard the SS *Raffaello* provided the setting for introduction of the new Alfa 1600 models to the USA market. Star

of the whole show was the new 1600 Spider with three examples on display. Two of the cars were on the top deck available for driving and being driven occasionally by members of the Factory Racing team who were on hand, resplendent in blue blazers.

"The pictures in this issue of the *Owner* do not do even 50% justice to the tremendous attractiveness of the new Spider. The car is simply overwhelming when actually inspected."

Enthusiasm aside, the completely new suspension was really an adaptation of the Giulia sedan front suspension to the new bodywork. This fact was hinted at later in the *Owner* review: "Construction costs and stocking requirements have been reduced by using identical modules wherever possible. Excepting the GTA, all models use the same basic driveline components, suspension, etc. *Please note that,* all *1600's now have Webers.*"

The *Owner* review concluded: "Consensus of the old-time Alfa types assembled at the party was that the new Spider was the most exciting Alfa production model they had yet seen. To quote one

American practice. This 1974 Spider had alloy wheels and square side-marker lights.

56

knowledgeable type, 'It sure makes the competition look antiquated.'"

Antiquated, indeed. As the years have passed, the Duetto has become a much more familiar car, and we have now passed well into the time when they are recognized collector cars. In 1990, Duettos bring $9,000—$15,000, depending on condition. Compared to the newer cars, at least in the United States, they have the advantage of carburetion with which the owner can fiddle, while the Spica fuel injection of the later cars is intimidating.

In character, the Duetto was only a slightly refined Giulietta, which is, in fact, a high compliment. There were some notable improvements. The instruments were larger and more dramatic, the seats reclined, the top was more easily handled, the heating was superior and the bumpers were a rust-free stainless steel. Mechanically, the car had everything that made an Alfa Romeo desirable; including four-wheel disc brakes, twin overhead cams, two twin-throat Weber carburetors and a fully synchronized five-speed gearbox. Seating position was still high and, reviews notwithstanding, visibility was most acceptable.

The car carried the same suspension introduced on the Giulia TI, and so had a lubrication-free chassis (the driveshaft still required grease). The tires on the new car were soon changed to 14 in. in diameter, down from 15 in. on the Giulia and Giulietta cars. Since the rims on the new cars were wider, it became common for enthusiasts to switch rims from the Duetto to the disc-braked 1600 Spiders. The 14 in. rims, however, won't clear the Alfin drums of the Giulietta cars.

Alfa Romeo marketed the Duetto from 1966 to 1969, years that saw enthusiasm build only slowly for the car, which still looked awkward after several years' opportunity to become used to the

The rear air dam made a fine display surface for the Graduate logo on the 1984 spider. The Duetto had made an impression in the Dustin Hoffman movie, The Graduate. *A decade later, Alfa Romeo revived the image.*

shape. In retrospect, the Giulietta Spider body was a tough act to follow, and the Duetto had a little too avant-garde styling to overcome the classic appeal of its predecessor. Most criticism of the Duetto centered on the tail of the car. It may have been a logical design, but it was considered ugly for a long time.

In 1969 Alfa Romeo introduced an enlarged engine and renamed the series the 1750, in honor of one of the truly great Alfa Romeos of history. In the US market, the new cars were fuel injected and received minor trim changes, but otherwise continued unchanged.

Finally, for the 1970 model year, Alfa Romeo simply chopped the tail off, producing the Kamm-tail spider, which continues in production to the present.

In June 1968, Alfa Romeo released a 1300 cc version of the Duetto spider called the Spider Ju-

Not yet nearing the end of its production life, his 1984 Spider offered front and rear aerodynamic aids to help speed sales. This was the Graduate, a low-priced version of the car with steel wheels and few options. The front bumper had become imposing, thanks to crash-worthy legislation.

The cockpit of the 1984 Graduate Spider was luxurious and filled with electronics, including a digital clock. Seat material was plastic, but optional leather on the Spider Veloce.

Cromodora five-spoke alloy wheels were almost a classic fittment to Alfa Romeos. This was a Spider Veloce of the mid–1980s. In this photo, the trough seemed very high, making the car much fatter appearing than top lighting would normally permit.

nior. This car was not imported into the United States, but was intended to round out Alfa Romeo's lower-displacement line, which offered tax advantages in Italy. In 1974 and corresponding with the introduction of the Giulia Nuova sedan and GT Junior coupe, it released an updated Kamm-tailed 1300 version of the Junior that was also available with a 1600 engine. Thus, in 1974, one could purchase Alfa Romeo spiders with displacements of 1.3, 1.6 and 2.0 liters.

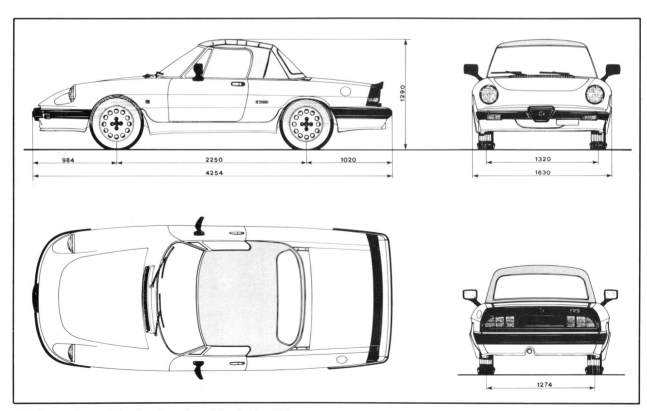

Alfa Romeo's specification drawing of the Spider Veloce revealed a lot of overhang, front and rear. This car also had sill skirts, another attempt to freshen the design.

4

Giulia Sprint and Coupe

The original Giulia coupe was little more than a slightly enlarged engine of 1570 cc in a 101 Series Giulietta Sprint body. It was introduced at Monza on June 27, 1962 with great success. This model was called the Giulia 1600 Sprint, and was produced until March 1964 when its engine was downsized to 1290 cc and the car became known as the 1300 Sprint. A total of 21,542 was produced.

The 101 Series Giulia 1600 Sprints were a more robust car than the Giulietta Sprint that they replaced. Their 1600 engine with a single Solex carburetor gave almost the same performance as the Giulietta Veloce. A five-speed gearbox was standard.

The cars were distinguished by a 1600 badge located just aft of the Bertone nut on the front fenders, and a similar badge on the trunk lid. The car had large three-function taillamps with a back-up light at the bottom. Circular reflectors were added below the taillamps. Because a completely new sedan was introduced at the same time, it was clear that the Giulietta-bodied coupe and spider were both interim solutions and that an entirely new configuration was expected. At the time, enthusiasts also looked forward to Veloce versions of the Giulia, for they would clearly be outstanding performers.

Giulia Sprint GT

In September 1963, the Giulia engine appeared in a new 105 Series coupe body designed by a young Giorgetto Giugiaro for Bertone. The new coupe was called the Giulia Sprint GT. Following the lead of the Giulia sedan, the coupe was much more squared-off than its predecessor, and was distinguished by its notched back. It was the first coupe to be produced at Alfa Romeo's new facility at Arese.

Admittedly, even when it was current, enthusiasts realized that the Giulietta was going to be a hard act to follow. There is no doubt that Alfa Romeo had developed a favorite car in the Giulietta. The Giulietta Sprint coupe was especially loved, a fastback car of minimum displacement and maximum enjoyment. In practical terms, the odds of bettering the success of the Giulietta were poor, since the Giulietta had launched Alfa Romeo into successful serial production. The Giulietta had made the Alfa Romeo affordable for enthusiasts other than kings and movie stars. It had to be with some trepidation that management, after almost ten years, prepared to introduce the Giulietta's replacement.

While identical to the Giulietta Sprint from the outside, the Giulia Sprint had a different dash. Its instruments were white on black with a raised center and recessed numbers. The knee-bolster effect on the lower edge of the dash was also typical.

The real objection was that the profile of the new coupe did not continue the smooth fastback lines of the Giulietta Sprint. Certainly, my own reaction to the new coupe style was one of disappointment. When I recalled this fact as a columnist for the *Owner* magazine, I received a heated response from one member saying that the new bodystyle was most certainly an instant hit.

How time does cloud our perceptions. When introduced, the new coupe style was considered uglier than its Giulietta precedent. The turnaround in appreciating this bodystyle is remarkable, I think, in automotive history.

Remembering its doubtful acceptance, it's especially instructive to read contemporary road tests of the new Bertone Giulia Sprint GT. *Road & Track*, in December 1964, established a genteel approach: rave about the car's handling, its engine and transmission, but give only a factual description of the bodywork. Even through 1966, this formula was followed. *Motor*'s July 13 review of the new 1750 coupe did not even mention styling, concentrating instead on the car's superb mechanicals.

Certainly, first-year production figures show that the Giulietta-style coupe attracted many more buyers than the newer style: 3,388 Giulia 1600 Sprints were produced in 1963, compared to only 842 Sprint GTs.

When did we learn to love the GTV? Just as soon as the Alfetta coupe was introduced in 1975.

There's a working, if unspoken, rule that any new Alfa Romeo is considered devolutionary by most of the marque's enthusiasts. I suspect that the 6C1500 of 1927 was derided as a toy compared to the eminently reliable RL Series it replaced.

The body is now considered by some as one of the most beautiful cars ever produced by any maker, and it is this Giulia coupe that is now the cornerstone of the Giulia's charm: a true grand touring car, with a twin-cam 1600 cc engine carrying dual sidedraft Weber carburetors and giving the capability of traversing long trips at high speeds in absolute confidence and comfort.

Alfa Romeo did two things to correct the coupe situation. It reintroduced the Giulietta-style fastback coupe with a 1290 cc version of the Giulia engine in March 1964; that is, it virtually brought back the Giulietta. This model was called the Giulia 1300 Sprint. The car is significant in another way than in simply giving us back the Giulietta; it also established a precedent, unique to the Giulia line, of a proliferation of engine sizes for a single basic bodystyle. The tendency reached its extreme in 1974 when Alfa Romeo offered the coupe in 2.0, 1.6 and 1.3 liter displacements.

To keep the new bodystyle before the enthusiast, Alfa Romeo began campaigning, in 1965, GTA racing versions of the Giulia Sprint GT throughout Europe. The racing successes of the new bodystyle helped build public acceptance, as did a convertible model, the GTC.

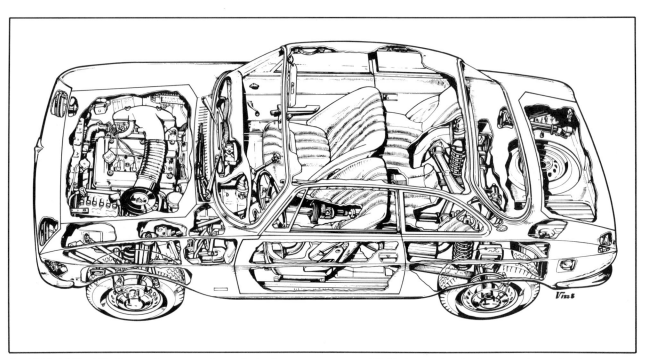

In 1962–1963, Alfa Romeo began work on designing a new coupe to replace the Giulietta-bodied Giulia Sprint, which had made its debut in 1962. This drawing of the new Giulia's mechanicals came from the factory archives.

Mechanical Specifications

The early sales fiasco of the Giulia Sprint GT coupe is a curious detail in the history of what has proved to be an overwhelmingly successful design. The compact body tucked in both fore and aft while a sharp crease ran along the side of the body adding both grace and lightness to the design. The greenhouse had a significantly greater glass area than the Giulietta coupe and helped provide a much more comfortable driving experience.

The seats of the Giulia coupe were deeply contoured and the dash was cleanly and efficiently laid out. Like the Giulietta coupe, the driver sat close to the floor with legs stretched forward, and there was a somewhat unnerving sense of sitting high in the car.

The Giulietta coupe was a breakthrough design in that it was the first car to offer true, low-cost, Gran Turismo capabilities. The grand touring car was intended to carry two people cross-country over a variety of roads with high average speeds, survivable comforts and good reliability. GT cars contemporary with the Giulietta included Lancia, Maserati, Ferrari, Porsche and Aston Martin. These early GT cars were far from ideal: Ferrari tended to stress higher speeds than comfort, while Aston proved slightly longer on comfort than reliability.

The Giulia added a significant gain in reliability and performance to the Giulietta Sprint's capabilities while offering superior creature comforts to almost any other true GT. It lacked only the absolute top speed of the much more expensive GTs.

The diminutive size of the Giulia Sprint GT and its derivations was another part of its charm (especially since the 2600 coupe was an almost identical design made larger). It was nimble on the road and encouraged a sense of oneness between driver and car—you truly "put it on" like a glove, and the fit was comfortable, indeed. The large expanse of legroom in the pre 1969 coupes was a novelty for the era and contributed to long-trip comfort for the passenger.

The Giulia Sprint GT was a true 2+2, meaning that there was a pair of seats at the rear that could be used (in an emergency) by two people. Because the coupe was capable of seating four, it could race in the sedan class in the United States. Thus, we watched Giulias warring with BRE Datsun 510 sedans on tracks all over the United States.

The driver position of most Alfa Romeos is quite different from many other cars, and demands an arms-out, legs-up approach. The new coupe was even more demanding in this respect than its Giulietta predecessor. An *Autocar* article dated October 9, 1960, commented on the position relative to *Willum*, a GT 1300 with British plates (WLM39G): "*Willum* . . . had been made for a particularly deformed specimen of the Darwinian ape who is

The Giulia GTV was introduced in 1967 with three more horsepower than the Giulia Sprint GT. Still, above all the GTV was a trim package upgrade over the Sprint GT with a new three-bar front grille replacing the Sprint GT's latticework grille. An ivory-and-green cloisonne Alfa Romeo quadrifoglio emblem was mounted on the C-pillar. These early cars had only two headlamps.

Italian Standard Man for most Latin car interior designers . . . [he] has very short legs, a stocky trunk and long arms. [In the GT 1300 he has] the right leg considerably shorter than his left; the accelerator pedal is therefore some way back from the brake and clutch. He is a strong enough fellow however, happily applying nearly 50 lb. of pedal effort over 6 in. every time he de-clutches. Not being as healthy, I found this tiring in traffic. Not being the same shape, my right leg had to remain partly unsupported and there wasn't enough rearward seat movement by about 2 in. My head brushed the roof. If I reclined the seat enough to clear, then I could hardly reach the wheel or gearlever."

A similar comment popped up in *Road & Track*'s August 1972 test of the 2000 GTV: "Other long-standing faults of the GTV's people accommodations are not corrected. The driver position, for instance, is something not a single staff member finds comfortable, and the trouble stems from the relation of seat, steering wheel and pedals as we have often pointed out."

The stock configuration for all of the early Giulias was a Solex twin-throat downdraft carburetor and five-speed transmission. The five-speed Giulia transmission was especially appreciated and a lot of Giulia transmissions have since been retrofitted to the Giulietta, which had only four forward speeds. Virtually all the Giulias imported to the United States were equipped with twin Weber DCOE carburetors, the same basic setup that graced the Veloce Giuliettas.

The initial Giulia coupe suspension, like the body, was identical to the 101 Series Giulietta. However, with the new 105 Series bodystyle, both front and rear suspensions were revised.

The GT Veloce engine bay. Power-boosted brakes were an innovation for this model: the booster diaphragm was in the upper left-hand corner. Note that the camshaft cover was dished to clear the air cleaner plumbing which ran over it.

The 105 Series Giulia front suspension had a lower A-arm, with trailing and transverse links locating the top of the suspension geometry. At the rear, a large T-shaped member controlled the side-to-side motion of the solid axle. While early Giulias had three-shoe drum front brakes (with 2¾ in. wide shoes), models built beginning late in 1963 featured Dunlop disc brakes on all four wheels. In 1967, the brake system was changed from Dunlop to ATE, a much more refined system.

Lubricated suspension points were eliminated in favor of permanently lubricated fittings and

The GT Veloce interior offered plenty of space. It did not have the center console of the later models. Several seat styles decorated the GTV interior. The original, shown here, offered shallow buckets with rather plain trim.

The GTV dash was a single concave plane of real wood veneer. It was appealing because it suggested a no-frills sports car of great capability.

rubber bushings. Early failures of some sealed joints prompted brave owners to add grease fittings, hoping to relieve squeaks and seizures. If you own a Giulia that has grease fittings added, it's important to maintain them regularly. You may wish also to dismantle the joint at some time to verify that the spindle on which the bush fits was not damaged by the drill bit when the fitting was added. The most failure-prone suspension link is the forward joint located near the headlamps in the fenderwell. Rough roads will cause this joint to fail rather quickly. Fortunately, its replacement is quite simple.

Giulia Sprint GT Veloce

In 1966, Alfa Romeo felt that it was an opportune time to reintroduce the Sprint GT and so offered a virtually identical "new" model, the Giulia Sprint GT Veloce, now known universally as the GTV. This time, the magic worked; 6,128 were produced in the first year and the bodystyle became widely accepted.

The GTV developed 109 hp compared to the 106 hp of the Sprint GT. Part of the horsepower increase can be attributed to some basic research into the gas-flow dynamics of the cylinder head. Alfa Romeo had been experimenting with various port sizes and found that a slightly smaller port increased fuel mixing because higher velocities were involved. As a result, the 1966 GTV has smaller inlet ports than the previous model.

In its February 24, 1967 issue, *Autosport* magazine compared the new Sprint GT Veloce to the Giulia GT: "The GTV employs the same body shell, suspension and transmission as the Giulia GT, but the power output has been increased by 3 bhp (theoretically—it certainly feels more). Yet surprisingly there is simply no comparison between the GT and the GTV, for the very minor alterations make the Veloce a much better car. Around Lake Garda the improvements were not that noticeable but the cars were brand new.... The GTV is the latest and the best of the current range of Alfa Romeos I have driven, the Giulia TI Super being my previous favorite."

Handling has always been one of Alfa Romeo's strengths, and the GTV offered exceptional handling. In the *Road & Track* test of July 1967, we

Initial reaction to the new Giulia coupe body styling was lukewarm at best, and so Alfa Romeo attempted to promote the new series by taking it racing in the hopes of winning the enthusiast's heart by winning races. In 1965, the GTA was introduced, based on the Sprint GT and GTV. No other manufacturer has created an all-out race car that so nearly duplicated the appearance of a regular production car. Only the plain grille, skinny doorhandles and the unique, magnesium-alloy wheels indicated that this was a special car.

read that "even a Porsche owner ungrudgingly approved the entire Alfa gestalt, and spoke highly of its quick, precise handling and instant recovery through a badly chuck-holed stretch of dirt road. And a former Chrysler engineer tried a brief test ride, returned wondering 'how the devil do they do that with a live rear axle,' then forthwith demanded more time for a really thorough examination."

Giulia GTA

The Giulietta Veloce showed us how the factory thought a racing Alfa Romeo should be built. The GTA, a GTV look-alike, represents the auto maker's graduate seminar in going fast. As dramatic and beautiful as the Zagato-bodied Giulia race cars were, they were not the mainstay of Alfa Romeo's fortunes on the track. That honor fell to the GTA, where A stood for *alleggerita*, which translates to "lightened." The car was introduced at the 1965 Amsterdam auto show.

It's my contention that the GTA was first used to accustom the world to Bertone's notchback styling. The GTAs were wonderfully successful on the racecourse, winning the Touring Class Group 2 European Manufacturers Championship in 1966, 1967 and 1968, and frequently humbling cars of much larger displacements.

In spite of their undoubted racing successes, of all exotic Alfa Romeos, the GTA is perhaps the most practical. Several enthusiasts have used them as streetable passenger cars.

While the original Giulietta Veloce retained much of the stock sheet metal, the GTA's body was more extensively modified with aluminum panels so that only the structural members of the body remained steel. Even the top was an aluminum sheet riveted to the steel door frames. Since the

The GTA was campaigned aggressively throughout Europe and took home countless trophies. For the most part, the cars needed little modification to reach the starting grid as they came from the factory with a highly modified 1600 cc Giulia engine and aluminum-alloy lightweight body panels. This was Pianta's first-place GTA running in the second division group of the Jolly Club Turismo Championship held at Monza in 1968. Note the large tires and flared rear fenders.

aluminum was stamped using the same dies as the steel panels, the appearance of the GTA was almost perfectly stock.

The unique grillework and doorhandles were a giveaway, however, to this pursang racer. And I have always enjoyed the quiet pleasure of discovering the little row of rivets hiding behind the rain gutter along the roofline.

With the aluminum-alloy body panels and all sound-deadening material deleted, dry weight of the standard GTA was 1,639 lb., down some 450 lb.

from the GTV. The Autodelta race-prepped GTA Corsa weighed a mere 1,540 lb.

Mechanically, the GTA's most obvious differences were the twin-plug cylinder head and less obviously, the sliding-block rear differential locator.

The twin-plug cylinder head replaced the single, centrally located spark plug in each cylinder with one in front of and another to the rear of the narrow portion between the intake and exhaust valves. The primary purpose of fitting two plugs per

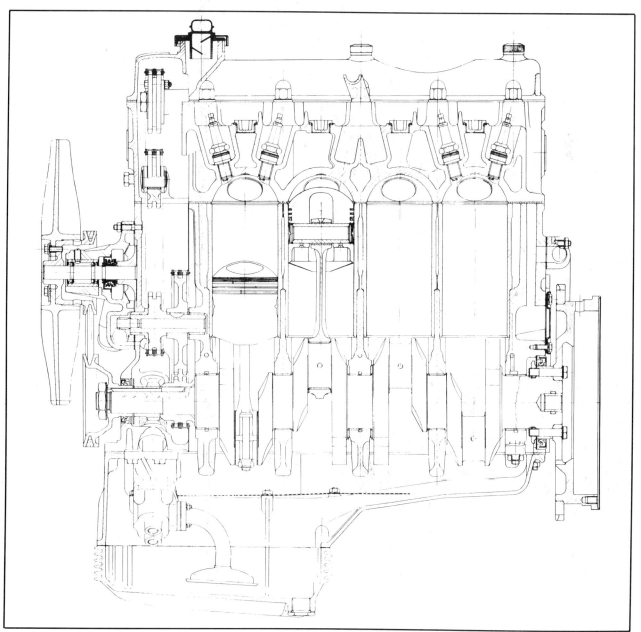

The most distinguishing characteristic of the GTA was its twin-plug cylinder head, which assured that the charge was fully and evenly burned even at high engine speeds. While every other part of the engine received *special attention to improve reliability there were no dimensional changes. Thus, most GTA parts were interchangeable with regular production items.*

A close-up of the twin-plug GTA cylinder head. The spark plugs closest to each other actually fire in different cylinders.

Autodelta: Alfa Romeo Racing

While Alfa Romeo would not have a true marketing department until near the end of the Giulia's lifespan, it did have a strong race department in the form of Autodelta.

From its inception, Alfa Romeo had raced its cars under its own banner and under the banner of independent race teams that were contracted to race for the factory. The earliest and most prolific of these was Enzo Ferrari's Scuderia Ferrari, based in Modena. In 1938, Alfa Romeo brought the racing effort within the factory walls, forming a race department called Alfa Corse.

In the 1950s and early 1960s, the Giulietta became the mainstay of Alfa Romeo racing, campaigned by the works and by the numerous performance-tuning shops that were common throughout northern Italy. These tuners were known as the *preparatori*, or "preparers." Carlo Abarth was certainly the most famous of these, and he worked primarily with Fiat among other marques, although his tuned exhaust systems were available for Giuliettas as well. Chief among the Alfa Romeo tuners was Virgilio Conrero's shop in Turin that was at the leading edge of high-performance modifications for the Giulietta. Others in the ranks included the Scuderia Sant'Ambroeus' tuner Piero Facetti, former Ferrari test driver Enrico Nardi and Almo Bosato.

In 1963, with the arrival of the new Giulia, Alfa Romeo contracted its race work with a new competition firm known as Autodelta. The goal was to mount a consistent, intensive and organized attack on the FIA Touring Car class championship and to develop a race version of the Sprint GT.

Autodelta had grown out of the Alfa Romeo dealership run by Ludovico Chizzola and his brother that was based in Udine, north of Venice. Work began on developing the Giulia Tubolare Zagato for competition in unison with Alfa Romeo's new sports car development center based in Milan. Initially, the firm was known as simply Delta, but the name changed as the works grew in stature.

The fame of Autodelta rested primarily on the shoulders of its new chief engineer, Carlo Chiti. Chiti had been the experimental design engineer at Ferrari, responsible for the development of the front-engined Dino Formula 1 racer that won the world championship in 1958 and Ferrari's first mid-engined Grand Prix racer that Phil Hill took to the championship in 1961. Chiti left Ferrari in 1962 as one of the leaders of the famous palace revolt, and helped found ATS to build sports and race cars for Count Volpi's Scuderia Serenissima. He came to Autodelta in 1963.

In 1965, Alfa Romeo selected Autodelta as its official factory race development wing, and the shop moved to Settimo Milanese, nearby the new Arese factory. In 1966, Autodelta became part of Alfa Romeo.

Chiti provided the genius that spurred Autodelta. During the lifespan of the Giulia series, Autodelta worked with the factory in creating and testing race versions of the TZ, TZ 2, GTA, GTAP, GTA-SA, GTA Junior and the GTAm.

With Fiat's purchase of Alfa Romeo, Autodelta was brought further into the corporate fold, being renamed Alfa Corse, a revival of the race team's name of the 1930s.

cylinder was to ensure that all the air-fuel mixture was burned in a controlled manner for maximum efficiency. In addition, the absence of a spark plug in the narrow channel between the valve seats removed one of the most common spots for stress cracking. Moving the plugs out of the way also allowed slightly larger valve-seat diameters.

The sliding-block differential was really a back-up device. On cars with leaf rear springs, the springs themselves are strong enough to locate the axle properly without additional suspension elements. However, a coil-spring suspension requires links in order to maintain the proper wheel geometry in a turn. The front-to-back, or lateral location of Alfa Romeo's rear axle was handled by two trailing track rods attached at the outboard ends of the axles. The front ends of the track rods attached to the body just behind the driver's seat. Side-to-side, or transverse location, was handled by a large T-shaped unit that attached to the body at two points on the rear-wheel arch and at one point near the top of the differential housing. Virtually all of Alfa Romeo's superior solid-axle road-holding ability came from the design of these links.

Alfa Romeo's standard rear-suspension links were set in rubber to reduce the amount of road

In 1966, a new race series for production cars was sparked in the United States as Trans-Am racing, and the Alfa Romeo GTA would go on to record some of its greatest victories in the series. In the first season of racing, Horst Kwech and Gaston Andrey tied to sweep the series championship, both running in GTAs against Ford Mustangs and Plymouth Barracudas. In later years, the American muscle cars would rule the series, but Alfa Romeos would take the 2.0 liter class trophies. Here is race action at Marlboro, Maryland, in 1966, with car number 37 driven by Sam Posey and Harry Theodorocropulous to first place. A second GTA followed.

The first-place overall trophy was awarded to Dick Davenport and his GTA at the 1971 American Road Race of Champions. Note the extensive wheel flares worked into the body.

The dashboard of the GTA spoke of the car's production-based identity with such amenities as the wood fascia plate and the carpeting on the floor. The gauges were easy to read and aimed straight at the driver, and the stock GTA steering wheel was a lovely aluminum-alloy three-spoke affair rimmed in wood.

vibration to the passenger compartment. For the racing GTA, improved transverse rear-axle location, and thereby better road-holding, could be achieved by adding a sliding block. In this setup, a sturdy tab on the back of the rear axle slid up and down in a grooved block attached to the body, eliminating any possibility of transverse movement. In fact, the GTA's solid-axle rear suspension was infinitely more successful than the more-exotic but underdeveloped independent rear suspension of the TZ.

The sliding block needed constant lubrication, of course, and so did have a drawback. You'll occasionally find racing GTVs with an extra transverse link (Panhard rod) added to the rear, which does essentially the same thing as the GTA's sliding block. The disadvantage of the Panhard rod is that, having a radius, it ensures some small transverse-axle movement over its working range.

From 1965 through 1969, only 493 GTAs were built, fifty of them with right-hand drive. There was no breakdown on how many of the Autodelta race-prepped GTA Corsa cars were constructed.

Giulia GTAP

Wanting to remain homologated for the 1600 Touring Car European race class, Alfa Romeo sought to further modify its GTA by constructing a series of cars with lighter-weight plastic-fiberglass body panels. Just as Autodelta built a series of four Tubolare Zagatos with fiberglass bodywork, the race team again did the modifications to the GTAP, with the P standing for *plastica*. While the aluminum-alloy bodied GTA Corsa tipped the scales at 1,540 lb., the GTAP weighed 115 lb. less at 1,425 lb.

The engine of the GTAP was modified in typical Autodelta practice with a large air plenum covering the ram tubes of the dual sidedraft Weber carburetors. The plenum was fed through a hole in the grille. The fusebox was remounted on the firewall to make room for the gigantic plenum. Enzo Giobbe

The engine was still the GTA 1600 unit but modified in typical Autodelta practice.

There are no records as to exactly how many GTAP cars were constructed, although the number is probably in the single digits.

Giulia GTA Sovralimentata

Early in 1967 a GTA prototype was created that had forced induction. The model was termed the GTA-SA, where SA stood for *sovralimentata*,

A rare GTAP 1600 cc racer prepared by Autodelta, the official factory racing group. The car was built in August 1967 for FIA Group 2 racing with fiberglass—hence the Tipo 32P "Plastica" designation—body panels to save weight over the aluminum-bodied GTA. The result was a dry weight of a mere 1,425 lb. This was believed to be the final GTA 1600 cc car built by Autodelta. Enzo Giobbe

Interior of the GTAP was partially stripped for further weight savings. The driver's seat was a fiberglass shell, and the speedometer was removed and blanked off, leaving only the tachometer. The side windows were sliding plexiglass sheets. Enzo Giobbe

literally "above the limit." It is hard to characterize this engine as either turbocharged or supercharged, for we usually mean exhaust-driven when talking about turbochargers and crankshaft-driven when talking about superchargers.

The centrifugal compressors—there were two—of the unit were turbines, but their drive was quite unconventional. An axial hydraulic pump was chain-driven off the crankshaft and the output of this pump was used to turn the drive turbine of the compressor. In practice, the unit acted as a crankshaft-driven turbocharger.

The purpose of this unique arrangement was to reduce the amount of lag normally experienced with exhaust-gas-driven turbochargers. Since the driving turbine of a turbocharger is powered by exhaust gases, there is a noticeable lag between pressing the throttle at low speeds and benefiting from the turbine boost. Some of this lag is unavoidable, since it comes from the need of the turbine to overcome the inertia of its mass and "spool up" to a speed where it can compress gases. Another source of the lag is the time it takes for the higher combustion pressures of acceleration to be expressed as higher exhaust-gas velocity; depending on exhaust gases just takes time. Finally, at low speeds, the exhaust-driven turbocharger is virtually inoperative because the energy of the exhaust gases simply isn't great enough to turn the turbine.

The oil-driven turbo was an effort to moderate the time lag and improve low-speed boost. The pressure differentials of the pump-driven oil over

Working with the 1600 cc of the GTA, Alfa Romeo created a supercharged version called the GTA-SA, with SA standing for Sovralimentato, translated literally as "above the limit." The cars were constructed for Group 5 racing, with ten examples built in 1967 and 1968. The twin superchargers were driven by a hydraulic pump at some 100,000 rpm. With compression of 10.5:1, power was 250 hp at 7500 rpm. The superchargers fed pressurized air into a box which pressurized the dual Weber carburetors.

the engine's operating range were much less than those of the exhaust gases, so the turbine tended to stay near speeds that actually produced compression, even when engine speeds were relatively low. The output of the compressors blew into an air plenum which supplied two sidedraft Weber carburetors. The result was a 1570 cc engine that created 220 hp at 7500 rpm for a top speed of some 150 mph.

The engine was similar to that of the GTA 1600 unit it was derived from, but the bore and stroke at 86x67.5 mm was much more oversquare than the standard 78x82 mm of the Giulias. Compression followed that of the GTA Corsa at 10.5:1.

With the GTA's aluminum-alloy body but adding on the weight of the dual superchargers, the GTA-SA weighed 1,716 lb.

A total of ten GTA-SA cars was constructed, destined to enter FIA Group 5 racing in Europe. In 1967, a GTA-SA won first place overall in the Hockenheim 100 mile endurance race. Other victories followed in France and Belgium in 1968, but the factory and Autodelta soon shifted their focus to the new, larger-displacement GTAm.

Touring GTC

When the Giulietta was first planned in the early 1950s, Alfa Romeo asked both Bertone and Pinin Farina to submit competing designs. The prototype Bertone Giulietta Spider survives in the United States, and there are several Pinin Farina coupes on the 1900 chassis to suggest what the losing coupe design might have looked like. Thus, we can imagine what Alfa Romeos would have looked like if the car maker had reversed the awards.

But Alfa Romeo settled for letting Bertone build its coupes and Pininfarina its spiders. The GTC, a thousand examples of which were produced between 1965 and 1966, is an exception to this rule and shows us how neatly the Bertone coupe could be converted to a ragtop. The car was introduced at the 1965 Geneva auto show, and was basically a strengthened Sprint GT coupe chassis

The GTA-SA supercharged 1600 cc engine. Below the distributor, the additional oil pump used to drive the hydraulic turbines was mounted. The two turbos were driven by an hydraulic pump to divorce turbine speed from exhaust gas energy. The result was a more even boost and better low-end performance.

with its fixed top removed for a soft top. The curious thing about the conversion, however, is that it was given to Carrozzeria Touring, and not Bertone.

Touring had been a favorite bodybuilder for Alfa Romeo up to the 1900 but had failed to enter the competition for the Giulietta or its descendants. In spite of the fact that Touring did not have a hand in Giulietta production, the Touring-bodied 1900 Super Sprint coupe of 1955 certainly anticipated the slender nose treatment of the Giulietta Pinin Farina convertible.

In the early 1960s, all of Italy suffered from worker strikes and Touring was stuck with an eighty-percent walkout. Its inability to meet existing orders led to cancellations and eventual receivership for the company. In 1965, Touring's total workforce was 263, compared to 403 only a year earlier. Production continued at surprisingly high levels during receivership, but the company was finally closed on January 31, 1967. Some of Touring's assets were purchased by Alfa Romeo.

Giulia 1750 GTV

Alfa Romeo had done the right thing by waiting patiently for its customers' tastes to mature,

and the 1967 GTV was received well enough to establish it as the standard Alfa Romeo coupe. In January 1968, it received a larger engine that was later introduced in the United States in 1969 with Spica fuel injection. The bore and stroke of the new engine were 80x88.5 mm and the total displacement, at 1779 cc, qualified the car to be called an 1800. Instead, recalling Vittorio Jano's masterpiece, the car was called the 1750. *Autosport* magazine, in its August 16, 1968 issue, did pause to compare the old and new 1750s: "the greatest change is ease of handling. The old supercharged car had to be steered with sensitive fingers and the gear-change demanded extreme precision. The latest model, in spite of having one carburetor choke per cylinder, is quite remarkably flexible and will pull hard at very low speeds. For this reason, it is an ideal dual-purpose car."

Horsepower was up to 132 at 5500 rpm and there was a significant increase in torque of 134 lb-ft at 3000 rpm compared to 103 lb-ft at the same revs for the 1600 Giulia. A hydraulically operated clutch replaced the mechanically actuated unit of the 1600 Giulia and the pedals became pendant rather than floor-mounted, although right-hand-

Exhaust side of the GTA-SA engine. The two braided stainless-steel oil lines would connect to an oil cooler in the car. Note that the capacity of the sump had been increased by the addition of a finned spacer. The bell-housing was a magnesium-alloy casting.

drive coupes retained floor-mounted pedals. A rear antiroll bar was also new. In the middle of the production run, the crank bearing journals were Tuftrided to increase durability.

Continuing with *Autosport* magazine's evaluation of the 1750: "The new engine gives a lot more performance, with improved acceleration right through the range and a maximum speed within two mph of the magic 120. The longer stroke is noticeable, the unit being obviously busy at 6000 rpm, and one would certainly not attempt to emulate the 8000 rpm of the early Giulietta. The extra punch is so great that this is a much better engine for touring, though it would be sacrilege not to make proper use of the delectable five-speed gearbox."

While the leading edge of the GTV hood had been raised above the plane of the nose, the 1750s were distinguished by a flat hood line. A wire-mesh grille with a single chrome bar carried four headlamps, and a different dash featured a large speedometer and tachometer carried in their own pods, while the water-temperature and fuel-level gauges were located in a center console, which also carried the shift lever and accessory switches.

The seats of the 1969 1750 GTV were perhaps the best—or at least the most attractive—of any fitted to the coupes. They were deeply contoured, and solid vinyl inserts formed heavy bolsters which allowed some air circulation while seated.

Giulia 2.0 Liter GTV

In mid-1971, the four-cylinder engine was enlarged still further to almost two liters. The bore and stroke became 84x88.5 mm, achieved by modifying the centerlines of the cylinders within the block, and larger valves were fitted. The new engine was fitted to the Spider, sedan and GTV. To signal the 2.0 liter version, the grille on the GTV became a series of horizontal bars from which the Alfa Romeo grille outline was embossed. A restyled interior featured different seats and a dash layout that put the smaller fuel-level and coolant-temperature gauges in their own pods between the tachometer and speedometer.

The 2.0 liter developed 131 hp at 5500 rpm and 134 lb-ft of torque at 3000 rpm. You will note that, initially, the larger 1962 cc engine developed 1 hp less than its 1779 cc predecessor. That was a nod to engine exhaust emissions which were beginning to

When the 1750 engine became the full-size Alfa Romeo, there was room to offer the Junior with a 1.6 liter engine, making it identical in specification to the original GT Veloce. The cap-type wheel covers dated this as a 1970–1971 vehicle, while the two headlamps and single chrome spear on the grille made it a Junior. You can't tell from the body work whether it had a 1.3 or 1.6 engine.

bedevil even Alfa Romeo. The series reached its nadir with the 1980-1981 Spiders which, in the United States at least, were so heavily emission-controlled that they became somewhat docile touring cars with an emphasis on comfort rather than performance. The performance deficit was largely rectified by the introduction of Bosch Electronic Fuel Injection (EFI) in 1982 on the four-cylinder spider and in 1981 on the new GTV-6 coupe.

The GTV was replaced by Giugiaro's restyled Alfetta GT in 1975, a change lamented by all true Alfa Romeo enthusiasts. The GTV continued to be marketed, however, until 1977 and the total production of the 2.0 liter model was 37,459.

By the time the bodystyle was retired, the GTV was growing long in the tooth, indeed. Even in 1972, *Modern Motor* magazine observed of the 2.0 liter GTV: "The Alfa Romeo 2000 GTV is a very good 1964

grand touring car—produced in 1972. In the old days, it surprised the world with (for then) revolutionary handling, with good ride, sensitive steering isolated from road shock and a remarkably clean, crisp, body style.

"Today it is the same—as it was in 1964. Certainly it has more power than its 1600 great grand-pappy and it has a few more refinements and creature comforts. But only a few more."

One of the most rapidly appreciating Alfa Romeos in the United States is the 1974 2000 Coupe. At current prices (Spring 1991) a good 1974 coupe is bringing nearly $10,000, almost double the value of a 1973 model in similar condition. There are several explanations for the phenomenon, all of which taken together may explain the price disparity between two adjacent years' cars. I say all,

When the 2.0 liter engine was introduced, all the GT coupes adopted a new grille and dash treatment. This is the final version of the GT Junior with grillework identical to the larger-displacement coupes. The 1.3 liter GT Juniors were 105 Series bodies powered by engines with 101 Series Giulietta displacement—the bores and strokes *were identical. These later engines were not exact replicas of the 101, however. They carried 105 Series numbering and incorporated the design improvements of the later-series engines, including smaller ports and camshafts versus those in the 1600 cars.*

because I don't think any single factor is responsible for the disparity.

The most significant contributor to its value is that the 1974 model marked the end of a bodystyle in the United States that was, next to the Giulietta Sprint Coupe, the most widely loved design of the modern era. I believe that much of the value of the 1974 coupe represents a cumulative respect for the series.

The last model of a series is frequently the most collectible. There is some kind of vague expectation that all the bugs have been worked out. Additionally, the 1974 is the most powerful of the Spica fuel-injected Alfa Romeos. It was also the first of the marque's coupes to offer Campagnolo aluminum-alloy wheels.

Giulia GTAm

As the stock Giulia engine grew into the 1750 and then the 2.0 liter, the GTA was able to take advantage of the larger displacements for even more power. The GTAm (for *maggiorato*, or "enlarged") is basically a GTA with a 1750 or 2.0 liter engine.

The 1750 GTAm was introduced in 1968 and the 2.0 liter version in 1971. Modification work was delegated to Autodelta, Alfa Romeo's racing arm, and more than forty GTAm cars were turned out. Most of the GTAms were fitted with wider tires to help improve traction. As a result of the wider tires, fender flares became common on the GTAms. Some of these were pop-riveted on and others were neatly faired into the bodywork.

Problems with the GTAm fuel-delivery system on the race engines were encountered. The stock Spica fuel-injection unit had an upper limit to the amount of fuel it could deliver, and I suspect that this limit was passed with the no-holds-barred design of the GTAm engines. Thus, instead of the stock Spica fuel-injection unit, many GTAm cars used Lucas Mk2 sliding-plate fuel injection. In the traditional design, the throttle plate pivoted

To keep competitive, the GTA's 1600 cc engine was enlarged, first to 1750 cc and then to a full two liters. With the larger engine, the car's name was changed to GTAm. The steel chassis of the 1750 GTV was used as the basis, with aluminum-alloy wide-arched fenders and fiberglass hood, rear deck lid and doors. The dry weight was reduced to just over 2,000 lb. Horsepower for the 1750 cc engine was 220 hp and 240 hp for the 2.0 liter. In all, forty GTAm cars were built by the factory in 1970 and 1971. This is the Hezemans 2000 GTAm taking first overall at the 1974 Monza four-hour endurance race.

The first and second series of GT Junior bodywork differed little. Models from 1967 to 1970 bore the side marker lights, hood scoop and the turn signals set into the front fender.

Beginning in 1971 and running until the end of production in 1974, the GT Junior was redesigned for a third series of bodywork, featuring small, round side marker lights, a hood that was smoothed into the front end and turn signals mounted atop the front bumper.

around the throttle shaft. At wide-open throttle, even though the plate was parallel to the throat of the carburetor, it still offered some restriction to gas flow. A sliding plate works like a guillotine and, at wide-open throttle, is completely withdrawn from the bore and offers no restriction at all to the gas flow. Its drawback is that additional space is required to accommodate the sliding plate. For maximum power efficiency, however, the sliding-plate design is most efficient.

With the arrival of the GTAm 2000 in 1971, Autodelta had tuned the heavily modified GTV 2000 engine to 220 hp at 7200 rpm for a top speed of 138 mph. By 1972, the engine was producing 240 hp at 7500 rpm, pushing the top speed over 140 mph.

To handle the additional horsepower and speed, 9x13 in. tires had been fitted, requiring the riveted-on wheel arches. Even with a majority of the body panels made in fiberglass and plexiglass mounted in the side windows, the GTAm weighed in dry at 2,068 lb. in 1971.

A total of forty GTAm cars in 1750 and 2000 form were constructed.

Giulia GT Junior

Giulia sedan, coupe and spider models were co-marketed with 1.3 liter engines. The displacement of the Giulietta at just under 1300 cc was no accident. In Italy, cars are taxed on engine size, and a tax break came at 1300 cc. Thus, when the factory introduced the 1600 cc Giulia it also put Alfa Romeo ownership into the next higher tax group. It regained its tax advantage and a whole category of buyers by reintroducing a sub 1300 cc vehicle.

In September 1966, Alfa Romeo invited the motoring press to its test track at Balocco to try the new 1300 GT Junior. This car carried the GTV body, but its grille featured a single chrome spear. Its engine had a bore and stroke of 74x75 mm and developed 89 hp at 6000 rpm. The Juniors were a desirable combination of comfort and performance. While they certainly did not have the top speed of their big brothers, they gave almost equal

The dash of the GT Junior also went through several series of revisions, beginning with the first series that had the gauges set into a single flat piece of wood veneer styled like the Sprint GT. Shown here is the second series *with two dash pods and a two-spoke steering wheel. The third series used a three-spoke wheel and the twin pods. The final series retained the three-spoke steering wheel but used a new dash layout with six dash pods.*

The 1300 GT Junior powerplant featured dual Weber carburetors and a cold-air box that almost dwarfed the engine. Note that this car had brakes with a dual hydraulic system working through a single booster.

The Giulia Junior series was introduced in 1966. From left, the GT Junior 1300, the 1300 TI and a 1600 Giulia Super at right. The 1300 cc series was designed to fit under an Italian automobile tax bracket, which was based on engine displacement. Like the GTV, the GT Junior was introduced with two headlamps, but used a single-bar grille. Wheels were stamped steel with chrome wheel covers. The early coupes had an interesting hood scoop cut into the front-end bodywork supposedly to feed air under the front edge of the hood. But, like the early Giulia Spiders, the hood scoop was blanked off.

performance otherwise. To put them into perspective, we frequently lament the passing of the simple, inexpensive bare-bones sporty car; with their small displacement and slightly Spartan interiors, the Juniors were just exactly that.

The Junior series spawned two especially noteworthy cars, the GTA Junior and the Zagato Junior, both of which later were also produced with 1600 cc engines.

In 1967, *Motor* magazine did a road test and found that "The 1300 is a light and easy car to drive, and fun too. If you want to keep ahead of the larger cars you have to use the gearbox, but mostly the engine pulls sufficiently well throughout its wide range to keep going at a very respectable rate; good roadholding keeps average speeds up on cross-country trip.

"In performance the GT 1300 is about as fast as the Giulia TI saloon.... Very few 1300 cc production cars can top 100 mph—the Lotus Elite and Renault Gordini being two that spring to mind—and it is quite a tribute to the Alfa, which is essentially a fast tourer, that it can do this quite easily. On motorways the comfortable cruising speed is around 85-90 mph which can be maintained up

hill and down dale all day without the oil temperature rising further than 170 degrees F."

Autocar, in its April 10, 1969 issue, found that "The GT Junior returned a mean maximum speed of 102 mph, compared with 113 and 116 mph for the 1600 and 1750 equivalents. Its best one-way was 104 mph.... As frequently happens, the use of a smaller engine does not result in significant gains in economy. The overall figure of 24.4 mpg, although good in relation to the car's performance and the way we drove it, is little better than the 23.9 mpg of the 1750 GT Veloce."

A Spider 1300 Junior was introduced in 1968 and produced until 1972. In 1974, when the current engine for the Sprint was the 2.0 liter, Alfa Romeo introduced GT Juniors with 1.3 and 1.6 liter engines, thus reprising almost the entire Giulia line in a single model year.

Giulia GTA Junior

The relationship between the GT Junior and the GTA Junior was tenuous; the competition version of the 1300 GT was actually based on the GTA 1600.

A competition version of the GT Junior was introduced in 1968 as the GTA Junior with a dual-plug cylinder head and 1300 cc displacement. Beyond the shared displacement, the GTA Junior was based more closely on the GTA's 1600 cc engine than on the GT Junior's. Bore and stroke of the GT Junior was 74x75 mm, while that of the GTA Junior was oversquare with a bore and stroke of 78x67.5 mm. Horsepower differed less, however, with the GT Junior's 1300 cc pumping out 103 hp versus the GTA Junior's 110 hp, depending upon state of tune. The GTA Junior came from the factory trimmed with the snake decal on the hood, quadrifoglio decal on the front fender and a wide white stripe along the side.

Beginning in 1968, Alfa Romeo sought to challenge the FIA European Touring Car 1300 class, and so set out to build a 1300 racer. The engine displacement would be shared with the GT Junior that everyone could buy, but the bore and stroke of the engine differed dramatically. For the GT Junior, the engine was slightly undersquare at 74x75 mm bore and stroke; for the GTA Junior, the engine was far oversquare, measuring 78x67.5 mm, the same bore as the GTA 1600 but with a shorter stroke.

Other GTA 1600 modifications were carried over to the 1300, including the dual-ignition cylinder head. Power was rated between 96 and 160 hp at 6000 to 7800 rpm, depending upon state of tune and Autodelta elaboration. Power for the GT Junior was 89 hp.

Like the GTA 1600, the GTA Junior was built with generous use of high-strength lightweight aluminum-alloy body panels. All sound-deadening material was removed and the side windows were made of plexiglass. Total dry weight was 1,672 lb.

On the racetrack, the GTA Junior followed in the footsteps of its big brother as well. In 1972, the car swept the European Touring Car championship.

A total of 447 GTA Juniors were constructed from 1968 to 1972 using both dual Weber carburetion and later, the Spica mechanical fuel injection.

Living with a GTA Junior
By John Hoard

I have owned GTA 1300 Junior serial number 775854 since 1971. This car is one of the street run of homologation specials, built in 1968. The model's parts book is a supplement to the 1300 Junior, and the car shares many items with the GT Junior. Body parts are generally 105.30 (GT Junior). Where the GT Junior lists early and late parts, the GTA Junior uses the newer ones. In my opinion, it is the best balance of trim level and styling in the long series of Bertone coupes. The body exterior looks like a 1600 GTA, except the GTA's chrome ID badges are replaced by decals on the hood and GTA 1300 Junior script on the rear deck lid. Interior trim is black vinyl, no space-wasting console, no cigarette lighter. The floor covering is a single layer of black vinyl with rubber foot mats. No sound deadener here!

I have never weighed my car, but light weight is obvious all over. For example, there are no cover plates where the rear shocks are removed through the back seat.

Early GTAs had aluminum floor pans, which turned out to be a problem for strength after a while. All GTA Juniors have steel floor pans and rockers, with the rest of the body in aluminum.

My car was bought at 50,000 km and is now nearing 200,000 km (about 120,000 miles). It has been used for daily transportation (except in salty winters) since I bought it. The engine has been rebuilt a couple times and was recently changed for a 1750.

The 1300 is thoroughly gutless below 4000 rpm, but runs to incredible revs freely. The standard cams are the same as a 1969 1750 US engine so power peaks at 6000 rpm. The close-ratio gearbox is a delight from 25 mph to maximum speed (about 110 mph), but the tall first gear makes starting from rest painful at best. For autocrossing, the technique is to rev to 6000 rpm and pop the clutch, producing about 5 ft. of black marks and a serious bog! The driveline is solid and has taken that sort of abuse with only two relinings of the clutch. The original light-steel flywheel and pressure plate are still there, as are the driveshaft U-joints. The rear axle has never been out of the car.

Handling of this car is the best I have ever driven—and I've had access to a number of exotic machines. The balance is perfect. You can brake deep into corners and apply power early on exit. Either backing out sharply or tapping the brakes while near the limit will bring the tail out gradually with easy control of satisfying drifts. Every good thing about other Alfa Romeos is simply magnified here.

Original wheels are 14x5.5 in. steel with unique welded-on caps visually similar to the bolt-on ones on a 2000 GTV. I have used BWA 14x6s and presently have 15x6 in. Minilites on it. Original tires were 165x14 in. Michelin ZAs, and I've used 185/70x14s and now 195/50x15s for the 1750 engine. With the 1750 engine, the power matches the handling and the car is unbeatable for a fun-to-drive feeling.

There have been a few problems over the years, however. One year I was forced to drive it through the Michigan winter. Starting the car at 10 degrees below zero with the miniature, 25 amp hour battery (the largest possible as the oil cooler, headers and air cleaner leave little room) is an interesting exercise. The starter won't turn the engine at all unless the clutch is depressed. Even then, you can count the cylinders as the starter works against compression. Unless it needs a tune-up, the fifth cylinder starts every try. It takes about two minutes past frostbite to get us enough torque to turn the transmission oil! The heater fan makes plenty of noise, so you can tell the heater is on. Actually, heat output isn't bad if you're above 5000 rpm. The aluminum body, of course, immediately conducts any heat out of the car.

The most troublesome component has been the twin-plug ignition. The distributor cap has rather small separation between towers and the vent system tends to get clogged with dirt and grease. The result is arcing to ground and some plugs dropping out. There is a noticeable loss of power when one of the two plugs misfires, degrading to bad surge if several go out. The cost of caps and rotors is daunting, starting at about $50 when I bought the car and escalating to nearly $150 locally (Italian prices are still around $50).

There are two sets of points of the same beautiful Marelli style used in Ferrari 308s and other Italian exotica; incidentally, the Ferrari list price is cheaper than Alfa Romeo's. Each set of points has to be set for gap, and then timed. This is done with the distributor on a bench, since the upper ball bearing makes access difficult. However, once installed, the points are fantastic. I once went five years without having to so much as regap the points. Finally I had to replace the points because the outer ply of the five-ply point springs rusted through and shorted out one set of plugs.

Another problem is the shift lever. In addition to the usual early 105 transmission rattle at 4000 rpm or so (caused by the reverse lock-out rod rattling inside the shift lever) the GTA's ultralight shift lever is made of a thin-wall tube welded to a cast elbow to attach it to the transmission. The tube likes to break off at the elbow. I once drove home from work all the way in third.

One final problem is wear in the bushing at the front of the driveshaft where it locates on the transmission mainshaft. I have had to replace both driveshaft bushing and mainshaft in order to cure a massive high-speed vibration.

Otherwise, the car is unbelievably reliable. The brakes have been relined every 15,000 miles or so but the discs are original. Both of the dual, clicker-type fuel pumps are original.

We drove it from Detroit to Los Angeles for the national club meeting on the *Queen Mary* in 1975, about 2,400 miles each way. Ran the time trials and all, taking the overall men's award, then drove it home. With three people, trunk full of luggage and all, we got 27 mpg at about 80 mph, and total oil consumption of about 3 qt.

5

Zagato Giulias

Alfa Romeo and Zagato are a team with a magic that is unsurpassed. The relationship between the two companies is old and close: the most famous and desirable Alfa Romeos have bodies by Zagato, dating back to the mid-1920s. Indeed, the simple

Carrozzeria Zagato had a long history of building lightweight bodies for Alfa Romeo chassis. A precursor to the lightweight Giuliettas and Giulias was this Zagato-bodied 1900 CSS coupe. As with the Zagato-bodied Fiat Abarths of the same era, the coachbuilders constructed dual bubbles in the roof for the driver's and passenger's heads, all in an attempt to keep the roofline as low as possible for good aerodynamics.

conjunction of Alfa Romeo and Zagato means a car of great distinction and value.

The most recent efforts of Zagato have proved most controversial, and not representative in my estimation of Zagato's best work. Stylists are still learning to cope with the science of aerodynamics and have not achieved a good balance between art and science. At the same time, Zagato has been pushed to the edge by Alfa Romeo's apparent insistence on a striking, if not jarring approach to styling. If one is to use the ES 30 as the rule, then it would be appropriate to say that the Zagato-Alfa Romeo conjunction produces interesting, if not beautiful, cars. But the very definition of the classic roadster derives from the Zagato-bodied Alfa Romeos of the Jano era. Those cars were unmatched for their flowing beauty and sheer animal magnetism. The Giulia also benefited from Zagato's best work: the Tubolare Zagato Giulia coupes were certainly among the most beautiful cars ever created.

Carrozzeria Zagato

Information about Zagato the man is hard to obtain, and much of what is available is in Italian. For those dedicated to his study, the book by Gianfranco Fagiuoli and Guido Gerosa (*Zagato*, Roma 1969, ACI/Editrice dell'Automobile) provided a boy-racer rendition of the details of Zagato's life.

Ugo Zagato was born June 25, 1890, at Gavello in the province of Rovigo, Italy. His father died before he was born and his mother never remarried, so Ugo was the last of five brothers.

It was a time of grinding poverty in the Italian countryside and the only escape available to a young man was to enter a seminary. Thus, Zagato received his basic education at the seminary at Rovigo. He was fourteen when he left, so he had the equivalent of a classic ninth-grade education.

Immediately on his graduation from Rovigo, he left to find work in Germany. He worked as an apprentice in Cologne for four years only to be recalled to Italy to answer military conscription. Some basic flaw in the system allowed him to serve about forty days in the military with the Third Bersaglieri of Livorno and then be discharged.

Ugo Zagato decided to remain in Italy and seek employment in the auto industry. This was in 1909—the same year the French firm Darracq decided to build a version of its car for the Italian market. The following year, the Milan factory was bought by Italian businessmen to build the ALFA.

Zagato didn't hire into the upstart firm, however. He chose to work in Varese, Italy, for Carrozeria Varesina, a company founded in 1845 to build horse-drawn carriages. The company was expanding into bodywork for automobiles and had a few clients in France and Switzerland.

To improve his skills, Zagato began part-time studies at the Santa Marta School for Designers in Milan. One should not get the idea that Zagato found himself in the mainstream of the Italian automobile industry; the locus for that center was most definitely with Fiat in Torino. That is not to denigrate Milan, however, where one could find Isotta Fraschini, which in 1909 was the second-largest Italian car maker after Fiat.

As the Great War approached, Zagato moved to Turin where he worked for Pomilio di Torino designing airplanes. It was there that he learned the lightweight construction techniques he would later apply to automobile bodies. In February 1919, at the end of the war, he returned to Milan to open his own bodyshop in Via Francesco Ferrer.

In the early part of the automobile's development in Italy, it was hard enough designing a running engine and a chassis to carry it; the clothing of the body was typically left to an outside firm. Manufacturers were quite accustomed to delivering running chassis to outside firms, which were usually retained by private customers to create

In the late 1950s, Zagato began modifying privateer racing Giuliettas for customers, building lightweight aluminum-alloy bodies on production chassis. In a short time, the Zagato cars were beating the best the factory had to offer, and so Alfa Romeo hired Zagato to construct a series of Giulietta Sprint Zagato cars. This is the d'Amico SZ at speed in the 1969 Targa Florio, still running strong some ten years after it was first built.

customized bodywork for the chassis they had bought. So it was that Ugo Zagato received his first commission to body a Fiat 501.

In 1920, Zagato married Amelia Bressello, whom he had met some ten years earlier. On February 27, 1921, a son, Elio, was born. Another, Gianni, was born on August 17, 1929.

Zagato's lightweight bodies became fashionable and his work prospered. In 1923 his company moved to larger quarters at Viale Brianza 10 in Milan. His work had come to the attention of Nicola Romeo through Vittorio Jano, an Alfa Romeo new-hire from Fiat. At Fiat, Giovanni Agnelli regarded Zagato as a kind of Michelangelo of bodybuilding, and the favorable reputation followed when Jano went to Alfa Romeo. Zagato was selected to build a body for Jano's first effort for Alfa Romeo, the P2.

For Fiat, Zagato was accustomed to laying his aluminum bodywork over wood, a classic approach not abandoned by the British until decades later. From his work on airplanes, Zagato realized that a lighter and stronger approach would be to lay aluminum over steel framing. It was this technique that he first used on the P2. A derivation of this approach, laying aluminum over a network of steel tubes formed to the shape of the body, was used by Carrozzeria Touring for its Superleggera, or "superlight," construction.

The success of the P2 prompted Jano to select Zagato to build sporting bodies for his first passenger car, the 6C1500. Similar Zagato bodies were constructed for the 6C1750 and 8C2300 chassis.

In the latter part of the 1930s, Zagato built sporting bodies for a number of clients, but he did not hold the dominant position at Alfa Romeo, which was now using the work of Castagna, Touring and Stabilimenti Farina for many of its production cars. It's ironic that much of Alfa Romeo's production efforts during the war were to build aero engines, which virtually eliminated any need for Zagato's services. During the war, Zagato built truck bodies for Isotta Fraschini. His factory was demolished by bombs in August 1943.

At the end of the war, Zagato opened a new plant at Via Giorgini, 16 in Milan to produce the Panoramic series of cars for Fiat. These cars featured rounded styling and a large glass area for excellent visibility. By 1949, he had added Maserati and Ferrari to his list of clients for Panoramic-bodied cars. Most of his production capacity, however, was taken up by Fiat for the Topolino.

Beginning in the 1950s, Zagato's name was once again linked intimately to Alfa Romeo. It was Zagato who constructed the bodywork for the world championship 1951 Type 159 Alfa Romeo.

Zagato was at hand to provide styling exercise for Alfa Romeo's first series-produced car, the 1900. In 1952, he created a prototype spider body for the 1900 and in the following year, the 1900 Super Sprint Zagato coupe, which went into production in 1954. Zagato's elegant fastback design for the 1900 did not remain exclusively Alfa Romeo's. Similar bodies were constructed for the Fiat 8V in 1953, the Maserati A6G and 212 Ferrari in 1954, and a few Aston Martins. In 1956, Zagato began production of the Fiat Abarth 750 GT series of cars and did no further work for Alfa Romeo until 1958, when a down-sized version of the 1900 SSZ body was created for the Giulietta.

The opportunity to create something on the Giulietta floor pan—a unit construction without a conventional frame—came when Dore Leto di Priolo crashed his Alfa Romeo Sprint during the Mille Miglia. A famous gentleman motorist, Priolo was nevertheless interested in winning, and so asked Elio Zagato to rebuild the Giulietta to make it as light as possible. Of course, Zagato would utilize aluminum body panels, but the fact that the car already had a steel body manufactured in unit with the floor pan meant that the bodywork had to be cut away and a completely new shell fabricated around a steel substructure.

Priolo's car became the SVZ prototype. In styling, it shared much with Zagato's other work of the era. Like the Fiat Abarths he was bodying, this SVZ had a double-bubble roof. Other touches were reflected from Zagato's Alfa Romeo 1900 CSSZ, especially around the greenhouse. Many styling cues came from the stock Bertone coupe. From the front, it might be mistaken for a stock Alfa Romeo, but only at a glance, for the grille sat quite low allowing the hood line to slope more aerodynamically than the stock car. But Zagato's efforts were only incidentally a styling exercise. The completed car weighed 1,657 lb. compared to the 1,978 lb. of the stock coupe, advantage enough for Massimo (Priolo's brother) to win the Coppa Intereuropa at Monza on September 2, 1956.

Nothing attracts attention like a winner. Soon, Zagato was besieged with requests for a lightweight car like the Priolos'. As great as these cars were on the track, they could never be competitive in the marketplace because the conversion work had to begin with the disassembly of a completed Bertone coupe. As the fabricator of the body, Bertone's product was created with much less labor.

The SVZ, however, became a focus of Alfa Romeo racing. It received the attention of the great Italian tuners: Piero Facetti and Stefanelli Vecchi in Milan, Virgilio Conrero and Almo Bosato in Turin.

The successes of the SVZ clouded the reputation of the stock Sprint Veloce, which itself was a lightweight car with aluminum panels and sliding plexiglass door windows. In a kind of retaliation against Zagato's success with the SVZ, Alfa Romeo asked Bertone to design a competing car. The result, the Sprint Speciale, was designed by Scaglione while he was at Bertone. Yet somehow, the design goal escaped Bertone. The SS was a wonderfully aerodynamic car, but it was fully appointed and steel-bodied. As a result it was never the racing success that Zagato's cars were.

Giulietta Sprint Zagato

It would never be economical to dismantle a complete car just to make another. In 1959, Zagato signed an agreement with Alfa Romeo that allowed him to purchase unfinished Giulietta Spider Veloce chassis from Pinin Farina, making his manufacturing costs competitive with Bertone. The new car, called simply the Sprint Zagato, was derived especially from two of the last SVZs owned by Miro Toselli and Ada Pace. It was introduced March 3, 1960 at the Geneva auto show. Zagato's labor cost was still enormous: 300 hours were required to build one car.

For the Giulietta SZ, Zagato carefully reconsidered the direction in which he had taken the 1900 CSSZ. The basic driveline dimensions of the 1900 demanded a rather vertical body, thus the engine sat high, forcing the envelope to be both high and narrow. The Giulietta, on the other hand, was the first Alfa Romeo to offer a design that was clearly wider than it was high. As a result, the

The frontal aspect of the Giulietta SZ was smooth for good aerodynamic airflow. The grille retained the traditional Alfa Romeo design, but it was mounted flush with the bodywork. Note the air scoop hung below the grille.

Zagato SZ bodywork looked very modern, while the 1900 SSZ was definitely of the classic mold.

Because the Giulietta's engine sat so low in the basic shell, the nose of the car could be a dramatic taper rising up to the windshield frame. Zagato made poetic sense of the possibility and added faired-in headlamps enclosed in plastic shells that followed the flowing lines of the fenders. Softly

A Giulietta-powered chassis undergoing testing before the Zagato body was installed. Note that the car rode so low to the ground that the exhaust system could not be run underneath and was instead routed around the car in a long, serpentine series of pipes.

The tail of the Giulietta SZ fell off in a smoothly rounded line so as not to disturb the airflow around the car at speed.

In 1961, Zagato began experimenting with a new body design on the Giulietta Sprint Zagato chassis that would become the forerunner to the Giulia Tubolare Zagato series of cars. Called the Coda Tronca, or "cut tail," the new styling reflected the Kamm design of a sharply cut-off rear aspect that actually provided greater down-force at the back of the car when at speed. Zagato lengthened the overhang at both the front and the rear of the car to aid the aerodynamics. This was the final version of the Coda Tronca SZ with streamlined headlamps covered by plexiglass.

rounded lines gave the impression of great aerodynamic efficiency. In the first of the Giulietta Zagatos, the rounded lines were repeated at the rear. The rounded front and rear, combined with a dramatic roofline gave the sheet metal a feeling of great tautness—and a rather football-like appearance.

Giulietta SZ Coda Tronca

The SZ Alfa Romeos were being hard pressed on the racetrack by the new Lotus Elite coupe from Colin Chapman. The Giulietta engine had been developed to its virtual limits by Virgilio Conrero and his competitors. As a result, if extra performance was to be obtained, it was clear that it would have to come from aerodynamic improvements.

Tests proved that the SZ was too short; to get better penetration for laminar airflow control, the nose and tail needed to be lengthened. Early tests revealed that a very long tail, however, caused steering difficulties on twisting roads.

Zagato decided to employ the revolutionary aerodynamic theories of Professor Kamm. The classic aerodynamic approach was the teardrop, in

The lightweight tube-frame Giulia competition car would be called the Tubolare Zagato, or TZ. Work began in 1959 on the car although the first body was not constructed until 1961. This drawing of the TZ prototype from Zagato was notable in that it featured rectangular front headlights and a rounded-off tail. Neither feature was retained on the production version.

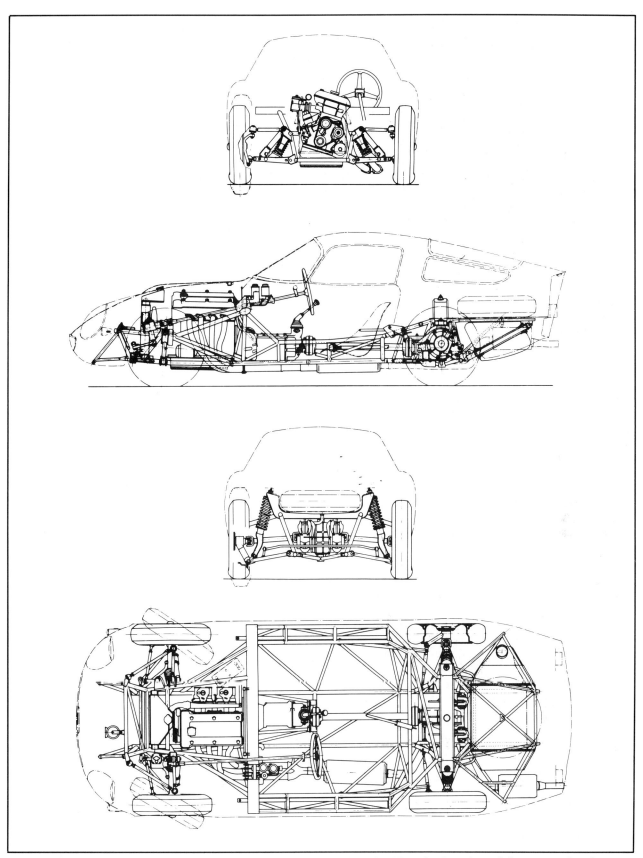

Mechanical profiles of the Giulia TZ detailing the canted engine and the exhaust system routed underneath the chassis. Note the location of the spare tire that was required by race rules.

which the tail of the car tapered gradually to maintain a layered flow of air over the body for as long as possible. Kamm realized that this extended contact between the body and the air actually increased drag, and proposed that a chopped-off tail, though it would cause a more turbulent termination of the flow, would provide less overall drag because the turbulence would affect a smaller area of the vehicle.

The final configuration was determined during a series of trial-and-error tests. Ercole Spada designed bodies with progressively longer tails which were evaluated during high-speed runs. The most successful configuration proved to be both narrower and lower than the SZ. The Coda Tronca, or "cut-tail," had only a slightly sleeker front and virtually the same greenhouse as the SZ, but its tail was chopped off abruptly, following Kamm's theory. In order to maintain aerodynamic penetration, and also to avoid sheer ugliness, Zagato provided a substantial rear fender overhang, making the Coda Tronca longer than the SZ. With this configuration, Spada and Elio Zagato reached 141 mph on the Milan-Bergamo autostrada, a truly remarkable speed for a car of 1300 cc displacement.

A total of thirty SV Coda Tronca cars were produced, although some owners modified their early SZs to the Coda Tronca configuration.

Giulia Tubolare Zagato

The ultimate Kamm application appeared on the 105 Series Giulia-based Zagato coupe, which carried a large, indented flat panel at its tail. The basic lines of the SZ Coda Tronca were continued, though the greenhouse gained some sheet metal and therefore seemed much heavier. The Tubolare Zagato, however, was actually not a development of the SZ, having been conceived within Alfa Romeo as project number 105.11 at about the same time as Zagato was rebodying Priolo's crashed Sprint Veloce.

In 1955, Carlo Abarth was working on the development of a box-type sheet-metal chassis that would provide superior strength and outstanding lightness. His idea was to create a light, Alfa Romeo-engined Abarth of 750 cc displacement. He actually built a chassis and presented it to Alfa Romeo for testing, according to Giuseppe Busso. The chassis proved too flexible, and it was reinforced at Alfa Romeo with a tube-perimeter frame. This is the chassis on which Carrozzeria Boano built the 750 competition prototype roadster.

Early in 1958, Abarth once again proposed an Alfa-Abarth, this time with a 1.0 liter Abarth derivation of the Giulietta engine and a tubular chassis designed by Alfa Romeo. The chassis work was carried out at Alfa Romeo by Ivo Colucci, under Busso's direction. The collaboration produced the Alfa-Abarth which was shown at the 1958 Turin auto show. However, production costs of the exotic car would have been too great, and Abarth asked permission to use a stock 1300 Veloce engine to lower costs. His request was refused. So perhaps in retribution, Abarth hired Colucci. (With Colucci's departure from Alfa Romeo, chassis development was assigned to Zava, who almost immediately left

An early production TZ in 1963. This car was serial number 002, and was raced by Lorenzo Bandini in the 1963 Fisa Cup in Italy. In addition to the different headlights and the cut-off tail, the definitive production car had a lip on the tail of the hood to control the high-pressure area at the base of the windshield, serving much the same purpose as the small plexiglass shield employed on the Sprint Speciale.

with Villa, an engine designer, to do consulting work for Autodelta and Euroracing.)

At the end of 1959 Satta proposed a light-weight race car to be built using the mechanicals of the as-yet unannounced Giulia. Based on Colucci's work for Abarth, Busso recommended tubular chassis construction. Zagato was the obvious choice to do the work, not only because he worked fast and reliably, but also because he had demonstrated with the SVZ that he had mastered working with a network of small tubes.

The TZ was completely designed by the end of 1960. The engine configuration was basically worked out by Conrero on a third prototype engine. He fitted Borgo pistons, changed the carburetion to 45 DCOE Webers (1964 Sebring cars had 50 DCOE 3 Webers), modified the cam timing and spark advance profile, ported the head and increased its compression ratio to 10.0:1. A 7.0 liter oil sump was obtained by fitting a 45 mm spacer between the stock sump and the block. The cars had a limited-slip differential, and their front and rear transmission castings were in magnesium.

The car did not use the basic body pan of its unit-bodied parent. Instead, a true multi-tube space frame was constructed, giving the car its name of Tubolare Zagato. A total of only 112 of these cars were built from 1963 to 1967. They are certainly the most desirable postwar production Alfa Romeo.

The entire front of the TZ tilted forward to provide ample access to the suspension and the powerplant, which in production trim was basically the same as fitted to the Sprint Speciale. The intake to the dual Weber carburetors was a ram system that increased manifold pressure as road speed increased. A true header exhaust featured four independent tubes that snaked around the chassis tubes.

The rear suspension was independent with top and bottom A-arms and coil springs. All in all, the suspension was certainly the least-developed part of the car. TZs are not known for their ultimate road-holding capabilities, though the number of racing wins shows that the cars demanded great respect. I have always suspected that the reputa-

The complete front end of the TZ pivoted forward, giving superb access to the 1600 cc Giulia engine. The engine was canted toward the driver's side to allow for a lower hood line. To assist airflow to feed the cylinders, the TZ used a ram air intake. The inlet for the ram air system was the huge plenum mounted in front of the radiator.

Another photograph of the TZ front end with the hood and the large air plenum removed. The tilted engine was obvious here, as well as details of the double wishbone front suspension. The front disc brakes were also visible. The tube-frame TZ chassis weighed only 137 lb.

At the rear, the disc brakes of the TZ were mounted inboard next to the rear differential, common Alfa Romeo race practice.

The Giulia TZ was successful in racing on the road and in hillclimb events, such as the 1964 Coupes des Alpes. This was Jean Rolland at the wheel.

tion of the TZ rear suspension suffers, like the Spica fuel injection, from inept adjustment rather than poor basic design.

The first two chassis were delivered to Zagato in January 1961 for the construction of two proto-

type spiders. The body was unusual: although the top was removable, the rear window was fixed, a design that anticipated cars such as the Lancia Beta Zagato. The result was too aerodynamically inefficient, and the hardtop was never removed

The Giulia TZ of Pelatelli/Angelo at speed on the Rome autodrome road course on December 19, 1965. The team took second place overall.

Endurance racing at the 1965 Nürburgring 1000 kilometers race with the Bussinello/Pianta team. Another TZ took first in class.

during testing. The prototype was outstandingly light: the bare space frame weighed only 137 lb. and with the top off, the entire car weighed less than 1,326 lb. The most troublesome unit proved to be the new rear suspension, which endowed the prototype with unpredictable handling.

Poor handling and unrefined aerodynamics kept the top speeds of the prototype to only 129 mph. The spider bodies were scrapped in favor of a coupe following the general lines of the Giulietta SZ Coda Tronca, which was introduced at just the time the prototypes were under test. Dramatic, rectangular headlights were a striking front-end feature of this first coupe. Speeds immediately rose to 133 mph.

Development of the TZ coupe continued during the early months of 1962. Although the rectangular headlamps were retained, the nose was lengthened and the rear inset of the Kamm tail was recessed even more deeply than on the SZ Coda Tronca. A lip was added to improve the Kamm effect. The final configuration was achieved in early

Le Mans, 1966. The Bussinello/Deserti Giulia TZ prepared to leave the pits. The car won first in class and thirteenth position overall, breaking the class record set by Jean Behra in 1958.

1963, after nine different prototype noses were tested for the car. Round headlamps were part of the final design.

After all the work, Alfa Romeo realized that it had no production capacity for the TZ. As a result, TZ construction was completely sublet. The chassis was constructed by Ambrosini at Passignano sul Trasimeno; assembly of the mechanical components and suspension went to Delta in Udine, soon to become the factory race team as Autodelta; and the body was constructed by Zagato. The final configuration of the TZ was shown in March 1963 at Geneva.

Make no mistake about it, the TZ is a race car through and through. Autodelta campaigned the cars with great success, as did other privateers such as Scuderia Sant'Ambroeus and Jolly Club. Yet, it was quite capable of being driven for everyday transportation. The seats were comfortable, although the heat and noise of the interior were much greater than on a passenger car.

In an attempt to further improve performance, the last four TZs carried plastic bodywork by Balzaretti and Modigliani of Milan. The plastic body was cast using a production aluminum TZ as a pattern, and so was identical, but it was both lighter at 137 lb., versus 203 lb., and stronger.

Giulia TZ 2

Studies for a follow-on car to the TZ began early in 1964. Giuseppe Busso wanted some modifications to the TZ chassis to get a lower roofline but still retain the independent rear suspension, which had finally been refined so that it contributed to the car's performance.

Like the last four TZs, the new body was fiberglass-reinforced plastic. The wheelbase of the new model was unchanged from the TZ but the rear window was a single piece of plastic, compared to the three-piece TZ. The lower profile mandated a dry-sump engine, with a 7.0 liter tank capacity. To gain more power from the Giulia engine, a dual-ignition head was fitted with larger valves and changed cam timing to give 165 hp at 7000 rpm.

In order to make a lower roofline, reclining seats were used and the driver assumed a slightly reclined position. Its low roofline gave it a menacing stance and it was clear that this was a car intended to go fast, indeed. The total weight of the car was between 1,370—1,392 lb., and it was called TZ 2.

The first TZ 2 was presented at the Turin auto show on October 16, 1964. In a press release for the show, Zagato claimed that the body was so efficient that a 1300 cc engine would be a perfect powerplant. Alfa Romeo would have none of it and insisted that the current Giulia 1600 engine be used.

To aid in cooling and to feed the giant air plenum, later Giulia TZ racers added a vent above the grille. This was one of the cars that ran successfully at Sebring in 1966, with a TZ 2 winning first in class. In the ongoing search for lightness, Alfa Romeo constructed three TZ racers in 1964 with fiberglass bodies that weighed a mere 148 lb., a substantial weight savings from the aluminum-alloy bodies that weighed some 203 lb. The car shown was an alloy-bodied car.

The TZ 2 is the most collectible Giulia-based Alfa Romeo. Only twelve were produced, and none were sold to private owners. As a result, with the exception of the Type 158 and 159 and possibly the

A Giulia TZ in vintage race form at the Riverside racetrack in a 1984 endurance run. Note the absence of body lean and the insistence of the rear wheel to remain vertical even under hard cornering. Tim Wise

Disco Volante, it is also the most valuable postwar Alfa Romeo. Clearly, the TZ 2 has now found its way into private hands (there is a privately owned Type 159, even), but the rarity of the car makes a market value almost impossible to establish. Considering the almost $500,000 value of the TZ and adding the TZ 2's rarity and desirability, a 1990 price approaching $1 million seems appropriate.

It is sad that the rarest and most desirable of all postwar Alfa Romeos should be so stillborn. Alfa Romeo did not develop the car, preferring instead to devote its efforts to the GTA.

Quattroruote Zagato

During the Giulia era it became popular to build imitation classic cars based on modern running gear. It was the era that saw the Volkswagen-based Bugatti and the V-8 powered, automatic-transmissioned SS Mercedes. These ersatz classics (one sees mind-boggling ads: "1927 Bugatti, VW

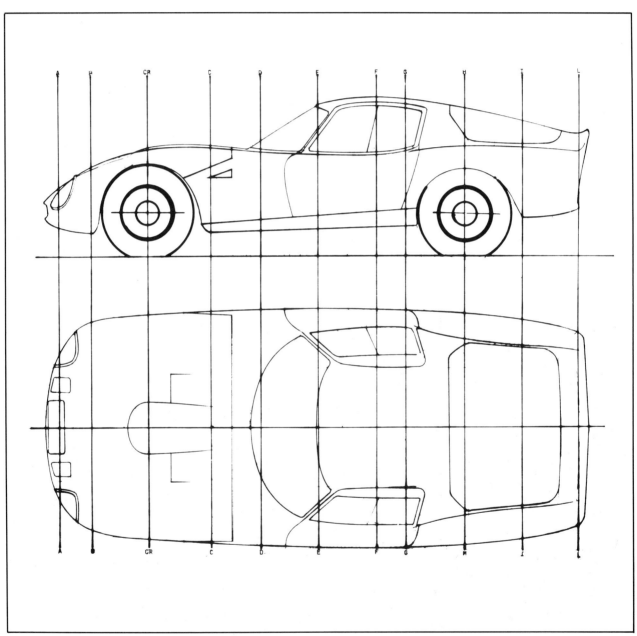

Alfa Romeo began work on the TZ 2 in about 1963 as a further modification of the TZ. The car was substantially lower and more aerodynamic than its predecessor and engine power from the 1570 cc Giulia motor had increased from the TZ's output of 112 hp at 6500 rpm to *165 hp at 7000 rpm. This early drawing from the factory archives was dated 1963, showing the development of the TZ 2 styling with air scoops in the hood akin to that of the Ferrari 250 GTO.*

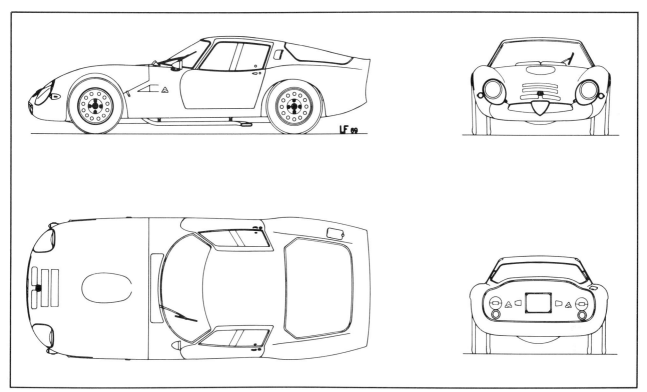

The final configuration of the TZ 2 was so low that the exhaust system had to be routed around the side of the car. Where the factory had experimented with fiberglass bodywork on the final three TZ cars, ten of the TZ 2 cars that were eventually built used the fiberglass technology.

While the aluminum-alloy TZ weighed a total of 1,458 lb. dry, the TZ 2 weighed only 1,370 lb. With the more powerful engine, the pound per horsepower ratio of the TZ 2 was 8 lb/hp versus the TZ's 12 lb/hp.

A Giulia TZ 2 outside the walls of Alfa Romeo's race operation, Autodelta. Note the cutouts in the plexiglass headlight covers to accommodate the low-mounted driving lights that were used for endurance racing.

A TZ 2 running test laps at the Alfa Romeo test track, Balocco, in 1966. Autodelta would experiment with different hood scoops and cutouts through the years to aid airflow, much as Ferrari did with its GTO.

A TZ 2 being prepped for a vintage race. As with the TZ, the 1600 engine was canted here toward the driver's side to allow for a low hood line. In addition, the TZ 2 used a dry oil sump with a separate oil tank mounted on the bulkhead, allowing the engine and subsequently, the hood, to be even lower. Just how low the car actually was can be seen in comparison with the MGA parked alongside.

running gear....") shared neither the road-holding ability nor the beauty of their namesakes. Indeed, the most outstanding feature of most of the retro-cars is their ugliness. Even Siata got into the game, with an 850 based, shoebox-shaped retrocar called the Spring.

Quattroruote, meaning "four wheels," is the premiere Italian car magazine. It is perhaps not surprising that its passions run high. It has disassembled cars for road tests, and it is not unusual for one road test to occupy almost as many pages as the entire editorial content of competing magazines. As a primary medium for advertisers, it's also not surprising that Quattroruote carries a lot of weight with Italian car companies. Thus, Quattroruote's suggestion to Alfa Romeo management that it should create a modern imitation of the 1750 Zagato was taken quite seriously.

The challenges for such an undertaking were daunting. The chassis of the 1750 was a thin, spare construction which provided, by twisting and flexing, much of the car's ride comfort. In contrast, the

*On its way to winning first in class, the Andrey/"Geki"
TZ 2 at the Sebring twelve-hour endurance race in 1966.
Ground clearance was minimal.*

*TZ 2 in the pits at the Roman racetrack, Vallelunga, in
1967. Autodelta chief engineer Carlo Chiti directed the
action from the wall. Chiti was one of the engineers to
walk out from Ferrari during the famous palace revolt.
He quickly found a home with the upstart car producer*
*ATS and subsequently headed Autodelta's race efforts.
The tubular contraptions surrounding the car were
jacks, custommade to lift the car mechanically with a
crewman's body weight.*

The Quattroruote Zagato was a factory-built replica of the great 1930s 6C1750 Zagato-bodied car. Using the 101 Giulia chassis in 1965 and the 105 chassis in 1966–1967, the 1600 engine and the minimal bodywork, the car weighed a mere 1,650 lb., and could out-accelerate many other production Giulias.

Giulia carried unit-body construction and its coil-spring suspension virtually dictated a wide, low body outline; the 1750 had neither feature. Finally, the 1750 was right-hand drive, and the retrocar would have to be left-handed if it were to sell in the United States.

The prototype Quattroruote Zagato (4R Zagato) was on the Alfa Romeo stand at the Turin show in April 1965. In profile, it was astoundingly

The clamshell front fenders of the Quattroruote Zagato didn't cover the modern suspension, which required an inboard attaching point rather high up on the body. In this view, it was clear that the line between the fender and the hood's side was quite high to accommodate the upper suspension link.

similar to the 1929 car. Amidships, it seemed at least twice as wide and the modern running gear peeked embarrassingly out from under the clamshell fenders. It was the only production Giulia to offer genuine wire wheels.

At 1,657 lb. the car was significantly lighter than the Duetto at 2,188 lb., but its top speed was limited by its poorer aerodynamics to only 95 mph, compared to about 110 mph for the modern roadster.

It is easy not to take the 4R Zagato seriously, lumping it together with the plastic-bodied jokes of the era. Nothing could be further from the truth. The 4R Zagato is the only replicar created by a manufacturer of its own product. And, since only ninety-two were produced, it is a collectible of demonstrable virtue. It is not nearly so beautiful as the 1929 6C1750 Zagato, on which it was modeled, but few other, even contemporaneous cars ever were.

It is appropriate at this point of retrospective to note that Ugo Zagato died at Milan on October 31, 1968. The company continued under the direction of his sons Elio and Gianni.

Zagato Junior

With the SVZ, SZ and TZ cars, Zagato had established good working relations with Alfa Romeo. He wanted to trade on this relationship to get the contract for a series-production car that would place him in the same league as Bertone and Pininfarina. He almost had his goal in 1963 with the 2600 SZ, but it had been plagued with difficulties. The 1965 4R Zagato, which proved trouble-free, still suffered from small production runs, since it was never intended to be anything but a low-volume item. With the Zagato Junior, he got his wish: some 1,500 of these lovely, steel-bodied cars were produced between 1969 and 1975.

The initial run of Zagato Juniors featured the 1300 cc Junior engine. Beginning in 1972, the 1600 cc engine was used. It was a measure of Zagato's diminutive capacity that in 1974 the total production of his factory was devoted to the Junior Zagato.

The production orientation of the Junior Z meant that it was a comfortable, fully equipped car quite capable of being driven every day. Its styling was attractive without being either cute or outlandish, its aerodynamics were superior and its drivetrain outstandingly reliable.

In the case of the Zagato Junior, Alfa Romeo not only hit the target, but did so several years ahead of its time. That is a testimony to the potential of the Alfa-Zagato team. The sorry fact is that Alfa Romeo did not have the capacity to capitalize on its success.

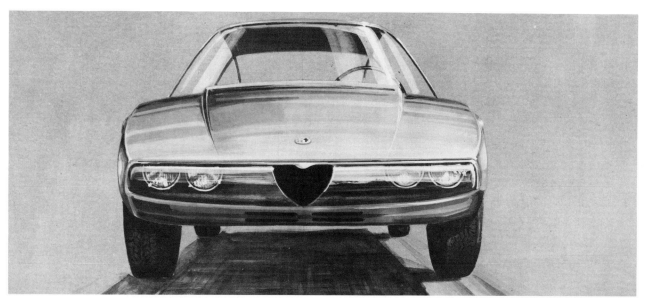

A 1970 Zagato drawing of the proposed Junior Zagato showed a much more sleek front treatment than made it to production. The headlamps were shaded by the body and illuminated the road through a plexiglass front nose. The lack of a bumper indicated that this design was still only a concept.

How it all turned out. This was the 1970 production Junior Z, which had gained bumpers and an extra row of slots in the plexiglass to improve cooling. The early cars used the 1300 engine.

In 1972, the Junior Z was available with the 1600 engine. The full profile view showed the beautiful lines of the car, which borrowed its profile from the TZ.

With the increase to the 1600 engine, the Zagato bodywork was modified to include larger doorhandles but was otherwise virtually identical to the original 1300.

Front and rear views of the 1600 Junior Z showed the car's compact, clean design. There were no bad angles.

The interior of the 1300 Junior Z was Spartan but efficient and comfortable. This early version had a two-spoke steering wheel.

The 1600 cc version of the Junior Z featured a slightly different dash and a three-spoke steering wheel.

6

Giulia Sprint Speciale and Others

There was a total of forty-nine models in the Giulia line, with a total production of 265,877. The model line includes right- and left-hand-drive cars, knockdown (CKD) cars shipped whole but disassembled to countries where domestic assembly has tax advantages, and six models with production of under 100 units. The rarest of these, the 1600 S with right-hand drive, had a production of three; the most popular, the Giulia 1300 TI, had a production of 140,684.

Giulia Sprint Speciale

The success of the Zagato Giulietta SVZ made Alfa Romeo realize that there was a viable market for an image car built on production components. Both Bertone and Pininfarina had much closer

working relations with Alfa Romeo than Zagato, so it is not surprising that Alfa Romeo allowed Bertone to design a limited-production dream car on Giulietta mechanicals. Nuccio Bertone had designed the Giulietta Sprint in a short time and under trying circumstances. The success of that car thrust Alfa Romeo into six-digit production figures for the first time in its history.

Prior to the Giulietta Sprint, Bertone had created a series of three aerodynamic studies on the 1900 chassis known as the BAT cars (Bertone Aerodynamica Technica). These three cars were numbered 5, 7 and 9. BAT 9 had a drag coefficient (Cd) of only 0.19, compared to 0.34 for the Giulia Super. The prototype Sprint Speciale had a Cd of 0.28. The BAT series of cars were a sensation. Not

An original concept drawing of the Giulietta Sprint Speciale showed that Bertone initially had a much more pointed theme in mind for the car.

The prototype Giulietta Sprint Speciale had a different nose treatment than the production car. The early grille design here said Ferrari rather than Alfa Romeo.

The front grille of the production Sprint Speciale was much more identifiably Alfa Romeo. The basic grille configuration had changed little from that of the prototype, but the addition of an Alfa Romeo grille and bumpers changed the front of the car. The Sprint Speciale was one of the few body styles to be translated directly from the Giulietta line to the Giulia line; this was a Giulia SS.

beautiful in any classic sense, the cars seem wildly disproportionate. Yet their flowing lines and large finwork nevertheless have a strong attraction, for they are clearly singleminded in their search for aerodynamic efficiency.

Many presume that the Giulietta Sprint Speciale proceeded directly from the well-known BATs. That was not precisely the case, though like the BATs, the Sprint Speciale gave away some beauty to aerodynamic efficiency, and the greenhouses of the BAT 9 and Sprint Speciale were similar. The true inspiration of the Sprint Speciale was the Alfa-Abarth 1000 GT, which was shown along with the prototype Sprint Speciale at the Turin auto show in 1958. This car was a true lightweight, with aluminum bodywork designed by Franco Scaglione and a tubular space frame with a heat-bonded plastic sheet for the floor pan. It is generally assumed that this Alfa-Abarth, though intended for serial production, was abandoned in favor of the Sprint Speciale.

In March 1963, Alfa Romeo introduced the Giulia SS, with only minor detail changes over the Giulietta version. Even with a larger engine, higher

The tail of the Sprint Speciale was truncated in the style of the Giulietta Sprint Zagato Coda Tronca. This was probably the worst angle to view the Sprint Speciale as the greenhouse appeared too high and the rear end seemed to miss the theme.

The front was probably the best angle for the Sprint Speciale as it showed its flowing lines to the greatest advantage. A convertible would have been beautiful. Note the plexiglass wind deflector mounted at the rear edge of the hood. At speed, the airflow over the sleek hood lifted the windshield wipers off of the window and so the wind deflector aimed the airflow around them.

The easiest positive identification of the Giulia Sprint Speciale versus the Giulietta was the badge on the fender. A similar badge, 1600 SS, was located on the flat tail panel. The Giulia Sprint Speciale was constructed on the 101 chassis.

The dash of the Sprint Speciale was typical Alfa Romeo practice. This angle showed the deep curvature of the windshield. The assist grip between the dash and the door jam on the passenger side demonstrated just how deeply the dash was recessed into the windshield curve.

compression, wilder camshafts and dual sidedraft Weber carburetors, changed gear ratios gave the Giulia the same top speed as the Giulietta Sprint Speciale.

Details of the Sprint Speciale were immediately familiar to Alfa Romeo owners, for there was extensive use of production components throughout. A unique radiator was required to

Sprint Speciales were just a bit too heavy for racing success, but that didn't keep owners from campaigning their cars. This was the Benchya Sprint Speciale at the Moroccan circuit in the city of Marrakech in 1967.

accommodate the lowered hood line, but the instruments and most of the interior furnishings were regular production items.

It's not clear exactly how sporting Alfa Romeo expected Bertone's design to be. In the literature on Zagato, one gets the feeling that Alfa Romeo may have wanted to quash the Zagato effort by offering a similar car itself at a lower cost. That would have been an easy assignment, for Zagato was having to buy complete cars to disassemble before starting its own bodywork. Evidence that this may have been Alfa Romeo's intent include the facts that a number of aluminum-bodied Giulietta Sprint Speciales were built, and the Weber-carbureted Veloce versions of the 101 Series Giulia engine were first introduced in the Sprint Speciale bodywork, at Geneva in March 1963.

If the plan were to outdo Zagato in the production of a light race car, Bertone certainly missed the mark. Although the Sprint Speciale has been raced, it is rather like the Mercedes 190 SL in having more sporting appearance than capability. What Ber-

With its excellent aerodynamics, the Giulia Sprint Speciale was a promising undertaking for land speed records. Hank Walker and his SS set a new record for the E/GT 1500 cc turbocharged class at the Bonneville Salt Flats. In an earlier normally aspirated SS, Walker set a G/GT record that stood for ten years. Hank Walker

A Giulia Sprint Speciale at the 1969 Targa Florio. For a long road course such as the Targa, the Sprint Speciale made sense with its durability, good high-speed stabil- *ity and comfortable racing ergonomics. Here it was leading an Abarth Simca and a Fiat.*

For the 1967 World's Fair in Montreal, Alfa Romeo was requested to construct a special show car. The result was the Bertone-penned prototype that became known as the Montreal. Based on a 105 Series Giulia chassis, the Montreal used a four-cam V–8 engine from Alfa Romeo's Type 33 race car.

tone did succeed in creating was the ultimate small GT. I've been fortunate enough to take a 100 plus mile freeway trip in a Giulia Sprint Speciale and can say the sensation of traveling near 100 mph for mile after mile in quiet and comfort is memorable. There is almost no wind noise, and the seating position, large glass area and leather-trimmed appointments make traveling in an SS a journey in luxury.

All in all, I believe that the Sprint Speciale was a less successful design than the Giulietta Sprint. The Sprint Speciale followed the classic approach to aerodynamics: good penetration from a pointed front and back so that the laminar flow stayed with

the car as long as possible. The result was excessive overhang and a front and rear that did little more than just start and end. Its greenhouse seemed disproportionately tall and peaked too early along the profile view. The high greenhouse was a result of having to maintain adequate headroom within a shortened wheelbase because of the excessive overhang. The tail treatment seemed especially weak. Its tentative, squared-off configuration was a concession to practicality, not aerodynamics, as the prototype tail tapered to a small-radius curve. In contrast, Zagato, with the SZ Coda Tronca, used Kamm's aerodynamics more boldly to produce, arguably, a prettier car.

If I am somewhat mean-spirited over the Sprint Speciale's styling, I need to reassert that its basic concept is unarguably voluptuous. It was a

From this angle, there was a little bit of the Lamborghini Miura in the Montreal, especially around the B-pillar. The tail on the Montreal was especially clean. The large rear window eased rearward visibility, given the extensive side sheet metal, but made the car an oven in hot weather.

The Montreal with its hatch up and hood open. The BBS aluminum-alloy wheels were not standard, but add visual impact to an already dramatic car.

car whose individual components had a stunning fluid beauty, but the total effect was less than the sum of the parts.

Montreal

Most Alfa Romeo enthusiasts know the story about how the hit of the 1967 World's Fair in Montreal became a regular production vehicle in 1970. That it took Alfa Romeo almost four years to capitalize on a sensation was one measure of the firm's bureaucracy.

It was infinitely worth the wait. The Montreal was another Bertone design, but executed by Marcello Gandini, instead of Giugiaro, who had gone to Ghia. Even in its prototype form for the World's Fair, the Montreal was much more real-world than the BATs or, even, the Sprint Speciale. As a consequence, the production version differed only slightly from the show car.

I think the Montreal is wonderfully underappreciated. Wonderful, because it is still affordable.

It carried a unique V-8 engine derived from the Type 33 race cars in a show-car body, and had a production run of only 3,925—powerful, beautiful and rare. Yet, only a few years ago I turned down a good example for $12,500 and even today they bring little over $25,000. When one considers that he or she could spend the same for a Giulietta Veloce Spider, or many times that for a Sprint Speciale or TZ, the Montreal must be the bargain of the decade. A momentary bargain, perhaps, since published comments such as this can have a dramatic effect on the market. Since I do not currently own, nor plan to own, a Montreal, these comments should be taken as both objective and heartfelt.

Some caveats, of course. Montreal ownership is likely to be stressful, for few mechanics will recognize the car, let alone be competent to work on it. And most will probably be comfortable increasing their rates to Ferrari scale for any work on the car. Like all Alfa Romeos of the era, they rust. As high-speed tourers they steer heavy at low speeds.

The Montreal offered unique instrumentation, but a familiar steering wheel from the Giulia. The window winders were also stock Alfa Romeo production. The two large instrument pods in the Montreal held a circular tachometer and speedometer, segmented oil-pressure and water-temperature gauges, clock and so on.

No doubt the most interesting feature of the Montreal was its engine, a V–8 with a power output of 230 hp. This was a display engine that toured the North American continent in 1970.

There are some distinct advantages, however, to owning a Montreal over similar head-turners with Ferrari or Maserati badges. Many stock Alfa Romeo parts can be made to work (note, I did not say fit). The Spica fuel-injection system is little

The engine bay from the driver's side. The large air cleaner and Spica fuel-injection pump stand out.

The engine from the passenger's side. The ignition modules on the far-side fenderwell were not stock. The black oval reservoir between the ignition modules and the air cleaner held additional vacuum for the brake system. Note the cold air intake to the air cleaner.

more than two 1750 pumps bolted together with a single logic unit. The eight-plug Marelli distributor seems adapted from the twin-plug GTAs. The rear axle appears to be a stock unit with an extra sump bolted on.

You'll note that I'm hedging; instead of saying that it fits, I say "seems to fit" or "appears to fit." That is because I know of no one who has verified conclusively any of the similarities between the Montreal and its 105 Series stablemates. Knowing Alfa Romeo's ability to make up unique parts on a moment's notice, I'm especially wary of ensuring anyone that the Montreal shares a single bolt with the Giulia.

The most encouraging fact about Montreal ownership is that most of its parts are in the 105 Series, which is the same series as the Giulia. The Montreal is a 105 Series Alfa Romeo.

While the block is a derivation of the V-8, Type 33 sports car engine, Montreal heads appear to be derived from the 1750. There was a series of letters in the Alfa Romeo club magazine on just how sim-

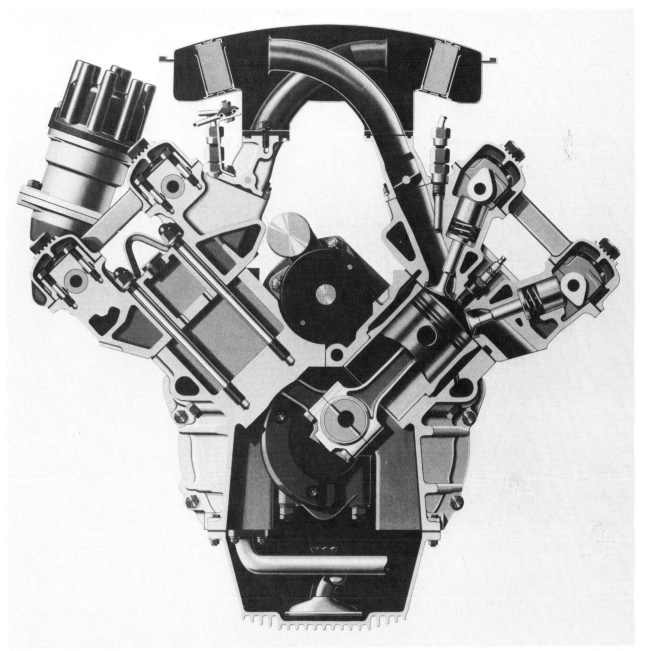

A cross-section of the Montreal engine. Traditional Alfa Romeo practice included wet-sleeve cylinders, hemi- *spheric heads with twin camshafts and Spica fuel injection.*

ilar to the 1750 the Montreal heads were. One accomplished Alfa Romeo mechanic, who served as a technical advisor for many years, had worked on many Montreals and claimed they were 1750 knock-offs. Not so, claimed Alfa Romeo's chief engineer in the United States when the Montreal was current. He stated that the Montreal heads were quite unique, with no relationship to the 1750.

It's fun to trace the derivation of a style. The Montreal had features that Bertone used in other cars. But there are no other Bertone cars that looked exactly like the Montreal, either; it was a surprisingly unique design. The prominent slats on the B-pillar (eight on a prototype, seven on the show car, six on the production model) had a forebear in Bertone's 1963 Iso Grifo, and the prominent B-pillar on a fastback was also found on the 1964 prototype coupe Bertone designed for Alfa Romeo. The idea of using the B-pillar as an air duct was also tried on the 1963 Corvair Testudo. The undulating fender line was found in the 1964 Canguro as well as a 1966 special built on a Porsche 911 chassis. The NACA duct on the hood was added to the production car. The prototype had a series of slats across the hood, similar in execution to the slats on the B-pillar.

The slatted headlamp covers were an attempt to do something interesting with the traditional round headlamps. A more successful, if involved, approach has been found with pop-up headlamps, but the Montreal's front remains certainly distinctive.

I've used "slatted" to refer to three items on the Montreal's exterior: the B-pillar, headlight covers and hood openings. If the design of the Montreal is to be faulted, it is that it came perilously close to gadgetry: all the vents and slats detracted from its basic form.

The interior of the Montreal was show car to the core. Two large pods carried the speedometer and tachometer, and a high tunnel separated driver from passenger. A short gearshift lever connected to the five-speed transmission. You sat low in the Montreal. Heavy low-speed steering lightened considerably at road speeds and the car came into its own just above legal cruising limits.

In a sense, the Montreal continued a line established by the 2.0 liter and 2600 Bertone coupes. All

A cross-section of the Montreal's Spica mechanical fuel-injection pump showed that it was basically a stock logic unit with two pump mechanisms end to end. This drawing was rare in that it showed the pump's piston mechanism in detail.

Like the Sprint Speciale, the Montreal was never really intended to be raced, yet owners have tried, even with occasional success. This was Dieter Gleich's car at the Nürburgring in 1973.

were intended to be luxurious, high-speed tourers. With 2.6 liters giving 200 hp at 6500 rpm (compared to 145 hp for the 2600), the Montreal offered a top speed of 135 mph compared to 120 mph for the 2600.

It is a shame the Montreal did not sire a line of high-performance coupes based on the V-8 engine. I have always felt that the Montreal could have been easily refined into a line of sports cars of outstanding character. In a sense it had one child: the sensuous Stradale, which was also Type 33 based. Only a very few Stradales were produced, a fact sorely lamented by all Alfa Romeo enthusiasts.

Canguro

In 1964, Bertone requested a chassis to build a show car for the Paris auto show. Giuseppe Busso sent a TZ 2 (serial number 101) and Bertone had

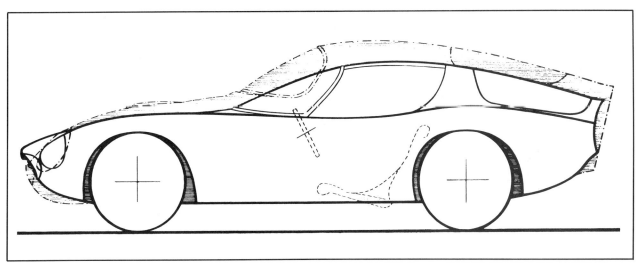

The Canguro was conceived as a significantly lower TZ. Here, the outline of the car was displayed in a Bertone drawing against a TZ profile. Bill Gillham collection

This Bertone drawing of the Canguro was signed by Giugiaro and dated 1964. Bill Gillham collection

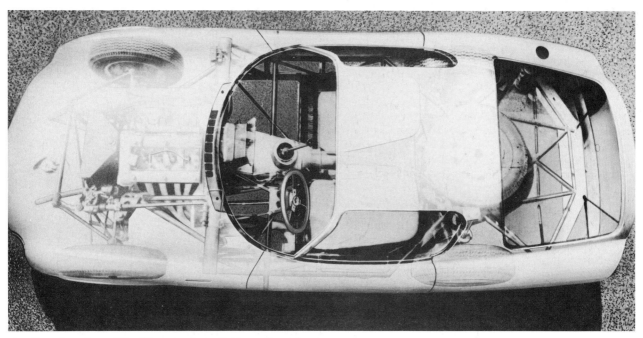

Another drawing of the Canguro from Bertone showed how the TZ mechanicals would fit in the bodywork. Bill Gillham collection

Giugiaro, head of his design office, create a body. Alfa Romeo decided against production.

From a design standpoint, the Canguro (Italian for "kangaroo") was a much more successful effort than Bertone's Sprint Speciale body. It shared the same wonderful fluidity but was not marred by a too-short wheelbase, awkward passenger compartment nor a compromised tail. Like the Sprint Speciale, its glass area was beautifully integrated into the lines of the body.

In retrospect, the Canguro probably suggested a direction Alfa Romeo should have taken. Giugiaro's design for the Alfetta coupe was much less aesthetically pleasing, though unquestionably more practical. On the other hand, practicality has never been Alfa Romeo's long suit anyway. The sensuous, flowing lines of the Canguro made it a masterpiece of design.

After its show-car duty, the Canguro kicked around the Bertone works and finally ended up minus running gear outside the shop in something of a designer trash-heap. Those who questioned its whereabouts were told that it had been destroyed. In a sense, that was true; when it was discovered by an American at Bertone, it was missing its hood and most of its mechanical parts. In fact, Bertone's staff had pretty much forgotten about the car until Gary Schmidt inquired of its whereabouts. He was insistent enough finally to discover the car, which was only partially complete. He is currently restoring it.

PF TZ 2

Pininfarina also asked for a TZ 2 chassis. Unlike the Bertone Canguro, the Pininfarina design was strictly for show. This car has suffered a much happier fate than the Canguro and has always been well cared for.

The Pininfarina TZ used TZ 2 mechanicals, and represented Farina's refinement of the TZ. The designer house asked for permission to construct a show car that would follow the basic lines of the TZ

Bertone's Canguro in the flesh, 1966.

Arguably the most beautiful Alfa Romeo ever conceived, the Canguro had exquisite lines.

2. After its show-tour duty, the car was sold and is currently in the hands of a Japanese enthusiast collector.

Scarabeo

Two of the three Scarabeos remain with Alfa Romeo. One coupe is on display and the other Spider stored in the museum at Arese. OSI has a 2600 sedan also in the museum, but the Scarabeo (Italian for "Scarab") is a much more dramatic piece. The Scarabeo used a GTA engine, but the car was mid-engined, with the transmission and powerplant in unit behind the seats.

For some time, the designers had been experimenting with the idea that driver position could significantly affect vehicle performance. I can

The rear of the Canguro picked up some of the TZ, but with a unique grace. The car is currently being restored

by Gary Schmidt. It is missing its nose, engine and transmission. Bill Gillham collection

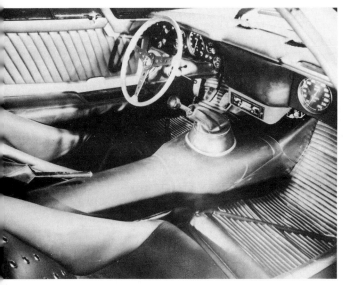

The interior of the Canguro was strictly show-car, with custom seats, carpeting and a speedometer for the passenger's eyes only.

The nose of the Pininfarina TZ 2 employed a wide Alfa Romeo grille which blended nicely into the quarter bumpers. Earl Seifert

speak from some experience, having sat in several Alfa Romeo race cars, including the 159, which was a classic configuration, and the 512, which is the Auto-Union-like mid-engined car of the late 1930s. The 159 was tight but comfortable, with the engine up front and the driving wheels just behind your elbows. It's easy to imagine racing a 159, for it offers many passenger-car analogs, which is where we all learned to drive.

On the other hand, the experience of just sitting in the 512 was fearful, for you feel as if you were on the end of a blunt battering ram with little more than sheet aluminum and a few tubes between you and complete oblivion. Moreover, you're aware that the bulk of the car's mass is behind you, waiting to squash you like a grape in a head-on. Add to that the undoubted fact that the rear end is more than willing to pass you in a curve and you have a machine capable of providing protracted terror if not outright catatonia as soon as you release the clutch.

The TZ 2 bodied by Pininfarina toured the European auto shows in 1966. There was striking similarity to the prototype Sprint Speciale in this angle. Earl Seifert

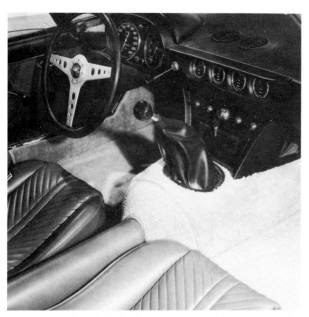

The dash of the Pininfarina TZ 2 showed the compromise between show-car and practical transportation. Lips on the dash shielded the row of auxiliary instruments from reflecting in the steeply-raked windshield. The long stalk protruding from the dash would never pass federal safety regulations. Earl Seifert

In 1954, Alfa Romeo experimented with a configuration of the 159 called the 160 that placed the driver at the rear of the car, similar to a contemporary dragster. The purpose of the placement was to improve the driver's sense of where the car was on the track without also inducing undue terror. It was felt that, if the driver had a better sense of control, he could be more aggressive in his driving and the net result would be a faster car.

The Scarabeo recalled the experiment with the Type 160 in that it attempted to place the driver as far back in the car as the mechanicals would permit. The engine was placed transversely, with the transmission attached conventionally in line with the crankshaft. At the end of the transmission, a conical gear was used to drive a short shaft diagonally to the rear to the pinion gear of the differential. Independent rear suspension was used. A spider prototype was constructed along with two coupe prototypes, and a short production run was planned.

In side view, the driver appears to sit no farther back than in a conventional layout, and plans for production were scrapped.

I do not want to leave the Scarabeo without a final suggestion of a road not taken. Like the Montreal, the Scarabeo had a fastback design with a heavy mass of body behind the doorjamb. If you can imagine a cross between a Montreal and Scarabeo, then refine that vision along the svelte lines of the Canguro and Stradale, and you begin to understand a styling direction Alfa Romeo could easily have taken with a mid-engined coupe powered by the Type 33 engine. Such a car might well have rivaled the 8C2900 B in beauty and excitement.

The Scarabeo was never intended for production, and its wraparound windshield and extreme front overhang were impractical. It was an attempt to see how a car would handle if the driver was placed as far back as possible on the chassis.

7

Giulia Engine and Drivetrain

The Giulietta engine was the design of Orazio Satta, who also designed the predecessor four-cylinder engine of 1900 cc. It's defensible to argue that all the twin-cam fours since late 1959 were actually the same engine, with only bore and stroke changes for progressively larger displacements; some casting dimensions changed, too, to accommodate the different strokes.

Some essential manufacturing details were amazingly consistent: all these engines have the same main-bearing diameter and cylinder spacing so that crankshafts from any model will fit in any other's block. Since the throws of the crank differed between displacements, the cranks won't bolt up to run, but the basic dimensions of the lower half of the Alfa Romeo block from 1959-1984 were the same, and the main-bearing shells were interchangeable between engines.

Cylinder Head

The Giulia cylinder head was a V-shaped aluminum-alloy casting that carried the combustion chamber, camshafts and valves. More happens in the head than in any other part of the engine. Its most important function is to control the passage of gases through the engine. It does this using valves, which are opened at the appropriate time by a pair of camshafts.

We learned quite early in the life of the internal-combustion engine that two camshafts were the best possible solution for working the valves. Over the years, as engine speeds have increased and the velocities of gases within the engine have risen, air's weight has become more significant. Inertia goes with weight and because it has inertia, once set in motion, air tends to stay in motion. Without being too obtuse, that means that a straight path is the most efficient path for air to flow through an engine. And, cutting out a lot of

suspense by not describing less successful designs, two valves with an included angle of about 90 deg. allow the air to flow in a virtually straight line through the engine. In order to operate the valves at such an angle, separate camshafts are needed.

None of this is new information. It was all worked out in the benchmark four-cylinder, sixteen-valve, double-overhead-camshaft Peugeot Grand Prix engine designed by Ernest Henri in

An evocative photograph of the Giulia engine's predecessors—and inspiration. On the left was a straight eight-cylinder Alfa Romeo engine of the 1930s, showing its tall stance, large oil sump and the double overhead camshafts. On the right, was a Giulietta engine that was more compact, primarily due to its having only four cylinders. The double overhead camshafts and the large oil sump were still there.

1912. Alfa Romeo fielded a Grand Prix car two years later that followed the same basic design, but it was not until 1923 that Giuseppe Merosi was again prompted to create an Alfa Romeo with two overhead camshafts. Merosi's successor, Vittorio Jano, set Alfa Romeo on a design course that continues to this day—a light, high-speed dohc engine, which is exactly what the Giulia has.

I don't mean to slight the remainder of the Alfa Romeo engine. It was, after all, a five-main-bearing, wet-sleeved design that used lightweight castings extensively, but it was the cylinder head design

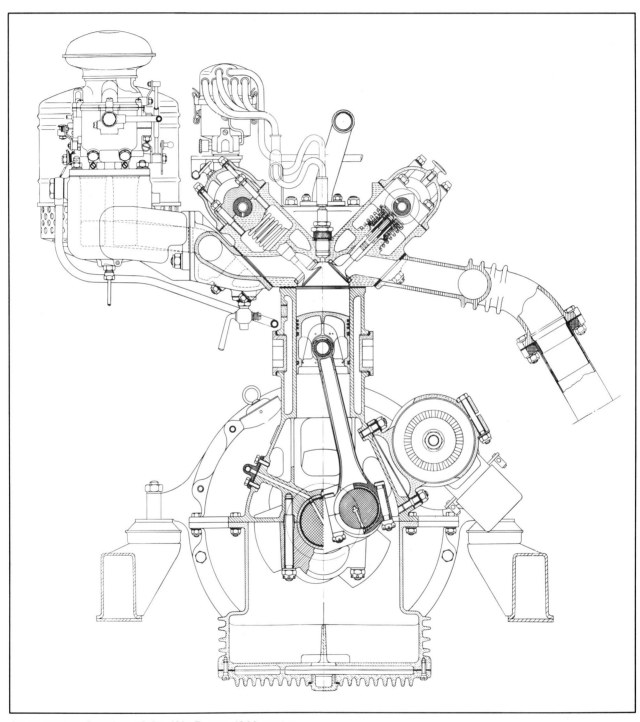

Cross-section drawing of the Alfa Romeo 1900 engine. The basis for the Giulietta and Giulia engine designs was all here.

that has most distinguished Alfa Romeo over the years.

The Giulia head was a labyrinthine casting with water passages provided wherever possible to keep the heat of combustion from melting anything. The head, more than any other part of an engine, has to dissipate heat within a restricted space.

The combustion chamber was a hemispheric depression in the head where the two valves and spark plug were located. The spark plug was placed virtually dead center in the chamber's depression so that the flame front of the burning fuel could expand uniformly in all directions over the top of the piston. Because flame propagation was so uniform in the Alfa Romeo head, the tendency toward power-robbing spark knock (uneven burning of the gases) was significantly reduced.

The Alfa Romeo combustion chamber was designed for power, but not low emissions. Its shape meant that only the inertia of the incoming and exhausting gases provided turbulence to maintain even atomization of fuel during the compression stroke. On modern emission-controlled engines, the combustion chamber is a wedge that "squishes" the charge around the chamber as the piston rises to compress it. Fortunately, emissions control was not a matter of importance to the Giulia (at this time, although, retroactive emissions laws are not impossible). And, rather than change

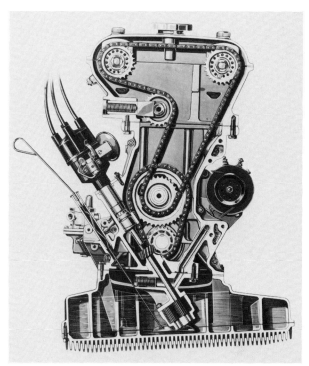

The Giulia camshaft and accessory drive arrangement were shown in this drawing. The short chain, which looped around the crankshaft, was the primary chain. The longer chain, which drove the camshafts, was the secondary chain. Note that the oil pump and distributor were driven off a common shaft.

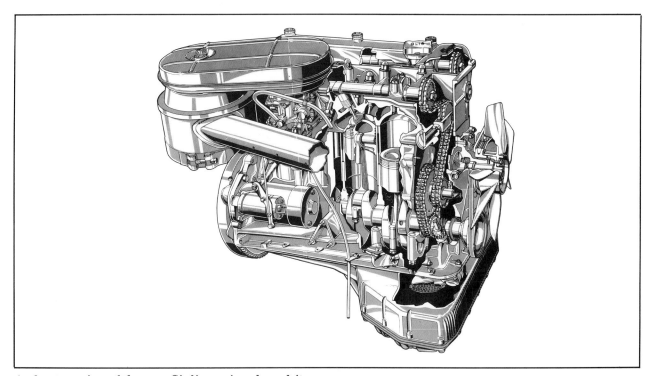

A phantom view of the new Giulia engine showed its major components. This engine, with its single Solex carburetor, was for the Giulia TI sedan.

the shape of the combustion chamber from the classic hemisphere, Alfa Romeo modified its intake system for fuel injection.

The head was sealed to the block with a metal-clad gasket. Some aftermarket gaskets used a fabric sandwiched between sheet copper, but the stock Alfa Romeo item was a fabric gasket with steel reinforcements around each combustion chamber opening.

The head gasket also sealed the six oil passages for camshaft lubrication. The actual seal was provided by small O-rings that were placed in head-gasket openings during rebuild. These O-rings proved to be the single most troublesome feature of the marque's engine, including the later V-6. On later Alfa Romeos, head-gasket sealing became a major problem. Generally, the Giulia did not share these legendary head-gasket sealing problems. I have had a single Giulia head-gasket failure, and that was a compression, rather than an oil leak.

Valves

The Giulia valve was basically a disc with a stem attached to operate it. When closed, the disc of the valve was seated against a steel insert in the top of the head's combustion chamber. When opened by the camshaft, the valve was held about 9 mm off its seat so the intake or exhaust gases could pass. Because the valve provided a narrow opening for high-speed gases, a lot of fluid-dynamic science was applied to the exact shape of the valve and its seat. Current practice uses three different planes ground around the circumference of the valve's head, but only one matches the angle at which the seat is ground. The shape of the slope as the valve

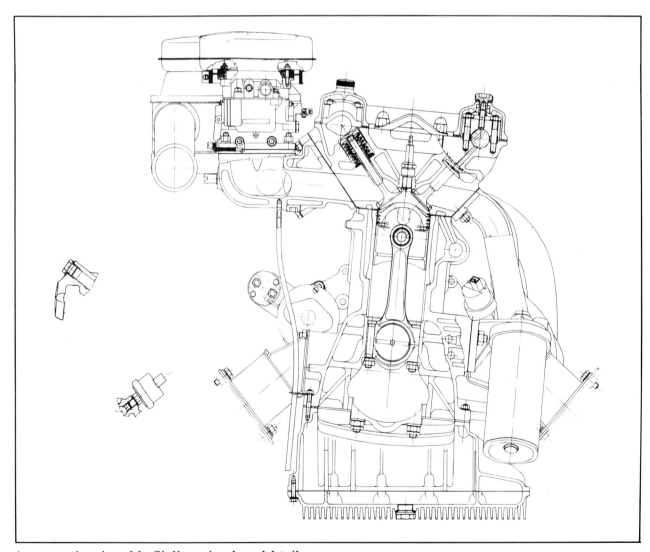

A cross-section view of the Giulia engine showed details of the connecting rod, piston and valvetrain. This was a TI engine with a single Solex carburetor.

The intake side of the Giulia engine with a single Solex carburetor. The distributor had been removed. Note the location of the fuel pump low on the block toward the front of the engine.

The exhaust side of the Giulia engine with the cartridge-type oil filter. Note how the mounting face for the transmission was reinforced with three heavy cast-in ribs.

The same engine as above, rotated 90 deg. to show a front view. The extra-wide sump was heavily finned to help cool the oil.

disc joins its stem was another aerodynamically important feature, though, in practice, much less important than the surfaces of the valve seat.

The Giulia's valves did not work in the bare aluminum provided by the head. Instead, bronze valve guides were pressed into the head to ensure a long-lasting surface for the valve stem to bear against. A small amount of oil was permitted to leak onto the valve stem for lubrication. This oil was overflow from the camshaft bearings, which

The Giulia camshaft cover was a light aluminum-alloy casting. Note the cast supporting web at the far right. The dished part of the cover was designed to allow room for the air intake plumbing.

123

With the camshaft cover removed, the twin camshafts were plainly visible. The chain had been removed to show the side-by-side drive sprockets.

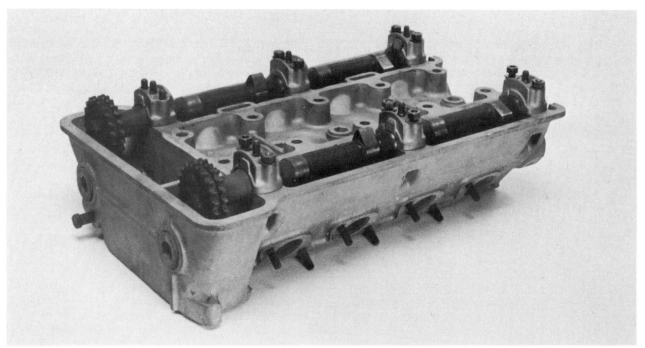

The Giulia cylinder head by itself as seen from the exhaust side. Note the prominent set of six camshaft bearings. The screw on the front face of the head clamped the chain tensioner in place.

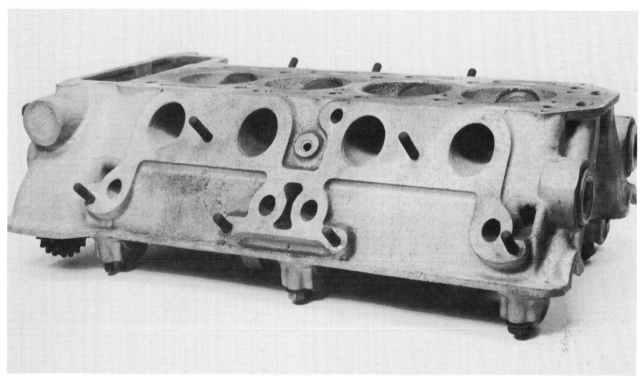

The cylinder head removed and laid upside-down. This was the intake side, so the four large passages carried the air-fuel charge. The four smaller holes near the bottom were water passages to the intake manifold.

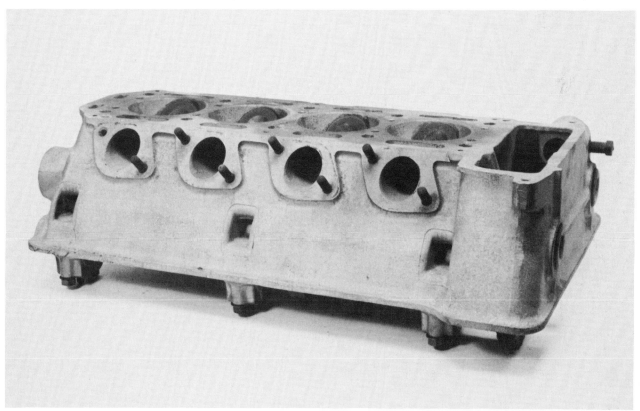

The other side of the cylinder head, also upside-down, showed the four exhaust ports.

The intake side of the cylinder head, showing the deep dish of the hemispheric combustion chambers. You can see from this angle the straight-through flow of gasses between the intake and exhaust ports.

was caught in galleries near the camshaft follower cups for camshaft-lobe lubrication.

Each valve was held in a normally closed position by a pair of springs. The small clearance between the valve and the camshaft base was adjusted using shims that were fitted over the tip of the valve's stem.

Camshafts

The Giulia camshafts were driven by a chain from the crankshaft and run in bearing surfaces machined into the aluminum part of the head; there are no camshaft-bearing inserts as there were crankshaft bearing inserts. The load carried by the cam bearings was quite low, and their large surface provided ample capacity. The lobes of the camshafts bore on the stems of the valves, so that the valves were opened as the camshaft lobe rotated.

In stock Giulia engines, the intake and exhaust camshafts had the same profile and so were interchangeable. This was not true of aftermarket high-performance camshafts, so it is a good idea to keep

A close-up view of the Giulia's combustion chambers. Note that the spark plug was offset somewhat from the center of the combustion chamber to permit the largest-possible valve diameters.

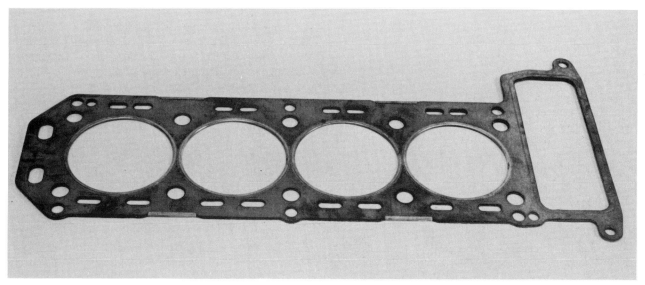

A metal-clad Giulia cylinder head gasket. The soft metal conformed to small irregularities in the head surface without sacrificing strength. This kind of gasket was *frequently thicker than stock to restore the proper compression ratio on engines that have had the cylinder head milled excessively.*

track of which cam goes where if they're removed from the engine. The rotating camshaft had four lobes that opened the intake or exhaust valves to admit or exhaust gas from the engine.

The profile of the cam has undergone much development over the life of the internal-combustion engine and it is the most exotic part of an engine. Engine performance is affected not only by how wide the camshaft opens a valve, but by how long the valve is held open.

In general terms, you can tell how "hot" a Giulia cam is by looking at it. If it is rounded, with a gradual curvature toward the tip of the lobe, it is a

mild camshaft that will produce low-end torque and not much high-speed power. If the lobe peaks sharply, the camshaft gives higher performance.

The intake and exhaust camshafts can be timed individually to the exact needs of the engine. This was a unique advantage of the Giulia's twin-camshaft design, which allowed a great deal of experimentation to extract the maximum possible horsepower or torque from an individual engine. It did not amount to letting you grind your own, but adjustable cam timing came very close to that.

Camshaft-timing adjustment was provided by two mating discs on the sprocket of the camshaft

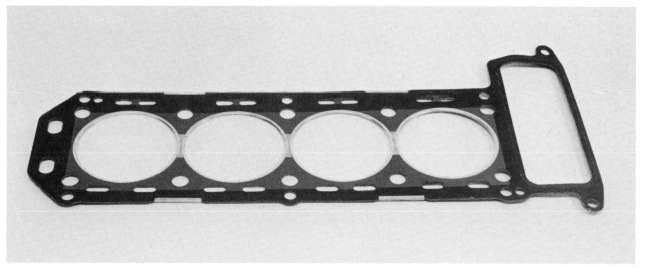

A composition Giulia cylinder head gasket utilizing metal sealing rings around each cylinder. Overall, this *fabric gasket was more compliant but weaker than the metal-clad gasket.*

Giulia intake and exhaust valves. The intake valve, sitting upright, always had a larger head diameter than the exhaust valve.

Components of the valve assembly included the valve itself, inner and outer springs, the disc-shaped retainer and two keepers which were wedged between the retainer and the valve stem. The assembly was held together only by valve-spring pressure.

that were held in place by a small through-bolt. One disc had one more hole than the other so that, as they rotated in relation to each other, only one hole could line up between the two. The advantage of this vernier arrangement was that it permitted changing camshaft timing in 1.5 deg. increments.

The clearance between the camshafts and the valve follower cups should be checked occasionally. The proper distance for the Giulia was 0.018 to 0.019 in. for the intake and 0.020 in. for the exhaust. In practice, you could go slightly closer to get more overlap and a wider opening. The minimum clearance was 0.012 in. under any circumstance for any valve. The exhaust valve was in more critical need of a wide clearance than the intake valve.

Always record valve clearances for reference. Over time, a valve clearance that was gradually closing up indicated a stretching valve head. Replace the particular valve and have the remaining valves inspected closely by a professional.

Engine Block

In contrast to the head's complexity, the Giulia block was a simple casting. Its primary purpose was to provide a solid structure into which the crankshaft and cylinders fitted.

The block was divided halfway down by a sturdy partition that was holed to accept the wet cylinder sleeves. Beneath the partition was a network of braces that helped contain the stresses of

The bucket-shaped valve follower fit over the tip of the valve, covering the springs. The follower had a slightly convex bearing surface, revealed here as annular wear.

128

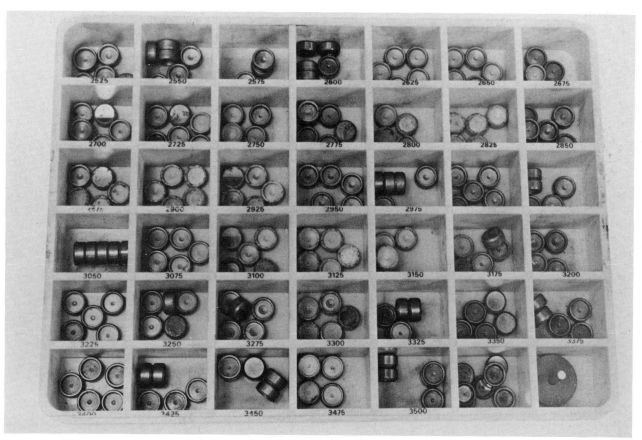

The numbered shim compartments visible in the image read (left to right, top to bottom):

2525, 2550, 2575, 2600, 2625, 2650, 2675

2700, 2725, 2750, 2775, 2800, 2825, 2850

2875, 2900, 2925, 2950, 2975

3050, 3075, 3100, 3125, 3150, 3175, 3200

3225, 3250, 3275, 3300, 3325, 3350, 3375

3400, 3425, 3450, 3475, 3500

Adjusting shims were used between the valve stem and the valve follower to adjust the gap between the valve and its camshaft lobe. A full set of shims, shown here, was mandatory for a dealership, but an unlikely luxury for the typical Alfa Romeo owner.

A cam lobe indicated the engine's stage of tune. A sharply-pointed lobe, such as the Giulia TI Super cam seen here, revealed a highly-tuned engine. Less highly-tuned cams have a more rounded lobe. The height of the lobe determined how wide the valve opens.

The camshaft ran on bearing surfaces machined into the head. Insert bearings were not required because the speeds and pressures involved were low. The camshaft could be removed easily from the engine after its three top bearing halves had been removed and the timing chain disconnected. The base of the camshaft lobe was also shown in this photo. The distance between the base and the valve follower cup was measured when setting the valves.

the crankshaft and improve its load-bearing capabilities.

The block was an interesting study in the use of curved surfaces to improve rigidity. It had few truly plane surfaces, in spite of the fact that the design could be quite slab-sided, indeed.

The cam timing mark was located on the forward cam bearing, seen here. The mark on the cam must line up exactly with the mark on the bearing.

Most blocks split the main bearing on the same plane as the gasketed surface where the block and pan mate. This was an economical arrangement because a single pass of a mill would finish a lot of surfaces that need machining. The drawback of this arrangement was that it put the weakest joint of the block in the plane (the main-bearing cap) of highest stress, and the bearing support by the block was limited to a radius of 180 deg.

The Giulia took the more costly approach of putting the main-bearing cap split deep into the block so that ample supporting webs could be cast into the block. The result was that the periphery of the block formed a sturdy "skirt" around the crankshaft, and the bearing support radius exceeded 200 deg.

Cylinders

The cylinders were slip-fit into the bores of the block and were sealed at their bottom by a slender rubber band.

It always amazed me how trouble-free this seal was. I have never had an Alfa Romeo that leaked coolant into the sump, and I have heard of only one in my thirty years of experience with the marque.

The cam drive sprocket was attached to the camshaft using a set of vernier holes and a locating bolt. If the camshaft was not properly timed, the vernier adjustment was used to get increments of 1.5 deg. rotation. The same adjustment could be easily used to increase valve overlap for improved high-speed breathing.

Pistons

Alfa Romeo pistons were made of a light aluminum alloy and had two compression rings and one oil control ring. For racing, the factory supplied a higher-compression piston with thinner compression rings. Under normal use, the stock pistons were more than adequate and would safely withstand higher compression ratios obtained by milling the head.

The piston pins were free-floating and were secured with small circlips on either end. The pin was splash-lubricated by oil in the sump.

Connecting Rods

The connecting rods were short and sturdy. Giulia rods had a slight offset between the center plane of the rod and the big-end bearing. During reassembly of an engine, it was important to observe the offset. The rod was properly assembled if it was centered on the piston pin with equal gaps between the rod little end and the piston pin boss.

Oiling System

Pressurized oil was supplied by the oil pump, which was driven by a gear near the front of the crankshaft. The driven gear was on a shaft that also extended up to end in a cup used to drive the distributor. The oil pump itself was a pair of gears that supplied oil at a nominal 55 psi to the bearings.

The oil pump pickup almost touched the bottom of the pan, reaching down into the pool of oil to pick up the layer closest to the cool metal of the deeply finned aluminum sump. Put another way, the oil pump pickup was sized to the sump. Since there were several sumps available for the Giulia engine, it was important to verify that you have the right combination if you were assembling an engine from pieces. The sumps of 101 Series cars were narrow and deep; 105 Series cars typically had the hammerhead sump with its large, baffled cooling surface.

Drilled passages in the block carried oil to the crankshaft's main bearings. Drilled passages in the crank carried the pressurized oil to the rod-bearing journals.

In the crankshaft, the drilled oil passages were sealed using soft-metal plugs. On the Giulia, there never was a tendency for the plugs to loosen. The plugs on later Alfa Romeos will fall out and cause a drop in oil pressure.

Crankshaft

The Alfa Romeo crankshaft was legendary for its strength, in part because there were five main bearings, a bearing between each rod. Crankshaft failure was virtually unknown, even in engines that were raced long distances.

One way the crankshaft would fail was when there was a loss of lubrication resulting from oil that had emulsified with coolant. This failure was caused when the head-gasket O-rings failed, and coolant was forced into the oil passages after a hot engine was shut down. Potentially catastrophic, this failure could be identified early enough to avoid trouble simply by watching for a light-brown sludge on both the dipstick and the underside of the radiator cap.

At the front of the crankshaft was a gear to drive the oil pump and distributor, and a sprocket that drove a short chain to the intermediate sprocket. The intermediate sprocket drove a longer chain to the cams at half crankshaft speed. The longer chain was held in tension by a spring-loaded idler located in the head.

This idler should be tensioned occasionally. The official procedure was to rotate the engine backward at least one revolution (put the car in second and push it backward), then loosen the tensioner lock bolt on the head and retighten it.

I have never trusted the factory procedure because you have no assurance that the few turns you give the lock nut in fact free the tensioner so its spring will work against the chain. I prefer instead to remove the cam cover and use a large screwdriver to wedge the idler sprocket to its proper tension. Then, when I retighten the lock bolt, I can also test that the sprocket is locked in place without having to put blind force on the lock nut.

A warning: If someone does put too much force on the lock nut, the tensioner will be wedged open and will not release for adjustment. You can't check for this condition unless the cam cover is removed.

The cam drive chains were housed in an aluminum timing cover that bolted up to the front of

Alfa Romeo took special care to cool the exhaust valve. This close-up showed the oval water passage which cooled the exhaust port.

The Giulia TI Solex carburetor and manifold. The Solex had two throats, with the second staged to open during higher engine speeds. A single Solex was the best carburetor setup for low-speed and optimum drivability.

Two sidedraft carburetors distinguished the Giulia Super and Veloce engines from the lower-power Solex setup. The installation shown here used the Dell'Orto carburetor, a common Italian substitute for Weber.

the block. The water pump and tachometer drive were mounted to the front of this cover. Occasionally, one would like to remove this piece to ease access to the cam drive chain or to replace the front oil seal around the crankshaft. In theory, by removing the pan and the head, it was possible to then remove the front timing cover. In practice, however, it was not a practical operation. Any repair requiring the removal of the cover should be made with the engine removed from the car.

Carburetion

The stock Giulia intake system consisted of a single, heated manifold carrying a two-throat Solex carburetor. Giulia Veloces had an abbreviated manifold that was really little more than a spacer for the two sidedraft DCOE Weber carburetors.

There was probably never a Giulia owner who didn't covet the Veloce's dual-Weber setup. There was no doublt that the single Solex carburetor undercarburetes the Giulia engine, but it did have the advantage of simplicity.

Several different kinds of Solex carburetors were fitted to the Giulia engine. The differences had to do with choke activation and control of the

Mounting Weber Carburetors on a Giulia Engine

In order to fit dual Webers to the Giulia engine with Solex carburetor, both the Webers and their manifold are required. If you don't have the Weber manifold, you're in for a major search. You can use a Spica fuel-injection manifold (not including the part that carries the throttle plates, of course) in conjunction with John Shankle's Weber-adapter kit (see appendices for supplier details). I have never tried this approach, but I see no reason why it could not be made to work with only a little effort.

On the Giulia, the lowest manifold mounting stud on the engine has to be replaced with a shorter one to adapt a Weber manifold. The engine should be tilted using Veloce motor mounts. The carbs will fit without tilting the engine if you don't have an air cleaner attached, but that is truly inviting long-term disaster.

If you fit the Weber carbs, you'll need different cams, at a minimum. The carbs alone free up the top revs so the engine feels as if it has a set of new lungs, but actual performance will not rise significantly unless you do more to the engine. The obvious choice is to use Veloce cams, but if you can't find a pair, Shankle and a large number of other suppliers offer aftermarket cams in a wide range of grinds. But don't order yourself a set of hot GTA cams if you want to drive on the street. In general, you should order the mildest cams you think you can live with, not the hottest. You can learn to hate hot cams if you do a lot of city driving.

Having fitted new cams to your newly Weber-carbureted engine, you'll of course want to increase the compression ratio of the engine and then add a set of proper headers; then the rear-axle ratio should be changed and so on.

I've known owners who prefer to swap Webers for the single Solex. They gain some tractability, and the engine becomes slightly more convenient to maintain. If you can make the swap, pack up the Webers neatly and put them away. Avoid selling them, for a real Veloce Giulietta is a rare and desirable piece.

There were also several Weber downdraft carburetors that matched the mounting studs of the Solex manifold exactly. If you try to exchange a Weber downdraft, check to see that the throttle bellcrank is on the outboard side of the carburetor when the float bowl faces forward. The throttle shaft must point toward the engine, not run parallel to it.

The two-piece exhaust manifold paired cylinders one and four, and two and three. This arrangement assured that there was maximum separation between exhaust gas pulses in the exhaust pipe. This 101 Series manifold is fitted to the author's Giulia Super.

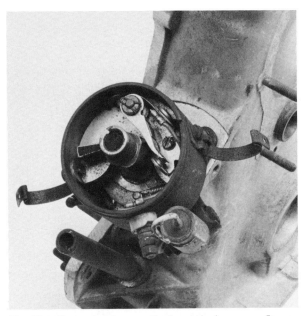

The distributor in place on the front timing cover. Its cap and rotor have been removed to show the contact points. Giulias typically were equipped with Bosch distributors: this unit happened to be a lookalike, workalike by Marelli.

secondary throttle plate, which was weighted to help it stay closed under partial throttle. Generally, all 35APAIG Solex variants were interchangeable.

Exhaust System

The stock Giulia exhaust system was a pair of cast headers that were similar to the one-four/two-three design of the manifolds fitted to later 1750 and 2.0 liter engines. The difference between the Giulia and later exhaust manifolds was the angle of the flange for the head pipe (no great challenge if you were fabricating something). The Giulia Veloce used true headers, fabricated from steel tube.

Original Giulia exhaust systems were virtual Abarth parts and had no internal baffling. If you're fabricating an exhaust system for a Giulia, use only straight-through glasspack and resonator units for silencing.

Ignition System

The Giulia ignition system was absolutely conventional, with a coil and distributor supplied by either Bosch or Magneti Marelli. The distributor had an automatic advance provided by weights

The top of the Giulia block with all four cylinders slipped into place. This photo showed clearly the water *passage cast into the block and the four oval passages which provided coolant to the exhaust ports.*

The block had been removed from the engine stand. Note the sturdy cast-in supporting webs between the main bearings and the block's wall.

The bare Giulia block, upside-down on an engine stand. This angle made clear just how deeply the crankshaft was recessed into the block. The hole almost dead-center on the front of the block was the bearing for the intermediate camshaft drive sprocket.

This photo showed how the mounting studs for the main bearing caps and the head were virtually inline. This arrangement helped reduce stress on the block by confining the clamping forces to a single, vertical plane.

This close-up of the main bearing surfaces in the block showed how bearings one, three and five were drilled for oil passages. Oil traveled to bearings two and four through the crankshaft itself.

A Giulia cylinder removed from the block. Though simple, this was a high-precision part. The cylinder was easy to re-bore, but the relatively low cost of the unit argued for its replacement, not repair. Thanks to its removable cylinders, 100 percent of the wearing surfaces of a Giulia engine could be replaced.

The piston top was marked with an arrow and should be installed with the arrow pointing in the direction of rotation. This piston was also stamped to show that it is 0.020 in. oversize.

and springs. The stock Alfa Romeo ignition system was perfectly adequate for the Giulia.

Most owners will want to adjust the gap of the distributor points. This is a straightforward procedure, eased somewhat if the distributor rotor is removed (on some models it's screwed on; don't lose the screw). The cap is held on by two blue-steel clips which are pried free with a screwdriver.

First, run an ignition file between the points to clean them of deposits. Rotate the engine until the

The stock Giulia piston was cast aluminum. The crown was partially cut away to provide safe clearance from the valves. A slight skirt extended downward to provide a large bearing surface for the piston's side-thrust.

Alfa Romeo rods were remarkable for their sturdiness. The rod was relatively short, with large small- and big-end bearings.

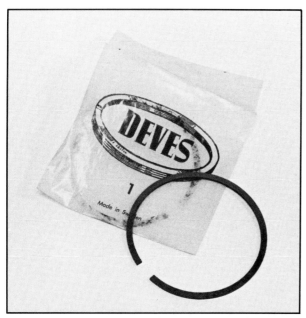

A compression ring, which fitted into the top groove of the Giulia piston. The rings were slightly expanded to fit over the piston during assembly.

points are fully open and use a feeler gauge to measure the gap between the points. It should be between 0.014 and 0.016 in.

If it is not, look closely at the points and identify the adjusting mechanism and locking screw. Loosen the screw slightly and then move the stationary point to achieve the proper clearance.

Be careful in returning the rotor and cap to their original positions.

Cooling System

In order to overcome the heat of the exhaust gases that passed through it, the head was the first

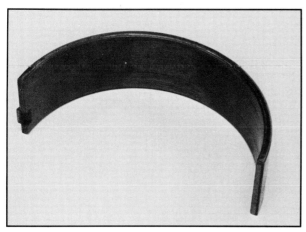

A Giulia rod bearing half. The tang on the lower left edge of the bearing fit in a groove machined in the rod and kept the bearing from spinning inside the rod.

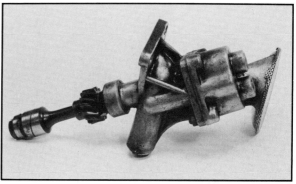

The Giulia oil pump was a complex casting. The oil pickup/strainer showed its right profile. The two pump gears occupied the rightmost third of the unit. The pressure relief valve pointed downward, and the crankshaft driven gear was on the shaft which faced left. At the tip of the shaft was the connector for the distributor drive.

The bottom of the Giulia sump was well finned to help cool the engine oil.

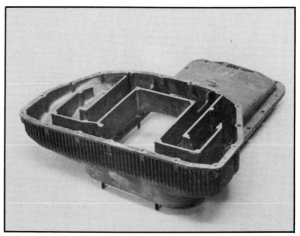

With the finned portion of the Giulia sump removed, the baffled oil passages were revealed. The baffles assured that the oil traveled for as long as possible over the cool sump bottom.

A large oil gallery ran the length of the Giulia block on the exhaust side. The oil pump fed pressurized oil to the hole on the front machined surface of the block in the center of the photo. Just below and behind the hole was the drilled passageway which carried oil to the front-most main bearing. Note that the oil-supply hole was visible in the shiny first main bearing surface.

part of the engine to receive cooled water from the radiator. From the water pump (located just below the head on the front timing-cover casting), cool water flowed alongside the engine through a tube cast into the block. It was directed through four oval-shaped holes in the head toward the exhaust valve seats. Thus, the hottest area of the engine received the coolest water. After circulating the

The forged Giulia crankshaft was fully counterbalanced and provided a main bearing on either side of each rod bearing.

In the center of this close-up photo you can see an open crankshaft oil passageway, which has been tapped for a threaded plug. The stock Alfa Romeo plug was simply a soft metal slug, which, over time, can loosen and fall out.

The front timing-chain cover was a light alloy casting. The large hole at its bottom carried the front crankshaft oil seal. The smaller hole above it was for the tachometer drive gear.

Preferred chain-tensioning practice: Use a large screwdriver to obtain proper chain tension. The clamping bolt must not be overtightened.

The back side of the timing-chain cover. The oil pump mounted to the bottom of the cover and fed oil through the cast-in passage running at a 45 deg. angle to the right in the photo. The oil then made a 90 deg. turn and exited the cover through the large hole midway between the dipstick and distributor mounting flange.

The engine oil filter was carried inside a large steel housing. An aluminum 90 deg. adapter mounted to the side of the engine.

The clutch driving disc was a concentric trio of circles. The clutch pressure plate had the largest diameter. Just above it was the spring-carrier assembly which also held the three clutch actuating arms. The bearing surface for the throwout bearing was nearest the camera.

head, the water passed through the thermostatic housing on the intake manifold and returned to the radiator.

The car's heater was also fed hot coolant. The two taps for the heater were on the water pump itself and the back of the head. A heater air-bleed valve eliminated any air in the heater system. If air

bubbles in the heater in the passenger compartment, you heard a distracting gurgle.

Accessories

The Giulia starter mounted with two bolts to the transmission bellhousing. Starters were made by Lucas, Marelli and Bosch for Alfa Romeo. The Bosch unit was the most reliable.

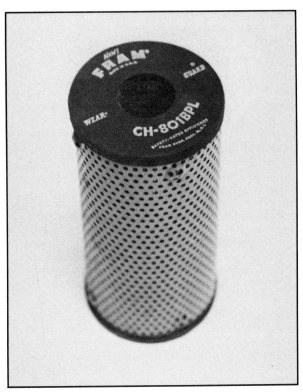

The pleated oil filter should be replaced every 3,000 miles.

The clutch driven plate had a splined center which slipped onto the transmission input shaft. The six coil springs in the unit helped absorb the shock of rapid clutch engagement.

Giulias used generators and regulators manufactured by Bosch, and these, like the starters, were superior to the other manufacturers' products.

Both the starter and generator were interchangeable between Giuliettas and Giulias. Since the Giulia units were more robust, they work well in Giuliettas, but Giulietta units were not recommended for the Giulia.

It was quite possible to fit a later alternator from a 1750 or 2.0 liter to the Giulia. This was not a difficult job, but it required some knowledge of electrics in order to get the wires hooked up properly. While the conversion makes sense practically, it detracts from the authenticity of a valuable classic. Similarly, the Giulia oil filter used a cartridge that was especially difficult to change when the hammerhead sump was fitted. Adapters are available to fit modern spin-on filters, but these again detract from originality.

When you change a stock Giulia oil filter, instead of trying to work the sheet-metal filter housing down to free it from its mount, remove the entire housing where it attaches to the block (two nuts) and then dismantle the filter on the bench.

Verify that the paper gasket is usable before you reassemble the unit to the block.

Clutch

The clutch is a device that connects or disconnects power. When you push the left foot pedal, you overcome spring pressure that clamps a fabric-faced disc (called the driven plate) between a heavy metal disc (called the driving plate) and the flywheel. The driving plate is bolted to the flywheel; the driven plate is splined to the transmission. When the clutch pedal is released, heavy springs in the driving plate clamp the driven plate to the flywheel, transmitting power from the flywheel to the transmission.

The advantage of this arrangement is that the fabric driven plate can slip without (immediately) burning up from friction. Its ability to slip allows you to transition between clutch in and out gradually.

American clutches are built with a robust idiot factor and can be slipped almost without harm. All early European cars (including the Giulia) presumed that the driver used the brakes, and not the

The main section of a Giulia five-speed transmission. The upper set of gears comprised the main and input shafts. The lower set of gears was the secondary, or lay, shaft.

clutch, to hold the car on a hill while waiting for traffic. As a result, Alfa Romeo clutches were significantly more prone to failure than was American custom. This doesn't mean they were fragile, but they did have a limit to the abuse they would take.

You can increase the clamping pressure of a clutch by fitting stronger springs to the driving plate, and lengthen driven-plate life by using a harder fabric. Fitting anything different from stock will involve trade-offs, and you can end up with a clutch that requires two feet to release, or a lining that slips easily or has a short service life and virtually no transition between on and off.

Later-model Alfa Romeos used a diaphragm-type spring instead of the multiple coil springs used on the Giulia. The flywheel diameter was larger on 1750 and newer Alfa Romeos, so the flywheels and clutches were not interchangeable to the Giulia unless a lot of other parts were swapped, including bellhousings and starters. The 2.0 liter flywheel was not only larger, but it also used a different bolt-mounting pattern to the crank and could not be fitted (practically, anyway) to the Giulia.

Representative components of a synchronizer assembly. Top left: the synchronizer shift ring. Top right: the synchronizer hub, which fit inside the shift ring. In the middle of the photo was a gear and at the bottom, parts of the synchronizer mechanism.

Transmission

The Giulia transmission was carried in a sturdy aluminum housing that split along the length of the housing. At the front of the housing was a large bellhousing that covered the flywheel and clutch assembly and mated the transmission to the engine. At the rear of the transmission was a short extension housing that carried fifth and reverse gears.

Originally, transmission gears were slid along a splined shaft into engagement with another gear. In order to engage, the two gears had to be turning at the same speed, or synchronized. (Reverse gear still involved sliding gears into mesh.) Driving a sliding-gear transmission takes much more skill and attention than most modern motorists care to develop. The synchromesh transmission includes small clutches that control gear speeds so that gear engagement is straightforward and can be completed without special skill.

In the Giulia transmission, all the action took place on the mainshaft, the rear end of which was referred to as the output shaft. The input shaft was mounted inline with the front of the mainshaft so that, when you first pulled the transmission apart, it appeared that there were only two parallel shafts. Not so: the big shaft with all the gears and synchronizers on it was really two pieces.

The input shaft carried a gear that meshed with a gear on the idler, or layshaft. The only purpose of the layshaft was to carry power from the input shaft to each of the transmission's main gears, which rotated freely around the mainshaft. All of the forward gears on the layshaft were always meshed with the gears on the mainshaft (remember that the reverse gear involved a slider).

Engaging a gear only required locking the desired main gear to the mainshaft. A collar that could engage the gear slide on a hub that was attached to the shaft, so the collar rotated as part of the mainshaft. The gear was locked to the shaft, then, just by engaging it with the collar. In the process of engagement, a small, expanding clutch inside the main gear was used to bring the gear up to the speed of the collar.

The sliding collars were moved using selector forks which were attached to a set of three rails that you moved using the shift lever. There was nothing in the transmission's basic design to keep more than one gear from being engaged at a time; indeed, some transmissions erupted in a hemorrhage of pieces when more than one gear was accidentally engaged. There was an elegant lock-out system used between the rails to ensure that only one rail at a time was used to engage a gear. Movement of the rail for reverse gear also turned on the back-up light.

Since the synchronizer clutch connected on only one side, but was manufactured with two working faces, turning the synchro rings around was the equivalent of replacing them. Clearly, you could only do this once before buying new rings. All Giulia transmission synchronizers worked well with EP transmission oil; early Giuliettas required non-EP oil. If you had a transmission apart, it was false economy not to replace all the synchronizers, bushes and bearings. The bushes between the gears and mainshaft were machined to size—you didn't just drop them in.

While understanding how the transmission worked was not out of range of the average enthusiast, rebuilding one may very well have been. Cleanliness counted, and a press and lathe were required tools for a complete overhaul. If the bushes didn't require replacement, you could take a transmission apart by renting a very large gear puller (about a 15 in. reach was required), but you wouldn't know if the bushes were bad until after you had the transmission apart. That is, you may well have found yourself with a disassembled transmission but without a lathe to put it back together again.

In point of fact, it was cheaper to buy a good used transmission than to rebuild one. You could use any Alfa Romeo transmission from the 101 Giulietta to the current Spider, but the Giulia bell-housing must be used to mate to the engine.

Driveshaft

Attached to the output shaft of the Giulia transmission was a large rubber donut that acted not only as a shock absorber for the remainder of the drivetrain, but also as a universal joint. The Giulia donut proved to be completely reliable, unlike the similar donuts that sullied the reputation of the Alfetta cars. They were all identical in design, but much less reliable in the newer cars. The Giulia donuts were long-lived.

The driveshaft was splined about halfway down the car, and the spline had a grease fitting that needed occasional ministration. Just ahead of the spline, there was a conventional universal joint and a rubber-supported steady bearing for the driveshaft. At the rear of the driveshaft was another conventional universal joint. Both universal joints required occasional lubrication (newer permanently lubricated joints were sometimes fitted).

All driveshafts required balancing. The Alfetta driveshaft was actually a part of the engine's rotating mass and so its balance was critical. The Giulia driveshaft was not nearly so critical in its balance requirements. Even so, if removed, it should be marked so it can be replaced in exactly the same rotational orientation to the transmission output shaft and the companion flange on the rear axle.

Rear Axle and Differential

Next to the crankshaft, the most robust piece on the Giulia was the ring-and-pinion gear set in the rear axle. The pinion was a cone-shaped gear that meshed with the circular ring gear. All the power of the engine was transmitted to this set and it had to withstand jack-rabbit starts as well as the continued pressure of 100+ mph tours. The set was really nothing more than a sturdy way of switching the twisting force of the engine from a lateral to transverse direction; that is, handling the 90 deg. turn from the spinning driveshaft to the spinning axle shafts.

Because so much power was transmitted, setting up the mesh of the pinion to the ring gear was a very exacting art and clearly beyond the average hobbyist. The pinion was moved in and out using shims, and the ring gear was located side-to-side with other shims to provide an exact engagement where maximum pressure was developed at the sturdiest part of the gear. Both the ring-and-pinion gear faces were curved, and it was usual to have the center axis of the pinion fall somewhat below the axis of the ring gear.

The ring gear did not drive the axle shafts directly. Attached to it was a set of gears that allowed the two rear wheels to turn at different speeds, a feature necessary for turning a corner without spinning one wheel as the outer wheel turns more times than the inner. This unit was called a differential which, itself, consisted of two ring gears and two pinion gears. The pinion gears meshed with the ring gears and limited the rate at which the two ring gears turned in relation to each other. The net result was not two-wheel drive, as many may think. Actually, only one rear wheel controlled the power that the Giulia put on the road.

The center universal joint for the Giulia driveshaft. The X-yoke design allowed the shaft to transmit power at an angle.

143

As long as both wheels had equal traction, then the power was divided equally between the two. But the standard differential played us false as soon as one wheel lost traction, as in snow or mud; then, the wheel without traction received all the power. That was exactly the opposite of what was wanted.

Limited-slip differentials were used on only a few racing Giulias, so a detailed examination here is a bit out of place. To simplify the operation of a limited-slip differential, a clutch pack is used to simulate traction for both wheels. Under normal-traction conditions, the clutches slip, allowing normal differential action. When one wheel loses traction, however, the clutch pack attached to its axle resists the axle's spinning and thereby simulates enough traction to coax some power from the car's differential.

You cannot tell from looking at a rear axle whether or not your Giulia was equipped with a limited-slip differential. The only way to check is to jack up one rear wheel and try to turn it with the handbrake off and the transmission in neutral. If the wheel spins freely, you do not have a limited-slip differential.

I have a Giulia Super fitted with a limited-slip differential from a later-model Alfa Romeo. The unit's more recent manufacture is revealed by the fact that both right and left wheel studs have conventional left-hand threads. On Giulias, the driver-side studs are right-threaded.

Brakes

A few of the first Giulia 1600 Sprints were fitted with three-shoe brakes working in large, radially finned Alfin drums. These cars had rear drum brakes like the Giulietta. The three-shoe brakes were full floating, so movement of one of the three brake adjusters affected the position of all shoes.

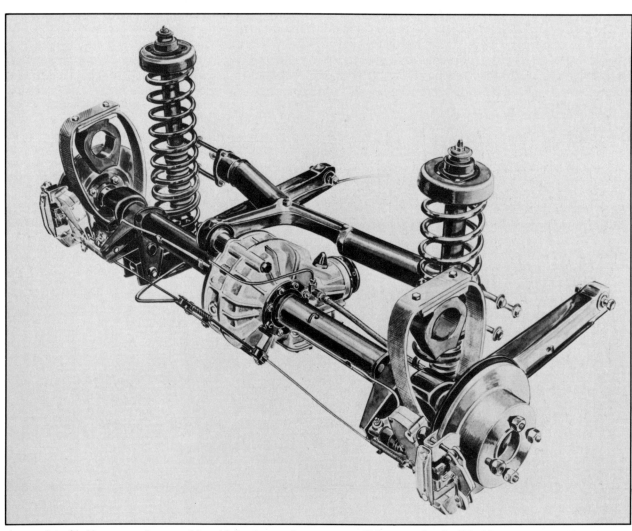

A complete Giulia rear-axle assembly with brakes and suspension locating links attached. The rear axle unit was light enough to be lifted by one person. Note that the differential housing was deeply finned for strength.

I have never been able to remember a clever way to determine which way to turn the star-wheel adjuster used on Alfa Romeo drum brakes. Since the drums were held on with only two (or three, in the case of the three-shoe units) taper-headed screws, I always found it easier to remove the drums to remind myself of how the adjusters work.

Rear drum brakes used a small square-headed adjuster that some person, surely, in the car's history will have mangled with a pair of pliers. The adjuster for the rear brake had a standard thread; it was screwed in to reduce shoe-to-drum clearance.

Disc brakes for the Giulia were initially Dunlops, and later ATEs. Parts for both were common with several other cars and a large parts store catering to foreign cars should be able to supply enough rubber to rebuild a cylinder.

The rear Dunlop disc brake design made the internal-combustion engine look intuitively simple. If you had a car with Dunlop brakes, studying the linkage of the rear unit yielded a pleasant afternoon of hilarious disbelief. Fortunately, they worked just fine.

ATE disc brakes used two pistons per caliper; they are not the cheap, floating-caliper design. If the car set for a long time, it's quite likely that a piston will freeze in its cylinder, reducing the braking effectiveness of the car slightly.

Frequently, you can unfreeze a stuck piston by forcing it all the way back into its cylinder and then working it in and out by alternately prying and applying the brakes. Remove the spring clip, but leave the pads in place and use a large flat-bladed screwdriver between the pad and the disc to force the piston into the cylinder. Then remove the screwdriver and apply the brakes. Repeat the operation several times to free the piston adequately.

Beginning with the Giulia, Alfa Romeo adopted power-boosted brakes. A large diaphragm with manifold vacuum on one side was used to add pressure to the brake's hydraulic system when the brake pedal was depressed. These boosters leaked occasionally, drawing brake fluid into the intake manifold and causing the car to appear to burn oil.

If the booster was broken or leaking, it was quite possible to run the Giulia brake system

A detail of the Dunlop rear brake. The brake cylinder ran parallel to the long spring and was attached to the C-shaped bracket to the right of the photo. The remainder of the brake was a series of levers that clamp pads against both sides of the disc.

The more-common ATE caliper assembly, shown here on the front suspension. A smaller, but otherwise identical unit was used for the rear. It was much tidier than the Dunlop rear brake assembly. Pistons on both sides of the discs provided the clamping force. The pads were held in place by the plus-shaped leaf spring located dead-center on the caliper assembly. The top and bottom of the leaf spring was held by two pins, clearly visible in this photo.

A Giulia Super brake vacuum booster. Note that the hydraulic lines had been connected to bypass the booster. This was not a desirable modification but, if the booster could not be rebuilt or another obtained, it was the only workable way to keep the car on the road. Higher brake pedal pressures were required.

unboosted in relative safety. Brake effort will increase noticeably, but not beyond the ability to lock up the wheels. Reconnect the lines (a female adapter is required) to eliminate the booster from the hydraulic system. Be sure to bleed the entire system thoroughly when you're through. Plug the vacuum line to the intake manifold.

When bleeding an Alfa Romeo's brakes, begin with the wheel farthest from the master cylinder (rear wheel on the passenger's side) and end with the wheel closest to the master cylinder. Brake fluid is a thin oil and can be harmful if it gets in your eyes. Wear goggles and be careful.

Most Giulias in the United States had four-wheel disc brakes, a feature that was first intro- duced for the TI front brakes only late in 1964. The Giulia Super was introduced with four-wheel disc brakes, a feature some manufacturers in 1990 are still representing as unusual (not true) and espe- cially desirable (true).

Steering Gear

Rack-and-pinion steering is renowned for its great feel and precision. Because of that, many people believed that the Giulia has rack-and-pinion steering. Not so. Two different boxes were used, one with Burman recirculating-ball design and the other with ZF worm and sector. Both offered some adjustment for wear, and neither was especially superior to the other.

The steering box operated one wheel directly and a track rod to another bellcrank arrangement on the opposite side of the car. The design meant that the tie rods to each wheel have equal length, and also made right-hand-drive conversion slightly more convenient.

8

Race Preparation

The image of Alfa Romeo is that it is a fast car which, off the showroom floor, is quite capable of sustaining racing stresses routinely.

There is a lot of truth to the image. As you will note, precious few modifications are made to the basic design in order to prepare an Alfa Romeo as a

GTA at speed during the 1967 six-hour Nürburgring endurance race. The drivers here, Bianchi/Rolland, took first place overall.

From the vantage point of this photograph at least, this Giulia TI 1300 appeared to be leading a powerful batch of sports racing prototypes. The venue was the 1967 nine-hour endurance race at Kylami in South Africa, where the team of K. B. Smith and Van der Heever here took an incredible third place overall.

The other end of the Giulia race spectrum, with an Alfa Romeo TZ taking first in class in the 1966 Jolly Hotel Trophy races in Italy.

winning race car. This is quite a different situation from the "stock" cars that circulate American tracks. Those cars have almost nothing in common, mechanically, with the sedans we see on the streets.

Note that in the following sections, I'll be listing Alfa Romeo part numbers where they may be helpful. Part numbers ending in .99 are not official Alfa Romeo numbers, but refer to unique parts available only through the old New Jersey-based Alfa Romeo International (ARI) distributorship, which is now a part of the Florida-based ARDONA organization.

As a starting point to setting up a Giulia engine for racing, the factory's preparation of the GTA offers an ideal benchmark.

GTA Engine: Cylinder Head

The stock GTA head was part number 10532.01.053.00. ARI supplied a prepared head, part number 10532.01.053.99, with the following modifications:

• Head thickness was reduced by an amount determined in conjunction with piston selection.

• Intake ports were reduced to 29 mm, with a 3 mm aluminum pipe driven into the port 25 mm or up to the beginning of the lower radius. They were tapered to match the inlet-port diameter just in front of the valve guide and epoxied in place. The smaller ports increase the velocity of the intake charge. Matching reducers were fabricated for the intake manifold.

• An 0.8x0.8 mm sealing groove was machined in a radius of 85.5 mm around each combustion chamber. An early cylinder head gasket, without mastic, was used (part number 10100.01.508.00).

• Water-passage size was reduced to lower water-flow velocity and improve cooling (two 6.5 mm diameter holes replaced each of the oval ports for intake-valve cooling on cylinders two and three), and the ten water holes that surrounded the combustion chambers were sealed.

• Intake guides were cut off flush with the port, and interior clearance was knurled to 0.001 in. The exhaust guides were not modified.

• An oil breather cap was used (part number 10511.01.037.00 or 10532.01.037.00).

• Carburetor-side internal diameter was machined to 45.5 mm.

• Air horns (part number 652.08.001) were used inside a cold-air plenum (part number 10532.08.204.00).

• Jetting for the Weber 45 DCOE carburetors was as follows:

The Giulia was even a success as a rally car. Here was the Ruiz 1750 GTV sliding hard through a corner. Bill Wood

In the United States, Alfa Romeos dominated their class in Trans-Am racing for years. Vic Provenzano and his GTA were the champs in 1970. Note the wider tires and the definite negative camber of the passenger-side front wheel. The clips around the windshield were Trans-Am regulation and the rear wheel-arch flare was an add-on.

GT Veloces distinguished themselves around the world. This was the Alec Mildren Giulia GT Veloce driven by *French in the 1968 Surfers' Paradise rally in Australia. He was first overall.*

Venturi 36
Main 150
Air 150
Idle F1255
Pump 35
Float level 48
Emulsion tube F16
Auxiliary venturi 4.5

Engine Block

If two-ring pistons were used on the GTA, the block height was reduced 0.8 mm and a corre-sponding amount was removed from the bottom of the cylinder liner.

The GTAm used a monosleeve design, in which the four individual cylinder sleeves were replaced by a single casting for additional strength. Some of these monosleeve assemblies found their way into other racing Alfa Romeos.

GTAm Fuel Injection

Many GTAm cars used Lucas Mk2 sliding-plate fuel injection with fuel control cam part number 10541.04.03/b. It and associated Lucas parts could

GT Veloces were always good in the snow because their weight distribution and fairly skinny tires gave supe- *rior traction. This was the Laurrusse/Dreyfus 2000 GTV in the 1973 Nieges et Glaces rally in France.*

An Autodelta GTA at the Italian Mugello circuit in 1968. Driver Riccardone captured first overall.

The Jean Rolland and GTA at the finish line after winning first place overall in the 1966 Coupe des Alpes. Note the two extra sets of driving lights and the grillework to protect the radiator.

Clearly, the Coupe des Alpes race was an up-and-down thing. The Baraillier/Verrier/Fayel GTA scored a first in Group 2 during the 1968 event. Runs such as the Coupe des Alpes gave excellent visibility to Alfa Romeo and helped establish the new GT Veloce bodystyle before the public.

be obtained from the factory. The guillotine throttle unit was part number 10551.01.060.99.

Giulia Competition Preparation

The Alfa Romeo Owners Club (AROC, see appendices for details) has always been a nuts-

The 1966 twenty-four-hours race at Le Mans with two Giulia TZs battling through a corner. The front runner here was the car of Biscaldi/Sala, which went on to second in class and fifteenth overall.

Alfa Romeo dealer Bill Knauz talked to Horst Kwech in the championship GTA which Knauz sponsored and Kwech prepared. Kwech formed AUSCA to campaign a series of racing Alfa Romeos which proved virtually the only serious competition to the Pete Brock 510 Datsuns of the era. Dave Trindler photo, Larry Ogle collection

Early testing of the new TZ 2 at Alfa Romeo's Balocco test track in 1966. The cars were developed by Autodelta, *and the race team's boss, Carlo Chiti, was at far left in the sweater.*

and-bolts group. It was originally formed to provide technical information to Alfa Romeo owners. Currently, four technical advisors are available by phone to answer member questions. In addition, the club magazine routinely publishes technical information.

It wasn't always so easy. When the club began, there was little information about the marque itself and virtually no technical information about the Giulietta. Consequently, a few individuals in the Chicago area got together to pool their knowledge and, about two years later, to write a letter to *Road*

The end of a successful day of testing, and the two TZ 2 cars were being rolled back into the transporter while *Chiti conferred with his test drivers. A pair of Autodelta GTAs were also being sorted out.*

The 1966 Targa Florio with the Pinto/Todaro TZ 2 at speed.

ALFA ROMEO, INC.
231 JOHNSON AVE., NEWARK, N. J. 07108
N. J. (201) 824-4949 • N. Y. (212) 227-6408
TWX 201/621/8285

WESTERN DIVISION
1700 DAISY AVE., LONG BEACH, CALIF. 90813
(213) 435-8351   TWX 213/549/1939

ALFA ROMEO GTA
Type 105.32

The GTA is a series production touring car. In answer to many requests we are listing below the details where the GTA differs from the Giulia GT.

Motor: 133 bhp SAE, dual Weber 45DCOE, 8 plug head. New crank, pistons, H.D. rods, and block. Dual distributor and coils. Large oil pump and pan.

Fuel System: Weber 45DCOE 14. Dual electric fuel pumps. Fuel filter and regulator. New intake manifold and linkage.

Exhaust: Large oversize steel tubing system. Sheet tubing headers.

Cooling: New water pump and radiator with provision for oil cooler.

Drive Line: H.D. clutch assy., new rear housing, "optional" gear ratio std., 5 speed. H.D. prop shafts with rubber joint reinforcement. New axle tubes. New rear center section.

Brakes: New racing calipers, non SERVO, racing pads, new m. cylinder and disc shields.

Wheels: Magnesium 6x14 std., new front hubs.

Suspension: Arms, pivots, springs, shocks, and joints are all new and different than std., G.T. Other differences include front anti-roll bar, rear alloy reaction triangle, limit straps, etc. Many parts derived from T.Z.I.

Steering: The box assembly is new. The steering wheel is wood rimmed. Track rod tubes, joints, and idler are also all new.

Electric: Lightweight generator, starter, and battery.

Body: Aluminum with plexi side windows. Lightweight steel chassis members. Lightweight instrument panel. Mesh grille with air inlets below main grille. Lightweight but durable SKAI interior trim. Bucket seats padded and upholstered. Light rear-seat cushions. Light door locks, handles and latches. Light carpets and rugs.

Right or left hand drive.

Price: P.O.E. $5,550.

FIA Homol. No. AR29 Tourismo

SCCA Sedan Class B

The US importer's spec sheet for the GTA, noting that it had been homologated with the FIA for Turismo or Touring Car racing and with the SCCA for Sedan Class B racing.

& Track inviting other Alfa Romeo owners to join. (A Detroit club had been organized earlier but did not join the Chicago group until somewhat later.) That letter was really the beginning of the national club, even though the Chicago chapter had members from all over the Midwest. One of the original members, in fact, was a dental student from Iowa, Paul Tenney. Other notable first members were Dick van der Feen of International Motor Sports Association (IMSA) and Bruce Young, the lead editor of *The Chicago Manual of Style, the* style book for authors and editors.

Paul Tenney became the first technical editor of the club. He collected virtually all the information one would need to race an Alfa Romeo successfully. One of my most indelible memories was driving his Giulietta Spider at one of the early Chicago conventions held at Bill Knauz' Alfa Romeo dealership. I thought Tenney's car was a souped-up Veloce until I popped the hood to discover a single Solex carburetor.

Tenney certainly knew what he was doing, and he compiled all the relevant racing information into a collection that was published by the club as the Competition Advisory Service (CAS). The CAS included conventional wisdom, official factory data and hard-won firsthand experience. It was Tenney's intent to update the information regularly, but the information covers only the four-cylinder engines from the Giulietta to the 1750. The CAS was reissued by the club in 1971 and is currently available from Alfa Ricambi in California (see appendices for details).

The CAS is divided into several sections, covering modifications to the head, block, lubrication system, ignition, electrical, exhaust, clutch, suspension, brakes and wheels. All the information is backed up by tables and illustrations, so that you are able to understand exactly how to make their Alfa Romeos more capable on the racetrack.

The introduction to the CAS best describes the scope of the document: "The facts are all here. If not, they just don't exist or were not recommended or proven. The experimentation has been done for you."

The first part of the CAS covers the general preparation of the engine, including Magnafluxing and balancing the connecting rods, crankshaft and valvetrain. Extensive balancing is suggested, including dynamic balance of the camshaft drive sprockets (with lock bolt included, of course). The intake and exhaust sets of valves are also balanced to match the weight of the lightest valve. (Note,

however, that you don't try to make the intake and exhaust valves the same weight; the exhaust valve is sodium-cooled and any machining on it to lighten it is potentially dangerous.)

The introductory section includes a multi-page reprint on blueprinting written by Dave Herrington for *Magic Circle*, a publication of Perfect Circle Corporation.

Cylinder Head Preparation

The cylinder head is milled to increase the compression ratio. For Type 101 and 105 single-plug heads, the head is milled 1.8 mm for an overall height of 110.2 mm.

With a milled head, a sealing groove has to be machined around the combustion chamber. For the Giulia 1600 engine, the groove is 85.5 mm diameter, 0.8 mm wide and 0.8 mm deep. For the 1300 cc engine, the groove has an 81 mm diameter. An early-type head gasket is used which has no mastic, and is slightly thicker. The groove causes the thicker head gasket to be embossed for an extra sealing surface, guarding against head-gasket failure.

The valve guides are cut flush with the port surface. The valves are machined to take a safety

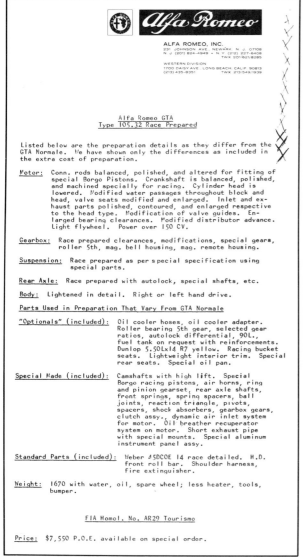

The US importer's spec sheet for the race-prepared GTA listing all the special preparation details as they differed from the GTA "normale."

International homologation papers passing the GTA for racing.

155

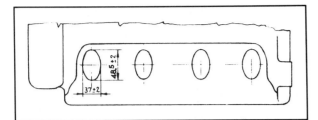

International homologation details on the GTA cylinder head intake specifications. The intake ports were described as 37 mm wide and 48.5 mm tall, plus or minus 2 mm.

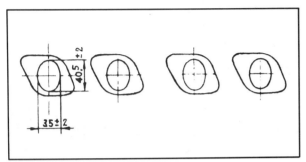

International homologation details on the GTA cylinder head exhaust specifications. The exhaust ports were described as 35 mm wide and 40.5 mm tall, plus or minus 2 mm.

ring, and special outer valve springs, part number 10511.03.313.03, are used with spring pocket number 10511.03.302.03.

The inlet ports are polished and smoothed to match the 45 DCOE bore, and air horns are fitted to the carburetors. Road-racing jetting is as follows:

Engine	1600	1750
Venturi	36	36
Auxiliary venturi	4.5	4.5
Main jet	150	150
Air correction jet	150	160
Emulsion tube	F16	F16
Pump jet	35	35
Idle jet	55F8	55F12
Air idle jet	90	90
Starter jet	65F5	65F5
Float valve	150	150
Float level	27–28 mm	27–28 mm
Float weight	26 grams	26 grams
Pump stroke	11 mm	11mm

The throttle butterflies are rotated so their notch is opposite the progression holes. The first (lowest) progression hole has a diameter of 1.0 mm; the second, 1.2 mm; and the third, 0.9 mm.

Engine Block Preparation

A groove is milled into the top of each sleeve to match the groove in the cylinder head. The resulting compression ratio is 10.8:2 if pistons number 10511.02.300.07 are used and the block is not milled. The compression ratio can be raised to 11.5:1 if the same pistons are machined using drawing number 10511.02.300.09 with the block

277.	Comando a mano		Automatico		A richiesta: comando a mano/automatico			
	Rapporto	Nº denti	Rapporto	Nº denti	Rapporto	Nº denti	Rapporto	Nº denti
1ª	2,54	$\frac{30}{23}$ x $\frac{35}{18}$			2,76	$\frac{30}{23}$ x $\frac{36}{17}$	3,30	$\frac{30}{23}$ x $\frac{38}{15}$
2ª	1,70	$\frac{30}{23}$ x $\frac{30}{23}$			1,78	$\frac{30}{23}$ x $\frac{30}{22}$	1,99	$\frac{30}{23}$ x $\frac{32}{21}$
3ª	1,26	$\frac{30}{23}$ x $\frac{26}{27}$			1,30	$\frac{30}{23}$ x $\frac{26}{26}$	1,35	$\frac{30}{23}$ x $\frac{27}{26}$
4ª	1				1		1	
5ª	0,86	$\frac{30}{23}$ x $\frac{21}{32}$			0,82	$\frac{30}{23}$ x $\frac{20}{32}$	0,79	$\frac{30}{23}$ x $\frac{20}{33}$
6ª	—				—		—	
RM	3,01	$\frac{30}{23}$ x $\frac{30}{13}$			3,01	$\frac{30}{23}$ x $\frac{30}{13}$	3,01	$\frac{30}{23}$ x $\frac{30}{13}$

International homologation details on the GTA transmission listing the stock gear ratios and gear teeth count at left, and two alternative sets of gears in the columns at right. The center column for an automatic transmission was left blank as no such gearbox was available.

milled 1.0 mm and the sleeve height reduced 1.0 mm by milling its lower mating surface.

Additional changes to the block include:

Component	Part number or description
Steel flywheel	10532.02.040.00
Rods	10512.02.020.00 (standard on some cars)
Reinforced rear main-bearing cap	10500.01.017.02
Oil pump	Nine-tooth gear (standard on some cars)
Oil pan (except 105 Series)	Stock Type 121 double-bottom
Type 105 wider sump	10500.01.211.03 (6 qt. capacity)
	10514.01.211.03 (7 qt. capacity)
	10514.32.211.00 (7 qt. capacity magnesium)
	10514.32.211.02 (10 qt. capacity magnesium)
Remote oil filter	10511.06.300.01

Front view of the Valco-prepped 1750 cc Giulia engine showing the custom-made pulleys, fabricated in aluminum alloy. Gary M. Valant/Valco

A 1750cc Giulia engine that has been fully competition prepped by Valco Enterprises of Dallas, Texas. The engine is ignited by a Crankfire system run off of the flywheel. The gearbox is a close-ratio five-speed Alfa Romeo transmission. Gary M. Valant/Valco

The key ingredients in building a sliding block rear suspension system in the style of the factory GTA rear end. This is the sliding block and steel pin. Gary M. Valant/Valco

Component	Part number or description
Oil cooler adapter	10516.01.014.00
Recuperator	10532.06.405.00 (meets FIA/SCCA regulations)

Ignition Timing

Fixed advance is 18 deg., and the maximum advance is 52 deg. at 7000 rpm.

The main pin plate for the sliding block GTA suspension is counterbored to accept the steel pin. The pin is then welded in position on the plate. Gary M. Valant/Valco

Electrics

The generator should be strengthened against centrifugation by epoxying the commutator and windings and then dynamically balancing it.

Lightweight prepared GTA generators are part number 10532.05.050.00.

Exhaust

Racing headers are available from Alfa Romeo, as well as most aftermarket Alfa Romeo stores. The official headers are:

101 Series	Part number 10121.01.071.00 and .072.00
105 Series	Part number 10516.01.071.00 and .072.00
1750 Group 5	Part number 10500.30.002.98 (an equal-length, ARI part)

Clutch

The lightweight TZ clutch disc (part number 10511.12.032.02) and pressure plate (number 10511.12.031.02) are used unless the stronger disc (number 10516.12.032.01) and plate (number 10516.12.035.00) are needed.

A stock plate can be made stronger using springs (part number 10516.12.031.01/11). These springs require a reinforcing ring on the spring cups.

The clutch throwout bearing is part number 10532.12.042.00.

The main support plate for the sliding block rear end with the steel pin installed. The upper hole allows for access to the rear-end differential to refill the fluid. The side notch is for the parking brake. Gary M. Valant/Valco

Transmission

A magnesium bellhousing is part number 10532.13.012.00. Heavy-duty shift forks for first and second gears are part number 10514.13.503.10 and for third and fourth gears part number 10514.13.504.11.

A heavy-duty rear transmission mount is number 1365.15402.

Sell Dentax 90 oil is recommended.

Driveline

The front driveshaft donut should be re-inforced using cover numbers 10516.15.032.01 and 10516.15.032.02, and spacer number 10516.15.318.00.

The dynamic balance of the driveshaft should be confirmed.

Rear Axle and Differential

A ZF Lok-O-Matic limited-slip differential part number 10510.17.043 should be used with axle shafts number 10514.17.300.00, which are stronger.

The 101 Series rear torque-mounting brackets on the axle tubes must be strengthened by making them box sections. Weld plates between the stamped-steel flanges front and rear, making cer-

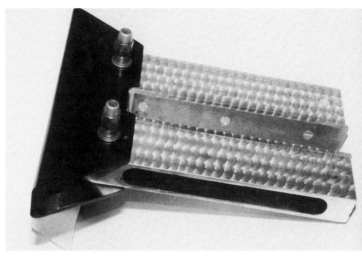

The sliding block guide is machined from a solid piece of aluminum alloy. Steel wear plates are then bolted to the inner friction surfaces. Gary M. Valant/Valco

tain that the front plate doesn't obstruct the trailing link.

On 105 Series cars, the rubber silentblocks in the trailing link should be placed with Heim spherical bearings.

Rear stabilizer bars should be added if not already in use. Stock 1750 bars are fine, but a 16 mm GTA bar is part number 10532.25.600.00, an 18 mm bar is number 10532.25.600.02 and a 20 mm bar is number 10532.25.600.03.

A variety of rear springs is available from the factory, and virtually all Alfa Romeo specialty shops offer aftermarket springs.

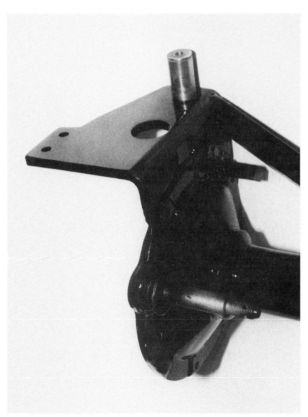

The main support plate is welded onto the differential housing and a support bracket is added. Gary M. Valant/Valco

The entire sliding block assembly is then mounted on the differential. Note the separate support bracket added to the right axle tube. Gary M. Valant/Valco

The sliding block and differential unit with a torque T replacement, ready to be installed on the car. Gary M. Valant/Valco

The entire assembly with fabricated support arms. The block guide had been added in place as well. Gary M. Valant/Valco

Front Suspension

Stock front springs can be cut ¾ to 2 coils, depending on the desired ride height.

The GTA used Koni shock absorbers part number 80-1551, or Alfa Romeo part number 10532.21.070.99 (ARI number).

Front roll bars of 1¹⁄₁₆ in. diameter are suggested. Shankle Engineering has a complete line of roll bars, as has Alfa Ricambi and several other Alfa Romeo shops.

If the car is lowered, knuckle extensions number 10532.21.118.01 and idler arm number 10532.24.020.00 (with arm part number 10532.24.201.00 and center tie-rod number 10532.24.401.01) should be used.

Brakes

If racing brake-pad materials are used, remember that the brakes must be warmed up before they become effective. It is dangerous to drive on the street with racing brakes.

If you plan to race an Alfa Romeo, the CAS provides a good look at successful Alfa Romeo racing practice. I want to emphasize that halfway modification efforts are not likely to be successful. If you're reading this chapter with $100 handy to spend for modifying an engine, forget it. The cheapest way to gain a guaranteed and immediate significant increase in power is to fit a nitrous oxide (NO_x) system. Curiously, I know of no Alfa Romeos modified for NO_x.

If you're looking for really cheap horsepower, put your money in the bank and simply remove the plastic fan attached to the water pump with a 10 mm box-end wrench (six bolts). You'll gain about 3 hp and an engine that can overheat in traffic. No one said racers have an easy life.

9

Giulia Restoration

Most Alfa Romeo owners are interested in the restoration process. Restoration was, by far, the single most-requested category in a survey conducted by the American Alfa Club. This is especially significant in view of the fact that *Road & Track* had just finished a three-part series on the restoration of a Duetto.

On the other hand, this finding was not surprising, since the approach used in the *Road & Track* article was to remove major assemblies and have them done by competent restorers. Restoration of this kind is management, not manufacture.

It is an approach that has much to recommend it, however. For those owners with little mechanical skill who still want to feel they've restored a car, delegation of the major work makes a lot of sense.

An overestimation of one's skills has ruined more cars—valuable cars—than any other single cause. The surest way to destroy a car is to present

From such humble beginnings wonderful cars are made. This Duetto has typical Alfa Romeo rust prob-lems. The rocker panel is completely rusted through and is hiding serious frame damage. Gary M. Valant/Valco

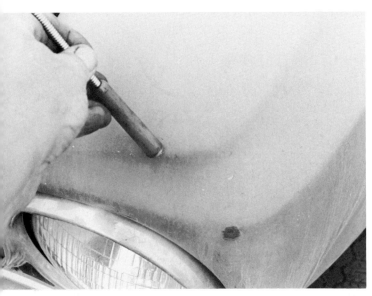

A magnet helps identify the presence of plastic filler material on the body. If the filler is very deep, the magnet will have almost no attraction at all.

it to a starry-eyed new owner who plans on a total restoration all by himself, and sees himself, only several weeks hence, standing with a 100 point car.

It happened to a car I owned—a 1900 Zagato. After several years of enjoying it, I concluded the time had come to sell it and buy another Alfa Romeo. The purchaser, a law student and enthusiast, decided on a total restoration of a running, complete car. He proceeded to dismantle it, portioning out the body to be done by a friend with a bodyshop, and saving the engine for another burst of energy.

I don't think the car has ever been totally reassembled, and that covers at least fifteen years. I've corresponded with the current owner, who never knew the car carried an originally fitted accelerometer, nor has any trace of its original unique markings, which I had carefully photographed to go with the car so it could be restored to its original condition.

Thus, my first observation regarding restoration is to be circumspect about the likelihood of a total effort's success, given your skills and resources.

Few people are capable of total restorations, emotionally, physically or financially. The tragedy—for many valuable Alfa Romeos—is that many people imagine that they are capable.

Restoration Budget

The first thing one should do before buying a car to restore is to make a budget. Add to the cost of the car all the items that will have to be purchased for its restoration.

• Engine rebuild: Budget about $1,200 for someone else to rebuild your engine if there are no major broken parts. If you do it yourself, you may be able to do it for half that. Remember that a piston-liner set is about $200 minimum, a set of bearings about $50, a gasket set another $50 and exhaust valves around $100 for the set. Add to this the labor of grinding a crankshaft and doing a valve job (around $100) and you are not far away from $600 just to rework an engine with no broken parts. If you need a water pump, oil pump, starter, alternator or distributor replaced or rebuilt, you'll exceed the $600 mark easily.

• Transmission rebuild: Bearings are expensive, and if you have a transmission down, you should probably replace them and the synchros. Maybe $300 to $400 as a ballpark estimate.

• Driveline: They're durable, and I've never had an Alfa Romeo with a bad ring or pinion. You'll want to replace the donuts, no doubt, and the brakes, including a rebuild of the hydraulics. You'll also probably need to replace the emergency brake cable. Set aside about $200.

• Interior: Plan to spend about $100 a seat, plus another $100 for the rest of the interior if you shop around. Carpet is extra, say another $100.

• Bodywork: You can hardly purchase the materials for a paint job for less than $100 anymore. Not counting your weeks of labor to prepare the body, you'll be giving up $1,000 before you get a decent paint job. Sure, your buddy will do it for half that, and you could do it yourself for less than that.

I'm sure it's possible to take issue that the prices I've quoted are too low; I don't think anyone will say they're too high. As a generalization, adding up the figures quoted, we have a ballpark range of $2,100 to $3,200 just for the major items. Forget wiring harnesses, a windshield and rechroming. For the sake of argument, let's settle on $3,000 cost to you for a somewhat decent restoration.

Now, what is it you're going to restore? Let's say a Giulia Super. Price one. Price a restored one. They go from $3,500 to about $8,000. Forget the top price for now, just take some middle ground, say around $6,000.

Now comes the tricky part. If you buy a running car with all the parts there, in somewhat good condition, you're going to spend the better part of $4,000.

Already, it's cheaper to go out and buy a restored one that you can drive today.

Put another way, money spent to restore your car beyond the average price of a restored car is money you are simply throwing away. If you wish, you may consider the difference the cost of pride ... or vanity. I know of several cars in which the owners have invested about twice the actual value of the car. The amount you invest in a car becomes a problem only when you have to sell it.

I have always sold cars to raise money. I may have fallen in love with another car—perhaps stumbled across a "once in a lifetime" opportunity—or had a need for cash. Either way, the car to which I had attached so much emotion suddenly became a commodity, no more, no less. You're never more aware of the market value than when you need to sell an oddball car and are trying to establish a fair price for it. All those astronomical prices you see advertised for cars like yours become grotesque jokes, because the only offers you get are about half the market value. It is at just such a time that you realize the folly of investing more in a car's restoration than it is worth.

There's another angle to mention. I have a friend who has a very rare car—one of ten—into which he has put $40,000 in a virtually perfect restoration. In fact, the car is probably worth the price. The problem is that it is a race car, and he can't bring himself to fling his $40,000 car around a track. As it sits, the car is useless, too valuable to race, and illegal for the road. He has it up for sale and can't find a buyer. Simply from a cash-flow standpoint, he's made an expensive mistake.

Reasons for Restoration

The first error in car restoration is believing that, no matter how much you put into a car, if you just wait long enough, the market will rise to your price. This idea is a good rationalization, but the fact is that the market is unpredictable, and, unless you're talking about decades rather than years, the idea is patently false.

My personal experience is that no car should be considered an investment. You can play with them, but don't expect them to earn money for you, ever. The few cars I've owned that did turn out to be good investments are now out of my price range by an order of ten.

I have a number of cars that will never be worth what I'll put into them to fix them up (notice, I did not use the word restore). I own them because I like owning them. They are costly luxuries, but I feel good having them. They have come close to breaking my bank, but somehow I manage to keep them, work on them and enjoy them.

Vanity has a lot to do with ownership for me. I think vanity is probably the only defensible reason for owning some cars, most certainly an Alfa

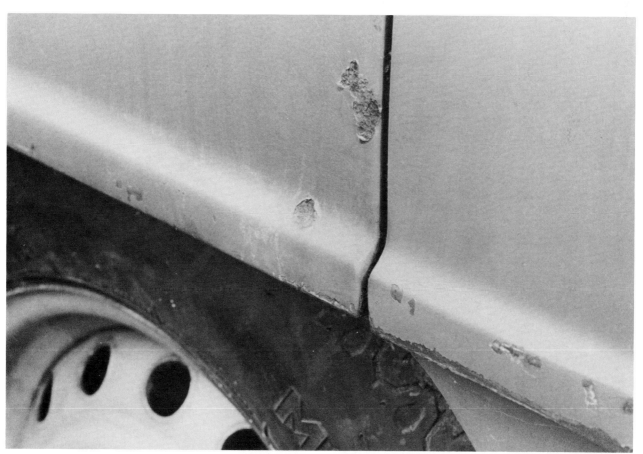

Incipient rust on a Giulia Super passenger's side rear wheel arch. On the door itself, the paint is scraped, but not rusted. You can easily tell the difference between *chipped and rusted paint because rust lifts the edges of the paint around the bare area.*

Romeo. Practically, you're better off with a Chevrolet. Vanity aside, I also enjoy working around the engineering that the car represents. I think Alfa Romeo engines are neat, and the people who designed them have a classic sense which I appreciate.

What are some other reasons why people enjoy car restoration? Craftsmanship is one reason. A garage full of machine tools allows this enthusiast to create a new Type 35 Bugatti with only a rusted rear spring shackle to begin with. Never mind the block is cracked; he'll cast up a new one in his backyard foundry. It's never quite clear what this craftsman does during the day to earn a living, but every evening he finds himself in his shop, buried in the details of a restoration. Never congratulate him on his work; he's left tool marks on one web of the new crank and is thinking of tearing the engine down to file them smooth. Of course, that will mean rebalancing everything.

The craftsman needs order and a goal. Restoration allows him to practice the first while reaching the second.

Another reason for undertaking a restoration project could be to fulfill an unrequited youth. The perennial youth loves startling the neighbors with midnight runs around the block with the mufflers off. So much the better if he's having a party and can scare the wits out of a passenger as well. As he stands by the car, the engine crackling as it cools, you realize the cloth helmet and scarf are the emotional diapers of this boy-racer. The fact that he's spent a ton restoring the car cannot disguise that his knowledge of it is limited to operating the major controls.

The boy-racer selects his car and restores it only to intensify the sense of youth and daring he needs to project.

Nostalgia can also spur on an enthusiast to attempt a restoration. Friends avoid mentioning the marque, for even the slightest opportunity sends the nostalgia buff into interminable stories about his experiences thirty years ago in a car just like the one he has now. The car is transportation for this enthusiast, but only metaphorically. It is a time machine. The real car may not run, but it still sits, shining in his mind's eye, on the showroom floor. All the better if Tazio Nuvolari were passing by when he first drove it away. In recapturing the past, the nostalgic enthusiast enjoys life without

Terminal rust on a neglected spider. To restore this panel, new sheet metal will have to be welded in place.

danger, for he already knows how it is all going to turn out. It was a time much brighter than now, and the car still retains its aura of Camelot.

A subset of this group owns cars that were too expensive when new.

Once the project is completed, the restorer bent on nostalgia recaptures safe and enjoyable experiences through his car.

Unfortunately, for some, the restoration of a car is merely an opportunity for conspicuous consumption. If this man is a bore, it is because he cannot stop complaining about how many thousands of dollars he has spent finding just the right hides to complete the restoration of the trunk. While the consummate model of this type wears a Rolex President watch, his net worth is irrelevant; appearance is all, and the car must be as conspicuous as possible. For this enthusiast, a car undergoing restoration is infinitely more desirable than a completed car, for it offers a continuing source of anecdotes punctuated by dollar signs. It is inevitable that this class form clubs where they can swap stories and impress young ladies. There are sexual overtones to the type, embracing virility and conquest.

Stupidity is a poor excuse for jumping into a restoration project. Sad to say, there are persons who don't know better. They've read a magazine or two, buy the first old car to come along, join a club and put a set of Taiwan tools on their Christmas list. A dismantled car may be an intermediate stage of the condition; the terminal stage is signaled when the body comes off for a plastic replica and the engine is exchanged for a Chevy V-8.

Some people wander into restoration by accident, which also describes the product of their efforts.

While the categories are perhaps overdrawn, they still represent the universe of those who restore cars. The secret is to know where you fit. To be able to identify why we want to restore a car makes the whole process more efficient and manageable. For many people, the car itself is only an incidental part of the experience. Since we have been trained through advertising to fall in love with cars, it's not too surprising that a restoration is an emotional, perhaps even profoundly emotional, experience. There should be some attempt to match the emotional need and the object of the affections. This may be an unique approach, but it is worth considering.

Selecting the Specific Vehicle

Obviously, for the ham-handed, a prewar Alfa Romeo is not the car of choice, especially if funds are short. The Giulia is currently the most economical and reasonable Alfa Romeo to restore (newer ones aren't an economically sound project), and

now is the time to talk about the things to look for in selecting a car to restore.

There's an inverse relation between your abilities and the condition of the car. If your mechanical abilities are poor, a good car must be selected. If you're an excellent mechanic, then you can save a little money and buy a car in truly poor condition.

It has been a hard lesson for me to learn, but always try to buy a car that is running. With a running car, no matter if it runs poorly, you will be able to check the steering, clutch, transmission, rear end and brakes. Be willing to spend several hours to get the car to run (if only for a quick ride) so the running gear can be checked.

The danger in buying a nonrunner is the lack of opportunity to check for proper operation of critical parts. Consider the car with a dead battery and leaking sump (the gasket at the bottom of the two-piece sump is leaking and it won't hold oil). You take a chance and buy the car. After fitting a new battery and pouring oil into the engine, the car starts and reveals no oil pressure, excessive oil burning and a seized water pump. Pressing on, since you'll have to rebuild the engine anyway, a short drive reveals a loud rear end, a tendency to steer to the left and a refusal to select any gear but first. You get the idea.

Even a running car can hide expensive faults. My 2.0 liter fuel-injected spider only revealed a leaking fuel pump after an engine rebuild (couldn't see the leak for all the smoke, before). That's over $100 for a replacement pump.

The biggest danger of purchasing a nonrunner is missing parts. For that reason, a disassembled car is a no-no under virtually all circumstances. Beware the car that is "ninety-percent complete." That represents 200 lb. of metal for a 2,000 lb. car, almost the weight of a bare engine. Moreover, you can bet the missing parts will be the most expensive or hardest to find, otherwise they'd still be there.

Assessing an Alfa Romeo for Restoration

You check the health of a running engine by wiping your finger around the inside of the tailpipe. If you get a black, oily goo on your finger, the car burns oil. Black smoke out the tailpipe means an excessively rich mixture, an indication that the carburetor or fuel injection is bad. White smoke is an indication of water in the fuel, probably from a blown head gasket.

Check both the oil dipstick and inside mouth of the radiator filler for a chocolate-malt-looking substance, which is a giveaway for a blown head gasket. This is a common problem for 1969 and newer cars, less common for earlier ones. Depending on the severity of the leak, the consequences of a leaking head gasket can be minimal or catastrophic. Only a teardown can verify the degree of damage. Signs that the leak has created a major problem include low oil pressure and smoking exhaust.

Any mechanical noises from the engine probably indicate a complete overhaul. Add $1,000 to your expenses.

On a Giulia, try to wobble the generator on its lower mount. This is a weak area of the engine's design. The rear mount will fall off, and the single remaining bolt will eat its way through the aluminum mounting boss.

Beware of fake Veloces. Twin Webers do not a Veloce make. The real thing had a special finned aluminum sump, high-compression forged pistons, special cams and a milled head. If an early Giulietta has Weber carbs, the body identification plate should read 750E (coupe) or 750F (spider). Later 101 Series Giuliettas and Giulias can best be identified by looking up the serial numbers in Evan Wilson's or Luigi Fusi's books.

Hint: Most original Veloces had a separate cold-air intake in the driver's-side grille, next to the turn indicator light. Looking into the grille, there should be a sheet-metal separation toward the smaller end of the ellipse. Also, the wire that goes to the electric fuel pump at the rear of the car should be wrapped as part of the wiring harness.

The transmission can only be tested during a drive. Any noise from the transmission indicates significant trouble. You test for transmission noise with a running engine and the transmission in neutral by pushing in the clutch. If the noise goes away with the clutch depressed, the bearing on the input shaft is probably bad, and you'll have to rebuild the transmission. If the noise increases with the clutch depressed, the throwout bearing is bad, and will require replacement.

Few used Alfa Romeo transmissions will shift into second gear without some clash. Learn to live with it, and don't rebuild a transmission just to fix the second gear synchro.

All Giulia transmissions have a shift lever with a telescoping, press-for-reverse feature and are housed in a two-piece case that is split longitudinally. The same transmission, but with four, instead of five forward speeds, also comes in long-

You can tell that this generator's mounting is worn because it doesn't sit parallel to the block. You can also make it wobble with your hand. On a Giulia, try to wobble the generator on its lower mount. This is a weak *area of the engine's design: the rear mount, if any, falls off, and the single remaining bolt eats its way through the aluminum mounting boss.*

wheelbase Giulietta spiders with a fixed-vent window. A Giulia with a nontelescoping shift lever has a nonstandard transmission, most probably one from a much later car.

A car-speed-sensitive vibration or noise during a test drive indicates an out-of-balance driveshaft (can be easily fixed) or a bent one (requires replacement). The same phenomenon can also indicate an out-of-balance tire, bent rim (look at them to see), binding brake or bent axle shaft. Giulia donuts (rubber joint just behind the transmission) do not give trouble.

A grinding sound from the rear that changes character as the car turns a corner or transitions from acceleration to deceleration indicates a bad rear end. Bad rears are uncommon on Alfa Romeos, and this will probably indicate very high mileage or abuse.

The wear pattern of the front tires will indicate the need for alignment, and might indicate worn suspension or steering parts. Generally, any non-symmetrical wear across the tread indicates a problem.

Most body inspection will be to find hidden damage, either from an accident or rust. Rust is the Alfa Romeo's biggest enemy, though the owner's gross stupidity is also a leading culprit. Rust, at least, is repairable.

Modern body repair involves smearing plastic over the damaged section and sanding it smooth to body contours. A careful repair is undetectable unless you use a magnet. The ideal tool is a magnetic paint gauge which is calibrated to show paint thickness; a standard paint coat is about 0.003 in. thick. Since fiberglass is nonmagnetic, any unaccountable loss of magnetic attraction along the body indicates that there's plastic underneath.

If the repair's presentable, you shouldn't worry too much. What you need to look most carefully for is rust damage.

The rear wheel arches are the first places to rust on an Alfa Romeo, followed by the rocker pan-

Use sturdy storage boxes, especially when storing heavy parts. If you plan to toss nuts and washers into a large cardboard box, put tape around the inside bottom flaps of the box to assure you won't lose the small items under the flaps. A first step is to set aside a storage area for parts. If you put the parts in cardboard boxes, label the boxes using a marker which is indelibly clear: the boxes may be filled with heavy parts for a long time, moved by myriad greasy hands and rained upon at least twice.

els. A Giulia is salvageable if the rocker panels are completely rusted away, and the wheel arches only a grotesque outline of their original shape. The rust problem is unbeatable in states such as Michigan, and the main job in selecting a car is to determine how much rust damage you'll have to repair.

The rocker panel area is a critical place to look. The external panels can be gone, but the structure underneath them should be able to withstand a healthy jab from a small screwdriver. If the substructure is questionable, check the area where the rear trailing link attaches to the body. If there is evidence of rust damage there, don't buy the car, for the rust is terminal.

The floor pan frequently rusts just about where the driver's heels rest. If the hole is not large enough to put your foot through, it's repairable without welding.

Rust propagates from the inside out, so by the time you see paint bubbling from rust, the metal underneath is in need of repair.

The interior of any car is probably going to be redone, so torn seats, mats and headlining are relatively minor items. The seats should be original, though, so don't get stuck with Triumph TR3 seats in a Giulia.

Giulia seats were rather fragile and tended to break around the hinge for the seatback. During restoration, you should have the seat checked for cracks in the metal support for the seat cushion near the hinge.

Broken curved glass could be a severe problem for a Giulia. Be cautious of buying a car with a broken windshield unless you know where to get a replacement; "I'll look for one" is not a good answer.

Clearly, the way you use this information is to attach a price to any defect. The sum of all the defects has to be added to the purchase price of the

A small plastic bin makes a find parts cleaner. This one is supposed to hold drain oil. A good stiff parts cleaning brush is essential. Never use gasoline to clean parts. Instead, make the effort to obtain a commercial parts-cleaning fluid.

car to estimate the total investment you'll have in a restored car.

Organization, Disassembly and Cleaning

By this time in the restoration process we have established a budget, a type of car to restore and a particular example of that type. In fact, at this stage, we'll assume that the car has been purchased and is sitting somewhat forlornly in the garage, ready for its restoration.

A first step is to set aside a storage area for parts. If you put the parts in cardboard boxes, label the boxes using a marker that is indelibly clear: the boxes may be filled with heavy parts for a long time, moved by a number of greasy hands and rained upon at least twice.

Moreover, you can plan that at least one box filled with both heavy major components and all the fasteners to the entire car will break as you're moving it, spilling irreplaceable parts in inaccessible corners of your garage.

To find them, turn out all the lights, and look with a flashlight, placed at arm's length so its beam just skims the floor and casts the longest shadow possible. As a last resort to find a small, irreplaceable metal part, vacuum the floor and then sift through the debris in the vacuum's bag with a magnet.

To identify parts, get some parts tags, or reasonable facsimile from a stationer. The worst thing is to label small components with masking tape—the surface is too smooth to take an indelible mark, and the tape is too fragile to withstand much handling.

A handy storage technique, if you have a baby, is to save glass baby food bottles for fastener storage. Just be careful not to store the bottles where they will break. Paper egg cartons (the Styrofoam kind melt in the presence of oil-based solvents) are handy containers for separating small parts.

Invariably during a restoration, I lose a box of small parts, mostly fasteners. Typically, I keep tripping over it, or moving it out of the way until the day before I need it. One way around this inevitability is to use the bolts to reassemble (loosely) the components they go with.

Some bolts and nuts should be used only as matched pairs. Head nuts, bearing retaining nuts, rod bolts and the flywheel bolts are less damaged if they are replaced on the same threads from which they were removed.

Consider that the car itself is the largest single item you'll have to store. For this reason, keep the car as whole as possible and in running condition for as long as possible. You will lose fewer parts, feel better about the progress of the restoration and be able to manipulate the car most easily. It should be rollable at all times. Plan to do brake, suspension and rear-axle work at a time when you know you can complete the job within a couple of weekends.

Fight off the temptation to take everything apart at once. The odds are, if you do disassemble the car completely, you will never see it together again.

There are alternatives to total disassembly, and I highly recommend them. For instance, you don't have to remove the engine to do a color change on the body. With the engine in the car, just spray what is convenient, around the top of the engine bay. When the engine is pulled later, finish the paint job. Similarly, if you have the engine out, paint the engine compartment and then finish the rest of the body once the engine is back together and in the car.

There is one instance in which total disassembly of the entire car is the only approach: if you're building a 100 point car for concours. Show standards require the virtual remanufacture of the car. The only way to do this is to take everything apart, fix everything at once, have all the chrome and paint done, and then reassemble the car, touching up the paint as you go. The outlay for this approach is severe economically, physically and emotionally. Most amateurs are not up to it, and that means you and me.

The incremental approach gives you bite-size projects and keeps the car more or less salable at all times, a fact of great significance.

For restoration purposes, a car is divided into several major categories, and your storage should reflect them: engine, transmission, rear axle, front suspension, rear suspension, exterior body trim, major body panels and interior parts. That is, keep the engine parts separate from the transmission parts.

Parts cleaning is one of the most time-consuming elements of restoration. Clean the item before it's disassembled, clean each part as it is disassembled and clean it again just before reassembly. There's an important exception to this rule, however. If you know you're going to take months to get to a part, leave it dirty to reduce the danger of rust.

I find that nuts and bolts are the hardest things to clean properly. Any dirt on a bolt will get wiped on the (clean) part it's fitted to, dirtying an otherwise clean surface.

Gunk, though popular, is a relatively weak solvent. Practically, lacquer thinner is the strongest solvent you should use in your garage, but be careful because its fumes are toxic. Industrial-strength solvents (like trichloroethylene) are available but very dangerous. The safest approach is to take extremely dirty major assemblies to a rebuilder to have them cleaned.

Glass-bead blasting leaves a lovely finish, but there is a danger that grit will inevitably get into critical parts and possibly ruin them. Use Gunk and a brush for internal mechanical parts.

I paint my cleaned engine with chrome aluminum. It's a bright paint and makes the block look brand new. A can of aerosol flat-black is good for touching up the radiator and miscellaneous bits. A can of bright red paint is handy to highlight things like the fuel-pump top stamping on a Giulietta, but that is a nonstandard trim if you're going after total authenticity in your restoration. Armor All will do wonders for the interior plastic, and make rubber parts pretty, too.

One of the hardest decisions in restoration is drawing the line between replacement and repair. I try to repair everything and replace nothing. I think one of the pleasures of restoration is making broken parts work again. I occasionally fabricate pieces, or adapt other parts to fit if I cannot make the original parts work again.

The decision becomes critical over an extensive restoration. You simply cannot replace everything with new parts unless you want a $40,000 investment in a car worth $7,000. There are some parts I never replace on an Alfa Romeo. Fortunately, I've never had to rebuild a water pump, an oil pump or a rear end. And I've never replaced wrist pin bushes. Now, these are all critical items, and you must make sure they are serviceable before deciding not to rebuild them. My point is, however, if you rebuild each item as a matter of course, the cost of your restoration will skyrocket. Why rebuild a serviceable transmission? If you need more convincing, just price the cost of replacing all the rubber on an Alfa Romeo.

One of the purposes of inspecting a car before you buy it is to identify what doesn't need rebuild-

This is the author's workbench, showing the tools required for ninety-five percent of routine Alfa Romeo work: a modest collection, indeed. A soft-metal hammer can be a real aid when you need to hit something without marking it. Alternately, a rubber mallet is a good, if lightweight, substitute.

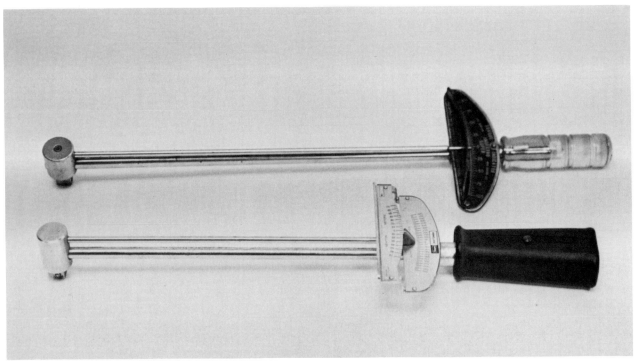

One tool for which there is no substitute is the torque wrench. The longer wrench measures pounds per foot; the smaller, pounds per inch. These are relatively inac- *curate beam-type wrenches. For maximum accuracy, take the reading only when the wrench is moving.*

ing. The consideration is part of the budgeting process, and should guide you as the car comes apart.

You should begin the restoration by fixing the most needed item first. This is probably going to be either the engine or the body.

Tool Supply

Before launching into the actual process, I want to say something about tools.

The number of essential tools for rebuilding an Alfa Romeo is quite small. Many required tools, such as valve spring compressors, are eliminated if you have a machine shop do your valves (few amateurs have a valve grinder). Bodywork consists of almost 100 percent expendable materials (com-

pressor and gun excepted). Some tools, such as the large gear puller required to disassemble the transmission, should be rented.

Now, I have a garage full of tools. In point of fact, I use very few of them and frequently, to take a ring compressor as an example, can do without them (the bottom of the cylinder barrel is beveled). So far as usual hand tools are concerned, a set of box-end or open-end wrenches and a socket set are just about all you'll need. I will say, however, that a hacksaw is essential to remove rusted bolts, and a snap-ring pliers has no substitute. My suggestion is not to celebrate an approaching restoration by purchasing $500 worth of Craftsman tools.

10

Bodywork and Painting

As a result of the original inspection when you bought the car, you should have a good idea how much bodywork will be required.

Bodywork is hard, physical labor. Initial bodywork (bending panels back to their original shape) can be downright brutal. Final bodywork is ulti-

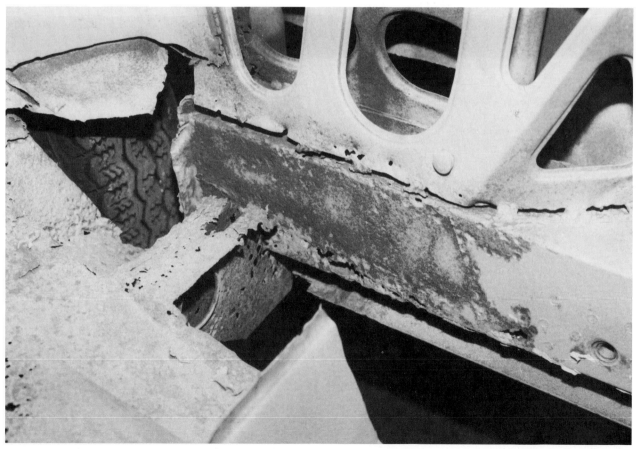

After this Duetto was fully disassembled, badly rusted panels were removed and the car was sent to the sandblaster. All suspect areas were sandblasted—but not the entire body. Good body panels may be damaged by over- *aggressive sandblasting—take care! This is the convertible top storage area and inner structure with extensive rust damage. Gary M. Valant/Valco*

When the Duetto returned from the sandblaster, the entire floor was removed as it was rusted beyond repair.

This is often the easiest solution to extensive floor rust problems. Gary M. Valant/Valco

A new battery tray was fabricated by working sheet metal over a wood form shaped to fit inside the old, rusted tray. A relatively hard wood and a router work wonders. In this case, the metal was formed over a wood die, the corners were welded up and the welds were ground away. Gary M. Valant/Valco

mately subtle. If you have an adventurous spirit, and can stand one fender looking significantly different from its mate, then there's no reason not to attempt bodywork.

Restoring the Body

The first step in beginning bodywork is to wash the car with a strong detergent. This removes any grease that would otherwise be sanded into the paint as you work.

At this point, you should remove any trim that could be scratched as you grind away rusted areas.

Chrome strips and badges are usually attached with nuts on an Alfa Romeo; lesser cars just stick them on with a glue. You must reach behind the panel on which the trim is located and unscrew its attaching nuts, which are on the order of 4-7 mm, flat-to-flat. This is not an easy job, for some of the attaching nuts can only be undone after removing other panels to reach them.

The chrome strips under the door of the Giulia Spider are held on by a bolt at either end and spring steel clips along the length. The grille pieces are bolted on, as is the chrome strip on the hood. Most other model Alfa Romeos follow this same pattern.

Generally, a close inspection of the chrome strip will reveal how it is attached. A slip of paper can be used to probe behind the strip to find where the attaching bolts are located.

Polish the trim pieces after you remove them. Use a Brillo pad to clean them up if they are not badly pitted. Though it is expensive, rechroming is the only acceptable repair for a badly tarnished or pitted chrome-plated part.

Remember that some Alfa Romeo bumpers (the Giulia Super comes to mind) are stainless steel, not chrome.

The next step is to grind away all the rusted areas so there is nothing left but shiny metal. With plastic fillers, this is an easy step to slight, for plastic will bond to virtually anything. However, if you try to bond plastic filler to a rusted section, water vapor will eventually creep between the porous metal and the plastic and pop the filler free. Be absolutely ruthless in removing rust.

The most frequently rusted exterior panels on an Alfa Romeo are the rocker panels and the rear wheel arches. The rocker panels can be removed by

The convertible top storage area has been repaired with sheet-metal patches that were fabricated and then welded into place. After the welds are ground down, the panel seams are sealed to halt water seepage or leaks. The whole area is then primed for painting. Gary M. Valant/Valco

Sub-floor repair of the Duetto in progress. Small plates of twenty-gauge sheet metal were cut into patches using paper or cardboard as patterns. The patches are then welded into place to duplicate the complex curves of the original factory panels. Gary M. Valant/Valco

Prior to fabricating a new floor for the Duetto, the remaining frame rails are prepped and cold-galvanized with a 3M spray that is applied to the rails prior to welding. Gary M. Valant/Valco

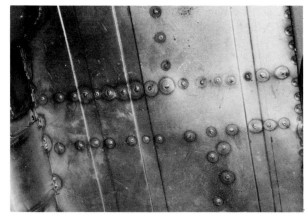

The floor panel is installed in the car and rosette welded to the frame rails. The tops of these welds will be ground down prior to sealing and priming. Gary M. Valant/ Valco

using a slender chisel to pop the spot welds holding the panels to the body. Typically, the lower attaching points of the rocker panels will already have rusted away, so a few deft pops along the flange below the doorsill will be enough to free the rockers.

The rocker panels are not a structural part of the body. Behind each, however, is a strengthening member that runs along the underside of the car, tying the front and rear wheel arches together. These two side members and the central transmission tunnel are the only sources of fore and aft rigidity in the body.

I've owned a spider on which both longitudinal members were completely rusted away. The car met its fate by being flipped end over end three times after running off the road at about 60 mph. The body was bent in the middle as if a giant had stepped between the seats, but was not the crumpled bit of tinfoil one might reasonably have expected. The transmission tunnel, in other words, has significant structural rigidity by itself.

The preceding anecdote suggests that even a badly rusted spider is salvageable. Perhaps the only unsalvageable spider I've ever owned was a Giulia Veloce which was so badly rusted underneath that

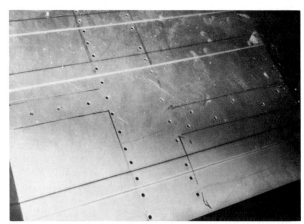

A large paper pattern is cut to replicate the floor pan. If the floor is to be made to closely follow the original contours, it will have to be fabricated in at least five pieces. For simple street restorations—or in this case, a race car—an adequate floor can be constructed from a single sheet. Note that we have marked where the panel will lie on the frame rails. Reinforcing beads are then pressed into the floor and ⅜ in. holes are drilled along the frame rails. These will be rosette welded. Gary M. Valant/Valco

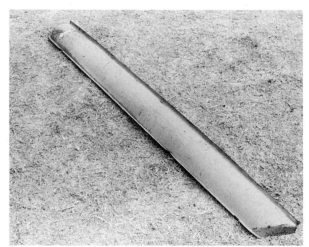

A replacement rocker panel can be fabricated from flat steel with a little patience. The panel is only spot-welded to the body. The rocker panels can be removed by using a slender chisel to pop the spot welds holding the panels to the body. Typically, the lower attaching points of the rocker panels will already have rusted away, so a few deft pops along the flange below the door sill will be enough to free the rockers.

the rear trailing links were pulling loose from their front attaching points. Restoration for that car would have required rebuilding the entire floor pan.

Whatever rebuilding is to be done to the undercarriage should be done now. There is no reason why the substructure of a unit-body car such as an Alfa Romeo cannot be rebuilt by welding in new metal. I've heard of only one person who has done it successfully, however, and he had to rewarp the body to get the doors to close properly. My suggestion is to use box- or C-section sheet metal to replace rusted components. Braze, rather than weld, wherever feasible and don't create any joint that will trap water.

I use a 7 in. grinding wheel to remove rusted sections. An 80 grit disc will work quickly on steel, and leave a surface that is roughened enough to encourage a close bond with a filler.

As you grind away, you will be uncovering the history of your car. All its various colors may still be preserved in layers, and strata of plastic filler attest to old and forgotten accidents.

Whenever you use a grinding wheel, no matter how coarse the grit, strive for gradual transitions in surfaces, not craters.

The prepared panels are clamped in place and welded in steps to minimize panel distortion. Wire welding (MIG welding) is preferred as it causes the least amount of panel distortion. Acetylene welding should be avoided if at all possible. Brazing is an excellent method; however, severe distortion can occur if too much heat is used. Unremoved brazing flux will also cause panel corrosion to blister up. Gary M. Valant/Valco

After all the rust has been removed, take a close look to see that the body panels line up the way they should. Now is the time to correct such basic misalignments.

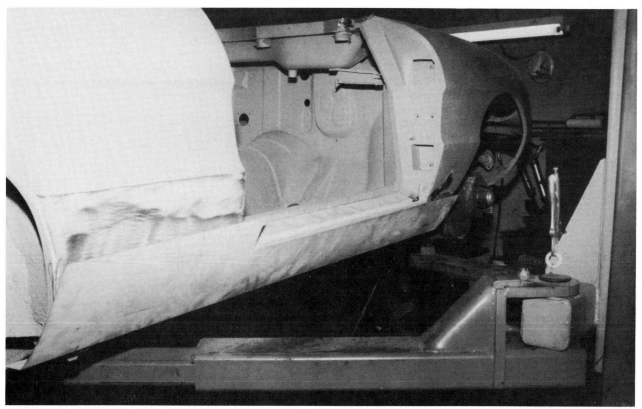

Rocker repair panels are available from most of the aftermarket Alfa Romeo parts houses. These panels typically extend beyond the wheelwells in order to take care of typical rust in these areas. The panel is fitted in position and the location of the excess material marked. The panel is then cut about 1/8 in. inboard of the marks so that the welding is done on the outside surface of the panel to be repaired. Gary M. Valant/Valco

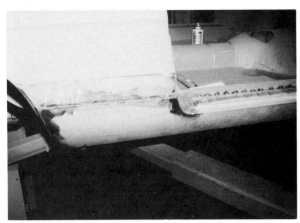

The rocker panel replacement welded in place. Excess welding material is ground off and the panel is finished off with filler. Gary M. Valant/Valco

Alfa Romeo archaeology: layers of paint and plastic filler are displayed during the sanding process.

Dent Repair

Doors, hood and trunk lids can be aligned by loosening the bolts that attach their hinges and shifting the panel slightly. Trial and error is the only way to achieve good panel alignment. You will be able to shim some hinges with washers to raise a panel to its proper height.

You may need to do some basic panel beating to bring a fender or door closer to its original surface. The goal is to add as little plastic filler as possible to the body, so you must take some time to get the basic sheet metal as straight as you can.

For those dented panels, a plumber's helper can do wonders. A door panel with a large dent may be helped by pressing a plumber's helper care-

fully in the center of the dent and then pulling quickly to pop the panel back to its original contour.

As a last resort, use a dent puller, which is a slide hammer attached to a sheet-metal screw. The metal is pierced with the tip of the screw, which is threaded in to form a secure attachment to the metal. Then, the slide hammer is used to pull the metal out. What usually happens is that a little

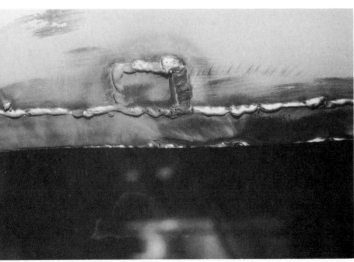

Small rust holes can be welded up by cutting out the rust and then welding a patch over the hole. As the patch cools, it will draw the metal together. After grinding, the surface of the repair should be level with or below the original panel surface. Gary M. Valant/Valco

For a full frame-off restoration, it's usually the easiest to have the body and the chassis sandblasted and acid-dipped to remove all of the old layers of paint and primer. After stripping the body on this 101 Series Giulia Spider, numerous patches of body filler were discovered, a testament to several front-end collisions. Instead of re-doing the patchwork, restorer John Kremer cut the front end of the body off ahead of the front wheels, cut the front end off of his parts car and welded it in place. This is the before photo. John Kremer

dimple of metal is pulled out, with the remaining dent still pretty much untouched. Quite a few holes are required to do anything significant to the panel with a dent puller. One advantage of a puller is that the multitude of holes it leaves act as a sieve to catch plastic filler and help form a secure physical bond between the filler and metal.

An alternate approach, if you have an arc welder, is to weld short stubs of rod to the panel and then pull on the rods to pop the metal into place. Grind off the rod after the basic contour has been achieved and smooth everything out with filler.

Metal is literally plastic: if you stretch it, you will end up with more metal than you began with. Metal-shrinking techniques are beyond the scope of an amateur restoration. For that reason, be careful how much force you use to get a panel back to its original shape. The proper technique is to use just enough force, applied over as large an area as possible, to encourage the metal to remember its original contour. That's the reason I prefer a shoe to a hammer for undenting. The hammer will leave you with a lot of dimples and stressed metal, where a shoe will just kind of nudge things back to their

A second pass of filler after the first has been rough-smoothed. The large spreader is used again.

general contour, which you will then complete in plastic.

If you're very ambitious, you might want to try cutting off damaged sections with a metal-cutting

Spreading the first layer of plastic filler. A large, flexible spreader is used to maintain a smooth surface. The

rough-finish file on the hood is used to smooth heavy ridges in the filler after it has dried.

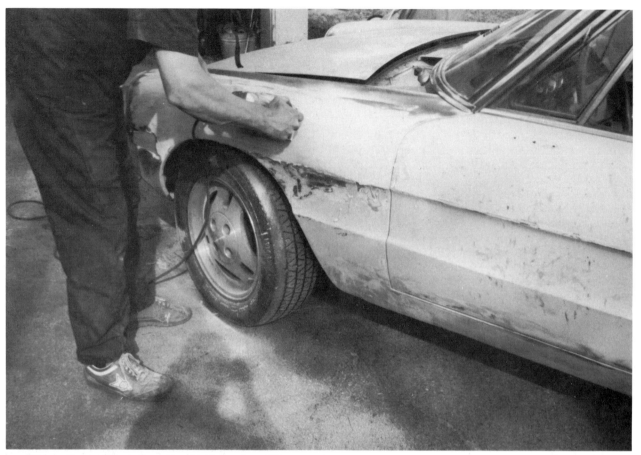

Rough sanding with an electric orbital sander will re-establish the basic contour of the body panel. This is a dusty job and a mask is mandatory.

The fender has been rough-sanded to shape. Hand sanding, using progressively finer grades of paper, is the next step. Begin with 180 grit and work toward 220 for the basic shape. Don't worry about pinholes at this stage. They will be filled with "green stuff" later. You may want to give in to a temptation to remove some trim pieces at this point and fill the holes with plastic. You have to understand that plastic only works well when it is thin and well-supported. Don't try to fill in a parking lamp mounting hole with a glob of plastic. It will fall out, eventually.

saw. This allows you to bang on them a little more conveniently. Once their original shape is restored, you tack-weld the part back on to the body.

Generally, any work with an oxyacetylene torch on a body is risky for an amateur. As the metal heats up, it becomes very plastic, indeed, and forgets its original set. Usually, when a torch is used, lots of wet rags are used to surround the area and reduce the danger of warping the metal.

Rather than resort to a torch, use mechanical means to fasten sheet-metal parts (pop-rivets are fine for unstressed panels) and cover the repair with plastic.

It used to be that plastic as a body filler was the last resort of an amateur. Only lead, heated to a plastic consistency and applied with a waxed paddle, was an acceptable filler. There is a legitimate reason for preferring lead over plastic. During changes of temperature, plastic fillers expand and contract at a different rate than steel. Over several years, plastic will peel off in chunks, while lead is a permanent repair.

The ease of use, however, has made plastic an almost universal body filler. The fact that its coefficient of expansion matches that of aluminum means that it can be used on aluminum-bodied cars without apology. The real danger of using plastic is that its ease of use encourages sloppy preparation. You can, in fact, fiberglass over rust and have a very presentable, if temporary, job. Because it is structurally a weak substance, don't depend on body plastics to do any more than fill shallow depressions. Keep the filler as thin as possible on the body; ½ in. thick sections can fall off over railroad tracks.

You may want to give in to a temptation to remove some trim pieces at this point and fill the holes with plastic. You have to understand that plastic works well only when it is thin and well supported. Don't try to fill in a parking lamp mounting hole with a glob of plastic. It will fall out, eventually.

The proper procedure is to depress the area immediately surrounding the hole (kicking is OK, but a ball-peen hammer is better) and then pop-rivet a piece of aluminum behind the hole. Fill the depression with plastic.

Never try to butt plastic against metal. Only gradual transitions between plastic and steel maintain good bonds.

The first application of plastic filler should approximate the final contour you need. You will probably spread two to three more layers of plastic over the first layer, sanding each until it is almost gone. A grinding wheel may be used to correct gross surface deformities in the plastic on the first pass, but subsequent layers of filler should be sanded with either an orbital sander or a sanding block.

You'll need all the help you can get to make a decent fiberglass repair. Don't pretend you're an

As with all Duettos, this one had been hit in the nose. The nose panel was not severely damaged, so it was worked and repaired without being replaced. With the floor pan and the rockers repaired, the car is ready to be prepped for painting. Note that the entire car was primed with a self-etching primer immediately after it returned from the sand-blasting shop. This prevents surface rust from forming on the body while the other repairs are in progress. Gary M. Valant/Valco

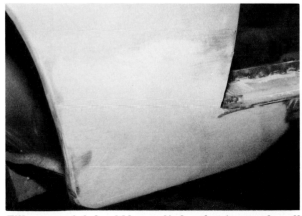

Filler material should be applied so that it extends well beyond the repair area. Filler should always be applied in light, thin doses so it doesn't crack or swell. The filler is then filed or sanded until it blends in smoothly with the original panel. The idea is to feather the filler out so that there is no step at edge of the repair. Gary M. Valant/Valco

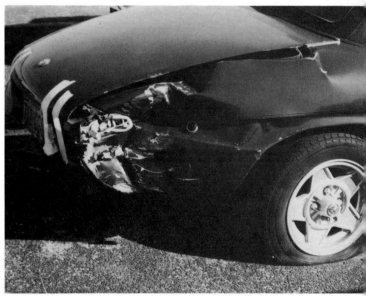

Sometimes you have to break all of the rules. A case in point: This Duetto had been severely damaged by sliding into an immovable object while it was moving at high speed. The entire rear end was shifted on the car and the trunk floor crushed. The front end, however, was repairable. The availability and price of duplicate panels almost rules out direct replacement of the damage, so in this case a better repair was possible by chopping the car in half and finding a rear half off of a donor car that had had a similar accident, only in reverse. Gary M. Valant/Valco

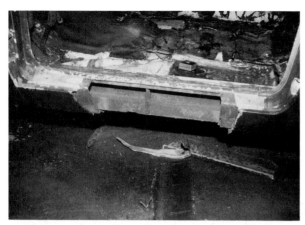

A portion of the rocker panel was cut away to expose the inner frame extension, which in turn is removed to expose the inside of the main frame rail. We measured everything and decided where to make our cut through the floor. In this case, the floor of the original car was in good shape so it was left intact. Gary M. Valant/Valco

Italian artisan skilled in the trade. Use straight edges and every other indicator you can think of to restore the body to its original contour.

I have found that the most helpful technique is to use light at a narrow angle along a panel. Move the car so the sun shines tangentially to a panel, highlighting high spots and shadowing depressions. Use a trouble light at night to identify surface irregularities. Remember that the plastic, after it is sanded, is a dull surface that does not show irregularities. Paint, on the other hand, is merciless, but it's too late to correct a wavy surface after it's been painted.

Body plastic comes in cans, accompanied by a little tube of hardener. There isn't any consistent technique of judging the proper ratio of hardener to filler; experience is the only true guide.

The ratio is not especially critical, providing you don't try to mix the whole can at once. To control the proportions of filler to hardener, always try to make the same-sized batch every time. Scoop out enough filler onto a piece of cardboard to make a couple of good-sized pancakes. For that amount, squeeze out a teaspoon of hardener. Mix the two with a spreader, trying not to trap bubbles of air in the mixing process. Don't try for a perfect mixture of hardener throughout the plastic; it will be further mixed as you apply it to the body. Just make sure there is a little bit of hardener throughout your lump of filler. You'll have from three to ten minutes to work with the batch before it begins setting up.

The main frame rail was cut behind the inner frame rail support, located under the front seat mounts. The donor car was cut ahead of this frame rail. The floor was removed and the frame rail support was removed while the inner frame rails were left intact. Gary M. Valant/Valco

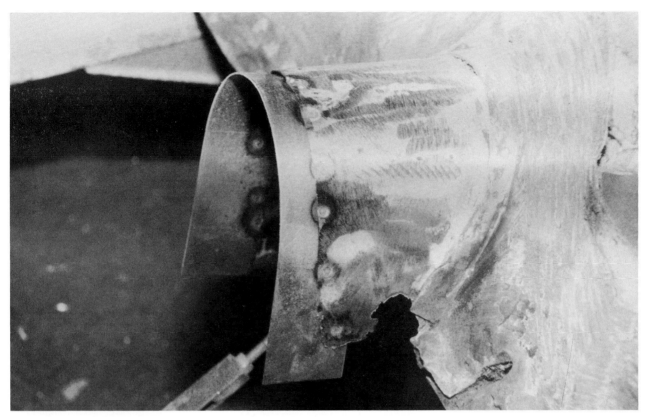

A reinforcing strip was welded inside of the tunnel section. Gary M. Valant/Valco

The main frame assembly must be carefully prepared so that all of the edges are clean and straight. Note that the cuts are staggered so that the welds will not all be in a single line. Gary M. Valant/Valco

The two car halves are brought together and ⅛ in. reinforcing plates are positioned inside the frame rail. A

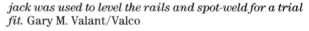

jack was used to level the rails and spot-weld for a trial fit. Gary M. Valant/Valco

Once we were sure that the trial fit was good—the doors fit the body—we began welding the frame. We left a ⅛ in. gap between the rails so that 100 percent weld penetration was assured. Reinforcing plates were added to the top and sides of the main frame rail. While welding the frame, slight upward pressure from the jack opened the top of the door gaps. If you weld from the bottom to the top, the final weld will shrink and pull the door gaps back together. Gary M. Valant/Valco

If you haven't added enough hardener, the plastic will not harden. After about twenty minutes, just scrape it off and start over.

If you've added too much hardener, the spreader will start to create a sandy surface as you smear the material. Stop, throw away the rest of the batch and take a break while the filler you've applied hardens. Then, make a new batch using slightly less filler and continue.

Paint Preparation

At this point in the restoration, the major bodywork has been completed: some trim and all rust is removed, the body straightened where necessary, filled with plastic to restore the original contours and sanded smooth. The work to this point has required physical labor, rather rough at first, but becoming increasingly subtle as the final contours are achieved.

What one fails to realize in an actual restoration is that most of the work has been accomplished at this point. It is somewhat incredible: the body is spotted with islands of plastic in a sea of colors, much like a topographical map but in fact the color history of the car, displayed as the most subtle irregularities are sanded smooth.

There is an urge to get on with it; to use primer to fill the remaining imperfections, give a quick wet sand and finally apply the color coat. Instead, this is the time for inspection and correction. The work that remains is physically easy and surprisingly quick. But the unprimed car is really the last opportunity to repair surface irregularities.

I've mentioned using a trouble light to evaluate the body surface. Hold it close to the body so its tangential light shows all irregularities, and then fix every one. This checking can be done in the evenings after work. Spotting putty, or green stuff, is used to fill small pits which result from air bubbles in the plastic or paint chips. After all the sanding is finished, wash the car with soap and water.

Next, prepare the area where you plan to spray the car. If it is a garage, cover anything likely to be damaged by overspray. Then, hose down the area and leave the floor wet. If you're painting outside, keep the hose running so the ground is wet while you're actually spraying the car. This will help reduce dust kicked up by the air from the gun.

I've painted a number of cars in a garage with good success. If you're using lacquer, good ventilation is absolutely necessary; otherwise, you'll have a buzz halfway through the paint job and the remaining half will show it. You can also kiss a significant number of brain cells goodbye. Don't use a fan to circulate air (and dust), rely on natural ventilation.

Lacquer is a much more psychedelic medium than enamel. The problem with enamel in an unventilated area is that every pore of your skin is clogged with an insoluble mist that just has to wear off. Soap won't touch it, and bathing in enamel thinner only makes the problem worse.

Whether you paint with lacquer or enamel, wear clothing that covers your whole body and—absolutely—wear a good-quality mask.

We should discuss the difference between lacquer and enamel now. If you're a beginner, I recommend lacquer. It can be sanded away if you get a run, and will polish to a very smooth surface if you're willing to expend the effort. Its disadvantages are several, however: it is more merciless than enamel in showing body defects, and it chips easily. It is quite thin, and can be polished away with relatively little effort.

Enamel, on the other hand, is a much thicker medium which dries very slowly, covers well and resists chipping. It is much less repairable than lacquer and a major run during spraying will probably be with the car until it is repainted several

Once the outer section of the frame rail extension was welded in place and rocker panels were installed, the *repair was complete. The floor from the original car was then rosette-welded to the frame. Gary M. Valant/Valco*

183

years later. When it is polished, enamel tends to give up its topmost oxidized surface, and a good polish job on enamel is literally a new paint job.

Modern acrylic lacquer tends to act much more like enamel, and acrylic enamel with hardener can be sanded like lacquer.

DuPont's Imron is a very sturdy enamel that requires its own chemistry. If you're fairly confident of being able to spray a run-free job with little orange peel (that means neither too wet nor too dry), then you should consider Imron.

Something about color. Months before you select the color, you should begin looking at cars to decide on the exact shade you'll paint. Forget picking from paint chips at the paint store; that's the most frustrating and hazardous method. There's no way you can identify the color of a car from a 1 in. square chip pasted to a page, especially when it's surrounded by several similar color chips. If you're a purist, just copy the paint number from the body, if you can find it, or ask for the proper color for your car at the paint store. As a last resort,

visit an accessory store with one of those spray-can displays for touchup paint. Buy several possible choices, take them home and spray a fender.

I've never been a purist for paint colors. Paint fades anyway, so one summer sun is going to give you an oddball color, like it or not. Furthermore, there is no one Alfa Romeo red any more than there is a Ferrari red. I chuckle at the ads for imports that say Ferrari red. My friend Norm Miller found that the most accurate red to match the original 1750 Zagato color was on a Coke machine.

Some more advice while we're talking about paint still in the can: buy cheap thinner (lacquer thinner, but enamel reducer) for the primer, but always buy the most expensive thinner you can afford for the color coat. Paints themselves don't vary that much in quality; thinner, on the other hand, does. Add some fisheye eliminator to the diluted paint to avoid spots from silicone polish that has penetrated the old paint. Generally, spend at least five minutes mixing the paint before it's diluted with thinner, and continue mixing another

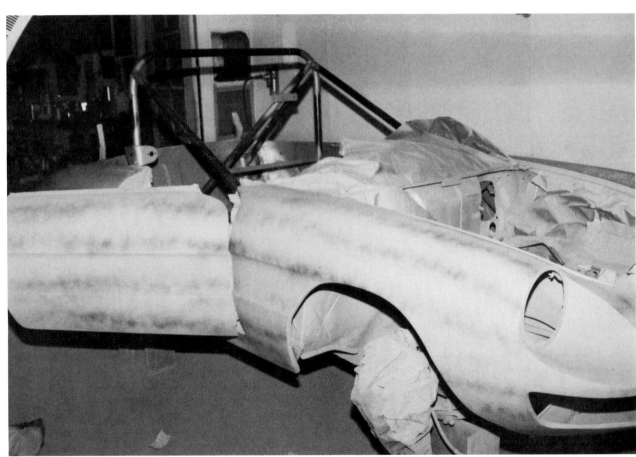

After all of the body repair has been completed, the entire car is shot with primer. High-solids catalyzed primer, such as Dupont Europrime, hardens quickly without relying solely on evaporation. The result is durable and covers small imperfections and grinding scratches.

After priming, a light coat of dark paint was applied to the car as a guide coat, which will later be sanded off. The guide coat reveals small imperfections that may require additional attention. Gary M. Valant/Valco

184

five after it has been reduced. Mix it for about a minute before refilling the cup on the gun in the middle of painting.

Pure, nonmetallic paints are the easiest to use. If you must spray metallic paints, mixing becomes even more critical and the paint must be sprayed at exactly the same distance, pressure and speed for the entire car. If you're not up to that kind of discipline, don't spray metallics.

The next major step will be to prep the surface, but the car should be masked first. Use regular masking tape, but don't leave it on for weeks at a time. Most cheap paint shops don't mask carefully. You should mask chrome with the same care you use to paint the car. Use a fairly narrow tape for the mask nearest the paint. Wider tape and newspaper can be used to cover convertible tops or windows.

After the car is masked, rub it down with a cleaner such as Prep-sol. Use freshly washed, lint-free rags and rub much as you would if you were giving your own body a rubdown with alcohol. After prepping the body, wipe it all over with a wax-impregnated tack rag to remove any trace of dust or lint.

Painting

You may have to spray a sealer over the entire car at this point. If you are spraying lacquer over enamel, then a sealer is necessary unless the enamel is very old (say, five years or more). The reason for this is that lacquer penetrates completely through all coats of paint. If it penetrates to

wet enamel, the enamel will react with the lacquer and pucker. Sealing is not necessary if you're spraying with enamel. If you spray sealer, let it set up and then wipe it down with a tack rag.

Immediately prime the car. Spray on at least two coats, waiting between coats for the primer to dry to the touch. Painters talk about wet and dry coats, and this is a good time to find out what that means. A wet coat flows into a single continuous surface just short of running. A dry coat has something of a powdery surface, OK for lacquer but not for enamel. I like to use a trouble light in my left hand when I'm painting with my right. By watching the reflection of the light in the paint, I can judge how close the paint is to running. The goal is to spray a coat that is wet just short of running.

Use the primer coat as practice for the color coat. Don't be afraid to make mistakes with primer—it sands easily. The difference between a professional and you is that he sprays paint all day long. This is your only chance to practice. Spray one pass so it runs, just to find out what happens. Use the primer coat to make any final adjustments to the gun. In other words, experiment now, because it's too late with the color coat.

Generally, a gun has two adjustments: pattern and mixture. Get them set by practicing with primer and then don't change the adjustments thereafter. You will rotate the horns on the gun to change the fan pattern from vertical to horizontal to paint doorsills and other vertical surfaces. You want a fairly large fan pattern, but not so large that

*The painted Duetto—in an Italian tri-color scheme—
before being finished and fully competition prepped.*
Gary M. Valant/Valco

One trick to match a new paint color to the original Alfa Romeo color is to find a section of the bodywork that is well-hidden from the sun's rays to use as a sample. Restorer John Kremer chose the glovebox door on his 101 Series Giulia, polished the paint and matched it with an available General Motors red by comparing the door and the paint-chip book in direct sunlight. Here's the freshly painted body on its way back to the workshop.
John Kremer

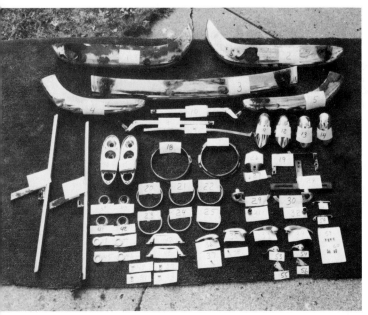

There is one important trick to learn before having trim pieces chromed. After the bodywork has been straightened out and all dents filled in, check to make certain that the trim pieces will fit to the body correctly. You do not have to have a component chromed, only to find out that the fit is not just right, forcing you to bend it to shape and destroying the expensive finish. Before sending the trim to the plating shop, it is a good idea to catalog all of the components so you have a record in case something is misplaced. John Kremer

the pattern is dry at either end of the fan. Set the mixture so the primer flows in a wet coat as you spray. The actual mechanics of gun movement are critical, so practice them during the primer coat. The gun should be moving whenever it's spraying paint. The proper procedure is to begin moving the gun from the left, then pull the trigger to start the paint. Release the trigger before you stop moving the gun. Never change direction while spraying paint. Always spray at the same distance and speed; in other words, act as robotlike as you can, and don't vary the parameters.

Spray two complete coats of primer. Go completely over the car once, working around the car a panel at a time. Then, start over for the second coat. It's not necessary to sand between coats. Once the second coat has set up and the thinner has evaporated sufficiently (about an hour for enamel, five minutes for lacquer) you can wet sand the car with 240 paper. During the sanding process, you'll discover depressions you missed in the basic bodywork. Fill these with green stuff and sand smooth. You'll also sand through the primer in several places. If you just go to paint, it's OK. If you sand through to bare metal you should re-prime the area and resand.

After the car has been wet sanded, go over the car, blowing water from trapped areas with compressed air. Be especially careful around masked areas and opening panels. Don't leave a single drop of water, for if water runs on your freshly sprayed paint it will leave an indelible mark.

Now is the time to clean the gun in preparation for spraying color. Wipe out the cup so it is clean, fill it with some thinner and spray the thinner against your hand until no trace of primer remains. Then, mix the color paint. The amount of thinner used will be different for primer and color. Follow directions on the can. If the weather is very hot, you will need to add retarder to the paint to keep it from drying too fast. You may also use different thinners depending on heat and humidity.

Wipe down the car with a tack rag and spray on the first color coat. This is the big time, and you're on your own. Just be careful and consistent. Begin by spraying all the corners and edges around opening panels. This ensures that visible edges get color coated, and helps eliminate the danger of runs. Then, go over the entire car, paying most attention to the flat panels. Let the first coat set up (fifteen minutes for enamel, no drying time for lacquer) and spray the second color coat. Some painters like to change the spray direction 90 deg. for the second coat. That is, the first coat is usually applied in horizontal passes along the sides of the car; for the second coat, make the passes vertical.

Whether you're spraying enamel or lacquer, the final finish is going to come out of the gun, not from later corrective work. So don't continue spraying a pebbled finish, planning to sand it out later. If something is wrong, stop and fix whatever is bad. Never touch the wet paint, and greet each run pleasantly, because it's going to be your friend for a very long time.

Wet automotive paint is irresistible to bugs over approximately a one-square-mile area. You may wish to invite an entomologist over if you're spraying outside. Again, grin and bear it. Above all, don't try to pick the little darlings out of wet paint with your stubby fingernails or a tweezer. I've found that the bugs, undisturbed, polish up fairly respectably. The gouges you leave trying to extract them are much more noticeable.

You hear a lot about wet sanding between color coats. I never could understand this with lacquer, because the topcoat melts the lower one anyway. I think it's literally impossible with enamel, which takes months to dry to a sandable hardness (enamels with hardener added are exceptions). If you must, use a tack rag between lacquer coats, but enamel simply gets two coats, untouched by human hands.

You may wish to do a third or fourth lacquer coat because lacquer is so thin. If you have enough paint, go to it. I've found that a gallon of lacquer will give me two good coats or three somewhat stretched ones. Don't be fooled, you couldn't measure the difference with a micrometer.

There is a real danger, however, in getting too much paint on a car. The Italians do this all the time and it results, after about five years of sunshine, in a paint job that looks like an alligator lived beneath it. If you're putting enamel over a car that's been repainted four or five times, you're better off with a single, wet coat.

If you've sprayed enamel with a hardener, let the car sit in the garage for a week. This will ensure that the paint is dry before you try any local repairs with 600 grit sandpaper. If you've sprayed lacquer, you may rub the car out after about an hour's wait. Rubbing with a sheepskin wheel is very tricky and I advise against it, especially on paint that may not be fully dry. Use white rubbing compound and a clean rag, generally trying to keep the strokes horizontal.

If you've really botched up a lacquer job, wet sand the bad spots with 400 paper, then wet sand everything with 600 paper. Spray any bare spots and resand with 600 paper, then rub the entire car

The body has been repainted and mated with the chassis, and most of the trim is in place. Restorer John Kremer's 101 Series Giulia waits to have its refurbished engine dropped back into the engine compartment. John Kremer

out with compound. Remove the masking tape after the paint is dry to the touch.

You'll probably want to stripe the car with an accent line. This is a tricky process in itself. If you try to press the tape onto the body with your finger, you'll get a wavy line. The trick is to hold the roll of tape in your left hand, with your right index finger holding the very end of the tape against the body. Pull slightly on the tape and let about 2 ft. of it adhere to the body by itself. Work in segments short enough that the tape doesn't sag. Once the tape adheres itself (slightly) to the body, check that it's straight and then rub it with your right finger, running along the tape lightly at first and then more firmly. Curves simply have to be done cautiously. You use your finger to trace the curve, positioning the tape under your finger and holding it slightly taut.

Don't wax the car for about a month after applying stripes. Wash it with soap and water before waxing.

This completes the restoration of the body. Generally, any enthusiast should be able to paint his own car with a little luck and a lot of care. More ambitious tasks are better left to those who know they can do them.

11

Mechanical Restoration

The mechanical restoration of the engine is considered the single most challenging part of a restoration project. The goal is to end up not only with an engine that runs well, but also looks like it's been restored. Thus, virtually any mechanical restoration will also include cleaning and polishing individual parts, and perhaps having some of the steel parts rechromed.

The intake manifold is secured with 13 mm nuts. On engines with a single carburetor, there is an attaching bolt underneath and in the center of the manifold.

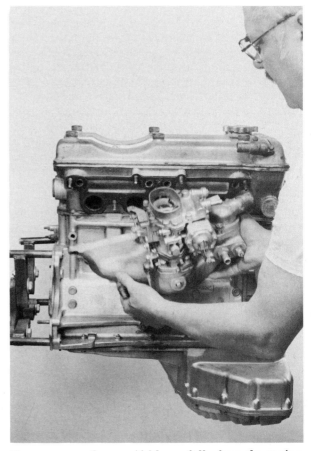

If you remove the manifold carefully from the engine, you may be able to save the intake manifold gasket. It can be re-used, if it is not torn, by coating it lightly with silicone gasket material during reassembly.

Alfa Romeo did not chrome plate any of its fasteners on the modern cars (except for the early Giuliettas, which had chrome-plated head nuts), nor were the aluminum camshaft covers ever polished to a chromelike finish. While there is some tendency to want to overrestore a car by adding chromed and polished pieces, there is a very subtle line between a restoration that is dazzling and one that looks like it was managed by a bordello decorator. As Giulias get older and rarer, it will be progressively harder to determine exactly what was original. To that end, when in doubt, keep a part finished as you found it.

It's foolish to attempt to describe intimately the restoration of the engine, since there are perfectly good workshop manuals devoted specifically to the task. Probably the most useful of the workshop manuals for the Giulia is the Intereurope manual, while the Autobooks manual is a close second. Chilton also publishes an Alfa Romeo repair manual.

All of these books are written to a format that is standard to the individual publisher, and there is some tendency for them to include boilerplate passages that are common to all the repair books in their line. This is not an especially bad practice, but it does mean that the boilerplate sections will ignore any peculiarities of your specific model, and so it is my intention to include those items here.

Alfa Romeo did not publish a proper Giulia workshop manual; however, the Giulietta manual remains the best single work for Alfa Romeo engine repair from 1956 to the present. If you can obtain it, along with the 101 Series supplement, you'll have the official factory line on repairing an engine.

Every manual, however, no matter how exhaustive, will fail to cover just that operation which hangs you up in puzzlement. The most common conundrum you'll encounter in mechanical restoration is trying to remember how something should go back together. Even if you're lucky enough to have a blow-apart illustration (that's a distinct advantage of having a parts manual for your car), you may be sure that the parts illustration you're critically interested in will have been smudged by someone else's greasy thumb, or they are printed so

A 14 mm hex wrench is used to loosen the cam cover's six decorative nuts.

Giulias were the first of the four-cylinder engines to add two 10 mm clamping bolts at the front of the camshaft cover. If you forget to remove them, you may break the cover trying to work it free.

reduced in size that even a magnifying glass will not distinguish between a rubber O-ring and spring-steel washer. The best defense against this is to make a lot of drawings during disassembly and store them where you'll be able to find them again when it comes time to put things back together. Be especially careful to make drawings that clarify potential reversals: Does the master link go on the inside or outside of the chain? Does the oil slinger go on the shaft before or after the gear? Just exactly how did that window-winder come apart?

Before You Begin

Troubleshoot the engine before removing it. Try to determine, before you begin, those parts which will absolutely have to be rebuilt. The purpose of this step is to avoid rebuilding perfectly good parts. If oil pressure is good and the water pump doesn't leak, you can avoid disassembling both pumps.

Never attempt a rebuild with the engine in the car. And always drain the engine and transmission of oil before removing them.

Engine Removal

Always remove the engine and transmission as a unit, and don't just disconnect the battery—remove it.

To make sure everything is disconnected before removing the engine-transmission assembly, work around the engine with your hand. Start at the back of the head and search for things attached to the engine. As you find them, remove them. The easiest items to miss are tachometer and speedometer cables, rear vacuum line to booster, starter wires, ground wire between body and engine, and back-up switch wires to the transmission.

It's easier to remove the exhaust manifold nuts at the head than to remove the manifold flange bolts at the bottom of the exhaust manifold. The bottom nuts will usually be rusted and break. The two lower nuts attaching the manifold at the third and fourth cylinders are most difficult to remove, since the foremost nut on cylinder four has to be removed one flat at a time. If your manifold nuts are 14 mm, the problem is compounded. Replace them with newer, 13 mm nuts for better access next time.

The camshaft cover should be removed carefully in an effort to save its sealing gasket. If not torn, the gasket can be re-used.

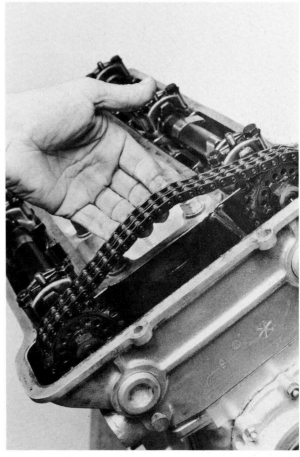

Loosening the chain makes it easier to remove the master link.

190

Disconnect the driveshaft at its companion flange (four bolts), not at the rubber donut. Remove the transmission mount cross-member and the shift lever before trying to remove the engine-transmission assembly. If you disconnect the tie-rod end of the transverse steering link on the passenger's side and also remove the sheet-metal clutch cover, you'll find it easier to remove the engine-transmission assembly. Remove the radiator to give yourself more working room.

In its traditional position, the engine-lifting loop is placed between cylinders two and three, where the engine by itself is perfectly balanced to swing level. This is elegant, but not at all practical. With the transmission attached, the assembly has to be rotated almost 90 deg. so the engine points almost straight up for the transmission to clear the body. Move the loop forward to the second row of studs (it won't fit on the front row), then use a sturdy rope sling between the loop and the crankshaft pulley. Position the lifting hook so that the engine-transmission assembly is lifted at a point approximately above the joint between the water pump and the timing-chain case.

The shift-lever stub will probably catch on the sheet-metal lip between the engine bay and transmission tunnel. A helper at this point will be able to hold the transmission tail down long enough to get it past the lip. Label all wires left hanging in the engine bay.

Clean the engine thoroughly before you lay a hand on it. Cleaning it with a solvent and then washing it down with water also ensures that it's cold enough to disassemble without warping a casting.

Undo the front crankshaft pulley bolt before removing the transmission from the engine. Slip the transmission into gear and block the driveshaft from turning. Remember to bend back the lock tab on the pulley bolt before trying to fit a socket over it.

Remove all accessories such as the distributor, generator and starter. Remove the oil filter by removing the two 19 mm mounting bolts at the block.

Engine Teardown

Before disassembling an engine, have these new items on hand: head gasket and its rubber

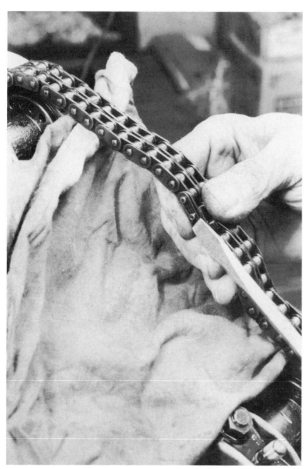

Always place a rag under the chain before snapping free the master link's clip. If the clip flies off, at least it can't fall into the engine. A large-bladed screwdriver works best.

Two 14 mm bolts are used to help clamp the front of the head to the timing-chain cover. They're easy to forget.

O-rings, main and rod bearings; piston rings; front and rear oil seals; timing-chain cover gasket; and all the blue-steel stamped locking tabs.

Disconnect the transmission from the engine. Remove the timing-chain link, remove the chain and then reassemble the link to one end of the chain.

Unbolt the head and lift it off. If the head won't come off, first check that you removed the two upside-down 14 mm bolts that hold the front of the head to the timing-chain cover. Don't try to pry the head off with a screwdriver wedged into the head gasket. Remove the spark plugs and feed some rope down a cylinder. Then, rotate the crank using the flywheel so the rope pushes up against the head, freeing it from the block. There is a special Alfa Romeo tool that is a steel-plate puller, screwed into a spark-plug hole and acting on the studs.

Set aside the head and work on it as a separate assembly. You'll need a specialized valve-removing tool which can reach down into the head casting to get the valves out. If you've never done a head before, it's better to send it out to a specialist shop. You must use a proper-fitting tool to drive valve guides in and out. You can make the tools easily on a lathe, but if you don't have the tools, don't try to replace the guides.

Check for alignment marks positioning the clutch assembly and flywheel. If there aren't any, use a chisel to punch a single mark that spans the clutch pressure plate and flywheel so the two can be reassembled exactly as they came apart. Then, remove the clutch pressure plate and clutch driven plate. Use the chisel to mark the crankshaft-flywheel relationship. Bend back the blue-metal locking tabs on the flywheel attaching bolts, remove the bolts and then pull off the flywheel.

Always remove the oil-pump blow-off spring and piston and verify that they move freely in the bore.

It's easy to forget the order of the front crank pulley, slinger, gear and sprocket, and the orienta-

A long extension handle is needed to remove the head bolts. They should be removed in a spiral pattern starting at the center of the engine and working out toward both ends of the head at equal intervals.

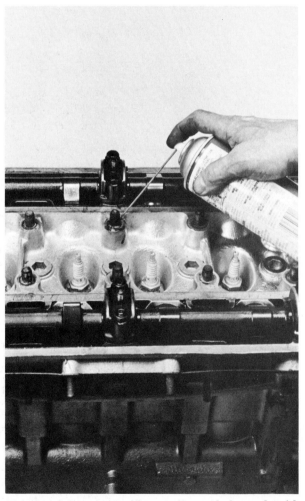

If the head doesn't come free easily, soak the studs with thin oil. Water frequently leaks into the stud passages; if the engine has sat for some time, the water will corrode the steel studs to the aluminum head.

tion of the gear. Make a drawing as you remove them from the crankshaft. Just in case you don't, the order is just as I've listed, and the gear slips on so its teeth are nearest the sprocket.

Engine Inspection

You can judge if the valve guide needs replacing by inserting an unworn (new) valve in it, holding the valve head about a centimeter off the seat and moving the valve back and forth, testing the stem-to-guide clearance. There will be some slop, but not much. If in doubt, send it out.

If you can catch your fingernail on a camshaft or crankshaft bearing, the bearing must be re-

ground. As a last resort, polish it with 600 grit sandpaper.

Be especially careful about checking the ring-to-groove clearance of the top ring. If the clearance is too much, you can have the top groove machined out to accept a number two compression ring, which is 0.5 mm wider.

Engine Reassembly

When reassembling the engine, be aware that connecting-rod offset is easy to forget. The rods at the ends of the crank have an offset that moves them farther apart; the rods at the center have an offset that moves them closer together.

The camshaft resists considerable pressure from the valve springs. That is why you should remove the camshaft bearing nuts in several incremental steps. Begin at the center and work outward, just as when removing the head bolts.

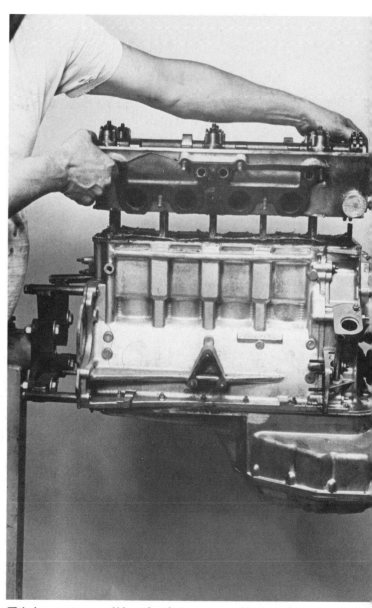

This is not as easy a lift as the photo suggests. The head is not heavy, but it is a challenge to free it from its studs evenly.

Numbers stamped on the shiny rod boss may be duplicates, but all the numbers must be on the same side of the engine.

Always stake the crankshaft oil plugs.

The orientation of the oil pump's distributor-drive slot is not critically important. You can always rewire the distributor to match.

Freeze the valve guides before installing them. One strong blow should get them ninety percent home. All guides must be installed to the proper depth, and you should work quickly on a guide to keep it from heating up too much.

Adjust the valves before you install the head. Write down the valve clearances before you start to replace shims. Unless you have a shim set or a large selection of shims, exchange the shims between all four intake valves in one session, then work on the exhaust valves. You can grind the shims to get larger clearances. If it isn't obvious to you how to do this, don't try.

At TDC (top dead center), the intake and exhaust lobes of cylinder number one should be pointing away from each other.

Assemble the timing-chain tensioner before you install the head. Let gravity help you keep the locking wedge in place on the tensioner as you slip it into the head. Compress the tensioner spring as far as you can and then lock it in the compressed position.

Always install the front oil seal before you put the front timing-chain cover in place.

Assemble the flywheel to the crankshaft before you put the pan on. Put a wooden hammer handle for the rods to press against when you tighten the flywheel bolts.

Put all the accessories back on the engine before you put it into the car. This is especially true of a Weber-carbureted manifold.

As a last act before lowering the complete engine-transmission assembly into the car, chase the motor-mount threads on the chassis, and selectively fit the nuts and bolts that most easily thread on. The lower two studs are very hard to get to, and it helps if you can run the nut on with your fingers.

If you've disconnected the exhaust manifold at the head, the engine will have to be properly tilted before you can slip the manifold onto its studs. With the engine settled on its mounts in the engine bay, put a jack at the tail of the transmission and

After the head has been removed you should take some time to clean the top surfaces of the block and piston. A shop vac is very helpful. Note the corrosion on the cylinder head studs.

The water pump is held on with nine 10 mm nuts. Check carefully that you remove them all.

194

use it to tilt the engine so the exhaust manifold will slip onto its studs.

Engine Run-In

Before starting the engine, disconnect the coil wire and use the starter long enough to see oil pressure on the gauge. If you've got a low battery, remove the spark plugs and push the car in gear until you see pressure.

Break in the engine using nondetergent, cheap oil. A new engine needs wide-open throttle, but not revs: don't take the engine over 3500 rpm for the first 100 miles.

Transmission

In general, you shouldn't attempt to overhaul a Giulia transmission unless you have access to a lathe and a press or gear puller with long arms. The lathe is required to fit the gear bearings to the shaft, and the press is used to dismantle the mainshaft.

The transmission is made up of a large number of interchangeable parts, and it's a challenge to work with the parts and not get them confused. When first opened, the transmission presents you with what appears to be miles and miles of gears. Disassembled, it's amazing how many parts can be fit into such a small case.

Fundamentally, the transmission is a collection of five modules of gears, paired front-to-back for the one-two and three-four sets. If you understand the operation of the friction clutch which

The water pump gasket is a thin paper which most certainly will be destroyed as you remove the pump. Don't try to save it.

A 38 mm (1.5 in.) socket is needed to undo the bolt on the crankshaft. The bolt captures a lock tab which must first be unbent. Never try to remove the bolt with a chisel or crescent wrench: you'll only destroy it.

gets the gear rotating at the same speed as the output shaft on which it rotates, and appreciate how the gear is locked to the output shaft with the shift collar, you have conquered about ninety-five percent of the transmission's mystery. The layshaft is simply a device to communicate torque from the input shaft, through the gear to the output shaft.

Probably the other five percent of the transmission's mystery is how the shift detent lock-out system works. This is a system of sliding balls and a rod which ensures that only one gear is selected at a time.

The transmission is its own best teacher. Study it carefully as you take it apart to understand exactly how everything works. By the time you have it dismantled, you should be able to reassemble it blindfolded.

If there are no broken gear teeth, overhaul will probably consist of renewing the clutches, bearings and seals.

The most important principle in overhauling a transmission is cleanness.

Rear Axle

In practical terms, Alfa Romeo rear ends never go bad. Of the approximately twenty-five Alfa Romeos I've owned, not one has developed a bad differential, or even had an outboard wheel bearing go bad. That is fortunate, for setting up a rear end properly is beyond the capabilities of most Alfa Romeo owners. The procedure requires special tools—and a lot of experience reading the gear pattern which is the final test of the setup.

If you have a bad differential unit, I strongly suggest replacing it with a used unit from a junkyard. Get the whole axle assembly, with the disc brakes attached, if you can. Check the outboard

The oil filter is held to the block with two nuts.

Once the bolt is removed, the pulley should slip off easily. It is keyed to the crank and so goes on only one way. The pulley shaft is the bearing surface for the front crank seal. If the surface is grooved or scored, the pulley should be repaired or replaced.

196

seals for leaking, fit new brake pads if needed and you've done about all you should.

Otherwise, let a professional repair the differential.

Brakes

You can rebuild a brake master cylinder with little effort. On the other hand, if you make a mistake, you can also kill yourself, passengers and bystanders, not to mention picket fences and fireplugs.

Working on the brakes is closer to working on an airplane than anything else you can do on a car: in both instances, you probably won't be able to interrupt your trip and hop out to fix what's suddenly gone wrong.

Having (hopefully) made the point, we return to the fact that brakes are essentially easy to repair, and repair kits are easily obtained.

The most likely problem you'll encounter in restoring the brake system is a frozen wheel piston. Sometimes, you can free it by forcing it back into its cylinder and then using brake pressure to move it along the cylinder. If the piston is hopelessly stuck, you'll have to take it to a shop to have it fixed. Don't

try to hone a disc brake wheel cylinder or sand its piston; replacing the sealing rubber on a disc brake is an easy job, however. Never try to separate the halves of a disc brake caliper.

The vacuum-operated brake booster is the most likely part of the brake system to fail. For a short while, Alfa Romeo offered rebuild kits for the booster but the fact that virtually no information is available about the booster is evidence that Alfa Romeo would just as soon you leave it alone.

Some Giulias are fitted with ATE brakes, and a few carry Dunlop. The front units of either are straightforward. The rear Dunlop unit, however, is a maze of linkages. Essentially, the rear unit requires occasional adjustment of the pullrod which connects the two actuating levers, a point not covered in any of the repair manuals.

Remove the filter whole: if you remove the element first, you'll probably spill dirty oil on the engine.

The fuel pump comes off in stages. First, remove the two 13 mm nuts.

Front Suspension

Giulia front suspensions come in two flavors, depending on whether you have a 101 or 105 Series car. The 101 cars had a suspension identical to the Giulietta: double A-arms. You can rebuild these suspensions by replacing the bushings at the base of the A (requires an adjustable reamer), and generally tidying everything else up, including replacing the outboard ball joints.

The 105 Series cars had a lower A-arm similar to the 101 Series unit, but the upper suspension consisted of transverse and trailing links.

If you have it apart, the upper tubular link can be made adjustable to provide camber adjustment. Cut the link at midpoint, shorten both tubes somewhat, then tap right- and left-hand threads into the inside diameter of the tubes. Fabricate an adjusting link from stock with right- and left-hand threads. Machine a hex on the link to ease adjustment, and use jam nuts to keep everything where it should be.

The upper link's foremost ball joint takes the most beating on a Giulia, and if you drive rough dirt roads, you can plan to replace the joint about once a year. You'll know it needs replacement by the resounding clunk every time you go over a bump. Replacement is simple, and a restoration should automatically include replacement of this joint.

Rear Suspension

Aside from cleaning and inspecting the rubber bushes that are part of the rear suspension, it's unlikely that anything will have to be done to the rear suspension for restoration. Giulia springs tend not to sag; nonetheless, it's a good idea to measure the two rear coil springs to verify they have the same unloaded height. Springs with different strengths are available from specialty aftermarket suppliers.

Inspect carefully the area where the rear suspension trailing arm attaches to the body. The area

As you remove the front half of the pump, you reveal the first push rod.

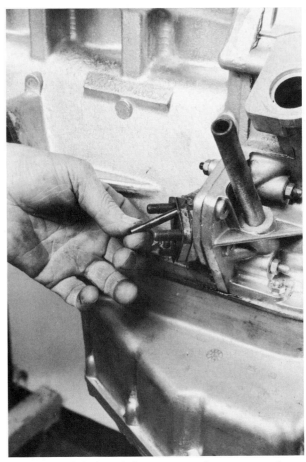

Pull the rod free and then remove the spacer and two gaskets from the mounting flange.

198

must be rustfree and perfectly sound. If the body shell is badly rusted, it is possible that the metal around the attaching point has been weakened. If there is any question about the strength of the area, replace the body's floor panel with new metal, welded in place.

If the Giulia Spider is going to be raced, consider strengthening the trailing arm's attaching point at the rear axle. Box the attaching arm on the axle housing to help resist side forces during cornering at racing speeds.

On factory-racing Giulias, the rear-axle assembly was further located transversely by a tongue attached to the differential and sliding in a groove attached to the body. These units were used on GTA cars, and if the Giulia you're restoring is going to have a life of racing, it would be worth tracking down a GTA to see the details of how the rear suspension was modified.

Alternately, you can fit a Panhard rod to the rear axle.

Fuel Pump

The mechanical fuel pump fitted to the Giulia is virtually troublefree. You can dismantle it by removing the stamped-metal top (it's spring-loaded, and held on by two screws) which exposes the one-way valves. The pump diaphragm itself is sandwiched between the two lower halves of the pump body. Rebuild kits are available, and the work is straightforward.

The Giulia fuel pump is driven by two push-rods, operated by a cam on the oil pump drive to the distributor. If you take the pump off and then reinstall it, only to discover it won't work, you have probably dropped the shorter of the two rods which is held in the fuel pump housing. Find it, remove the pump and replace the rod.

Some prefer electric fuel pumps. If you do fit an electric pump to the Giulia, verify that the fuel delivery pressure doesn't exceed about 3.5 psi.

With the spacer removed, you can then undo the three 10 mm nuts that secure the rest of the pump to the engine.

After the second part of the pump is removed, pull out the second pushrod. Keep all the parts of the fuel pump together in a bag.

Higher pressures can overcome the carburetor's float needle valve and cause the carburetor to flood.

Generator

The generator itself is a Bosch unit and virtually troublefree. The bottom generator mount is a stamped-steel yoke that fits snugly against a boss on the aluminum front timing-chain cover. If the long mounting bolt loosens, the boss can become worn to an oval; under extreme wear, the bolt can actually wear its way through the boss. Preventive maintenance is the only real insurance against wear, in this case.

If the boss is worn, press-fit a steel bush to renew the mounting hole.

A failure to charge, even with a good generator and regulator, indicates a slipping V-belt. If the red charging light stays on and gets brighter when the engine revs, the number three fuse in the fuse block is not making a good connection or is blown.

Starter

Like the generator, the starter is a Bosch unit and virtually troublefree.

Carburetor

Several variations of the Solex 35APAIG carburetor are fitted to Giulias, and rebuild kits for the Solex are easily obtainable.

The Solex may be replaced by any of several Weber carburetors which are members of the DFT and DGAV family, since the mounting holes are identical.

The Giulia used DCOE Weber carburetors on many models. These carburetors are infinitely rebuildable, short of catastrophic damage from fire or wreck. During 1986–1987, replacement DCOE carburetors were virtually unobtainable, due in

Like the water pump, the timing cover is held on by a number of unevenly placed nuts. It's easy to miss one; if you do, it will be easy to break the cover attempting to remove it.

Four of the cover's nuts attach it to the pan. As a result, the pan must be removed before finally lifting the timing cover free.

part to the popularity of the carburetor as a replacement unit for the 1750 and 2000 Spica fuel-injection system, and the fact that Weber production was kept busy supplying the carburetors as original equipment for several manufacturers. As a result, if you are unable to rebuild the Webers on your Giulia, you may not be able to find new replacement units.

Fortunately, two manufacturers supply bolt-on replacements for the Weber 40 DCOE: Dell'Orto and Mikuni. Both are well made and work as well as the Webers, though they look different enough that they're unacceptable for a concours where originality is judged. My Giulia Super is currently running Dell'Ortos quite happily.

During a restoration, there is an almost irresistible urge to throw away the single Solex carburetor in favor of a pair of Webers (or facsimile). I've swapped Solexes and Webers on an Alfa Romeo several times. Webers, because of their larger total venturi area, certainly make a more responsive engine, though they will not, by themselves, give much added power nor change fuel economy. The Solex-to-Weber conversion requires a new motor mount, manifold and air cleaner setup, different

The drain trough area of the pan is clamped with removable bolts.

The "hammerhead" portion of the pan is attached to the block by studs.

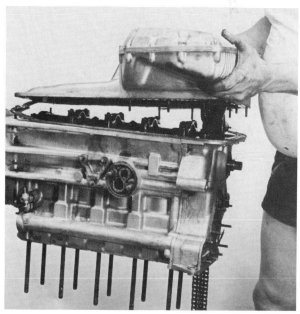

There are two nuts holding the pan to the rear of the block. After they have been removed, the pan can be lifted free. The pan gasket is sturdy and frequently can be re-used with the aid of a silicone sealant.

The oil pump is held to the timing cover with three bolts.

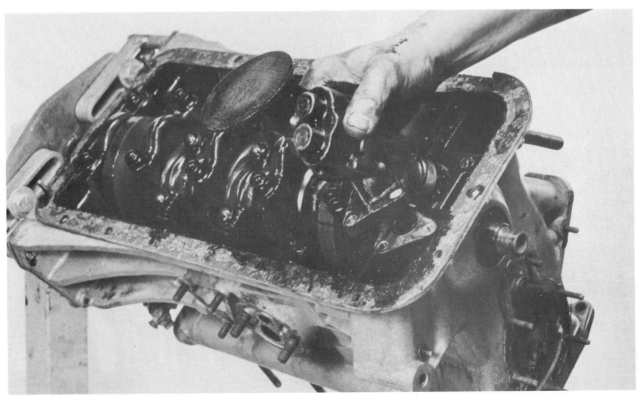

*The pump has to be worked out of the timing cover,
following the axis of the distributor driveshaft.*

After the oil pump is removed, the timing cover can be lifted off.

radiator top hose and a lot of work. Unless all these items fall easily to hand, the conversion is probably not worth the effort. To make the conversion truly worthwhile, you also need different pistons, the Veloce camshafts and a proper one-four and two-three header exhaust manifold.

An oil slinger is fitted over the nose of the crankshaft and should be removed next.

The oil pump drive gear, primary timing chain and idler sprocket all come off as a unit.

The bottom end of the Giulia engine.

This view shows the rod and main bearing nuts which are the next items to be removed.

The rod nuts are secured with lock tabs. Bend them back using light taps on a chisel as shown.

A long handle is needed to undo the rod nuts.

Look closely at each bearing as it is removed. If the crank journal is scored, the bearing surface will be deeply grooved. If a brown layer of metal shows on the bearing, then the bearing is quite worn and the crank journal should be checked for roundness. Never re-use rod or main bearings.

The main bearing cap nuts are secured with stamped-steel locknuts. Be careful not to bend them when removing them, for they can be re-used.

The rear main bearing cap also carries the rear main oil seal. The cap's nuts are secured with lock tabs.

The rear main bearing cap is hard to remove and easy to damage. Remove all the other main caps and lift the nose of the crank slightly to start the rear cap upwards. After worrying it up about 0.5 in., try to pry the two rubber seals free on either side of the cap. There is a special Alfa Romeo tool for removing this cap, but it can be removed with only a screwdriver if you're patient.

With the rear bearing cap finally removed, the crank will lift free.

Lowering the restored engine into the engine compartment. You need to have all components in place on the actual engine unit before putting it into the compart- *ment as there is little access to some parts when in place. This includes the oil-filter assembly, fuel pump and the complete transmission.* John Kremer

12

Interior Restoration

This chapter covers those interior items that can be restored by the average enthusiast. You should not try to remove the windshield from a coupe without professional aid. Similarly, I feel that head-

liner replacement, which involves glass removal, is not an appropriate project for the typical owner. There are, however, many useful items that can be restored by the enthusiast.

The underside of a GT Veloce rear seat shows its construction. The basic form is foam rubber, supported by *steel rods. The covering is held in place with wire loops and heavy thread.*

Seats

Replacement seat covers are available for many Giulia models, but I advise against trying to do anything more than slipping them over already existing upholstery. Upholstery, like painting, is a job that requires daily honing, and the occasional amateur is probably only going to botch it.

Nevertheless, there is a great deal of satisfaction in doing your own upholstery. If you use a reinforced plastic material, make certain that it is worth working on. There is no such thing as a cheap, good plastic; those two terms are mutually exclusive. The proper material is also probably the most expensive, backed with a deeply woven fabric and supple to the hand. Further, a durable thread is essential: Mom's spare spool of black cotton thread won't work here.

A heavy-duty sewing machine is required to stitch upholstery material. You must carefully take the old material off the frame, for what you take off becomes the pattern for what you put back on. Further, how you take it off is the pattern for how you put it back on. Note how the fabric is attached to the underside of the seats, and what hardware is used to attach it. You should obtain new hardware to use when you recover the seat.

It's possible that the foam material beneath the covers is crumbly. In that case, you can form new material from a block of new foam using an electric carving knife. The trick is to cut the material without deforming it.

If you are lucky enough to be able to observe an upholsterer at work for an hour or so (and perhaps, ask a few questions), you will be able to approach the job with greater confidence. That failing, there are several books available on the subject.

Side Panels and Headliner

Door panels are easy to refinish on the Giulia because they are essentially two-dimensional. In fact, you can make door panels from scratch using a good-quality brown fiberboard using the old panel as a pattern.

On the other hand, a headliner requires removal of the glass, and should be left to a professional.

Convertible Top

You can buy inexpensive aftermarket convertible tops from several sources. Replacing a top is a major undertaking, no question about it, but the essentials are quite straightforward. The top is

Strip the covering from the foam rubber form by opening the wire loops with a needle-nose pliers, as shown. New covering can be stitched to the framework using heavy thread instead of the wire loops.

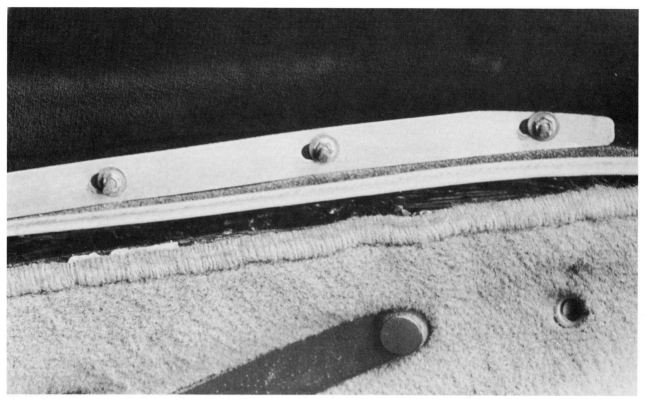

You learn how to install a new top in the process of removing the old one. Take plenty of notes. The convertible top is held in place at the rear by a metal strip and small studs. Soak the threads of the studs before trying to remove the nuts, otherwise, you're likely to break off the studs.

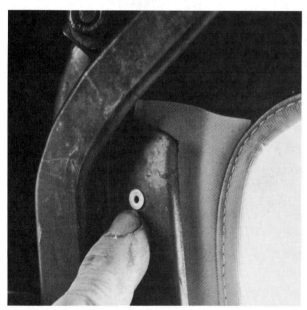

Original tops have a metal trim piece at the rear of the door glass, as shown. Drill the rivet out to remove the trim piece. You'll find that the top material is glued in place; pull the top material free and then scrape clean the surface to which it was glued. A guide wire loops through the top material from the base of the trim piece (shown) to the front bow. Thread it into the new top material with a length of sturdy wire as a guide.

glued or clamped in place. You remove it by carefully pulling it free of glue or carefully unclamping it by removing screws or nuts.

You should not worry about getting a top drum-tight. Rather, be concerned that you install it evenly from side to side and front to back. As the top weathers, it will tighten up, but no amount of weathering or waiting will square up a top that has been put down crooked.

Complete installation instructions come with every aftermarket top, so I will be brief here. You'll need a tube of trim cement, a pop-riveter and precious few hand tools.

As for the upholstery, you learn how a top goes on by taking the old one off. Note where and how it's glued to the top bows. When you begin to fit the new top, begin with the front bow. Square the new top material carefully and glue it in place at the front. Then, with the top partially erect, attach the rear of the top to the body using the clamping strip and its studs along the rear deck. After those two positions have been fixed, you can proceed to install the remainder of the top, running up and forward over the side windows.

Floor Mats

There is no substitute for the original rubber floor matting with the embossed Alfa Romeo logo.

There is commercial ribbed rubber matting that can be cut to fit, but that is not acceptable for a concours restoration. Most restored Alfa Romeos seen at national meets have replaced the rubber matting with standard fabric carpeting, properly bound all round with material that matches the upholstery.

Dash

The dash, which here is taken to include the instruments and electrical switches, is perhaps more of a challenge than the casual enthusiast should attempt. It's not so much getting the physical piece out, it's failing to scratch up the whole interior in the process, and then remembering where all those dangling wires go when you try to put it back in. No shop manual I know of deals with removal and replacement of the dash. I have removed the dash on a Giulia Super, as well as my 2.0 liter Spider, which is essentially the same as the Duetto. After having it completely free and attached only by a few wires (unlabeled), I decided that anything I needed to do would be as easily accomplished with the dash in situ as continuing its removal, and thus returned it to its proper position.

Be aware that the dash of the 101 Series cars is an integral part of the body structure and is not removable.

Instruments should be rebuilt by a reputable shop. VDO has an office in Winchester, Virginia, if you can't find anyone to do it locally.

Wiring

Some marques are notorious for poor wiring. Alfa Romeo is not. The Giulia is notorious for parking its fuse block out where its contacts are sure to fail, but the actual wires are quite sturdy. The fact has not deterred owners from hanging a veritable Christmas tree beneath the dash to accommodate CBs, radios, amplifiers, several generations of burglar alarms and miscellaneous auxiliary lights and horns.

If you can cut through all the add-ons, you may discover a perfectly serviceable wiring harness. Though you can purchase a new wiring harness for

The front of the top has a decorative cover which is screwed in place. Remove the top's latches (shown) and all the decorative Phillips-head attaching screws to pull it free. The front of the top itself is glued to the front bow.

The new top is first attached to the front bow and then to the rear. The most important check is to assure that the top is hung evenly side-to-side.

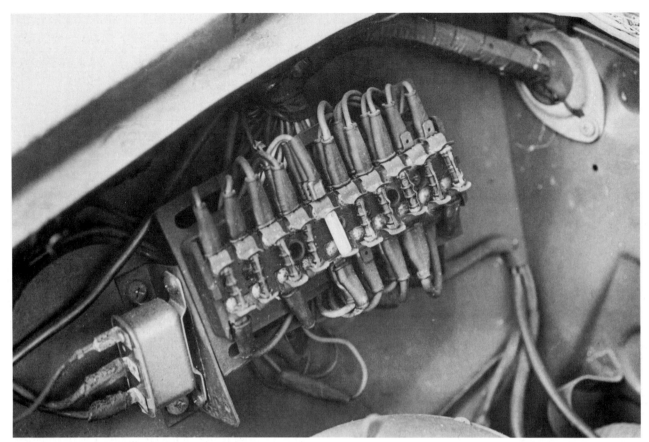

The Giulia fuse block, shown here minus its cover, is located on the passenger's side of the engine compartment. This is an ideal location to encourage corrosion.

Alfa Romeo learned: later models have the fuse block inside the passenger compartment.

There are two ways to re-carpet your Giulia during restoration. One route is to purchase new-old-stock carpeting—if it can be found. In the more likely case where NOS material is not available, you can cut carpet to size. When disassembling your car, make certain you save each piece of original carpet as it is invaluable as a pattern for cutting your own pieces against. John Kremer

the Giulia from the factory, the effort required to install it is probably daunting unless the body is completely stripped. If the only problem is wires that are too short from countless trimmings, then you can use a bullet-fastener set to renew the length of the wire. Alternately, you can replace any bad wires and then rewrap the harness in black vinyl tape to match the original. If you plan to do any extensive electrical work, you should purchase one of the kits that contain a collection of spade and washer electrical connectors and a special-purpose pliers for crimping the connectors to the prepared wire.

Any work on the wiring requires an intimate knowledge of the wiring diagram. Most Alfa Romeo shop manuals publish wiring diagrams which most nearly resemble a Rorschach test. The trick in using these diagrams is to use a magnifying glass and business card. Under the glass, place the business card so its edge follows the line in question, and ends just where the line does a right-angle turn. Using that technique, you should be able to follow a line from its origin to its end. Do not try to follow a wire any more than is necessary to draw it on another piece of paper. In other words, draw your own (enlarged) diagram. You will not have to reproduce the entire diagram, of course, just the part of interest to you. In the process of drawing the diagram, you will also come to understand which wires go where; that is the real purpose of the exercise.

You will probably find that the wires, especially in the engine compartment, have been painted or otherwise defaced so their true color is virtually impossible to determine. Solve this by carefully scraping the surface of the insulation with a razor blade. Be careful to scrape enough area to identify any coding stripes on the wire. Even with this technique, be aware that the color coding of the wiring diagram will probably not be accurate for the wires in your car. In that case, an ohmmeter must be used to verify the matching ends of each wire in question.

The first rule of troubleshooting wiring is to verify a good ground. Electricity has an annoying habit of wandering aimlessly through the system the moment its ground return is lost.

There is a short-checker, available at automotive tool supply stores, that uses inductance to trace a shorted wire. If you plan to do extensive patching on an extensively butchered electrical system, I recommend the short-checker. An electronic switch is plugged in to replace the fuse, and a gauge is then moved along the wire to detect exactly where the wire shorts to ground.

Summary

This rather long explanation has avoided much of the nitty-gritty detail that the experienced

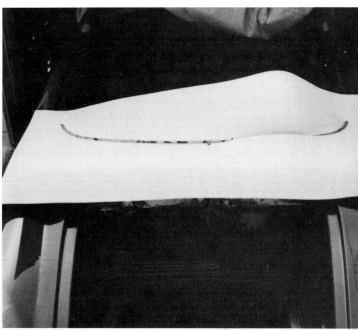

Underneath the vinyl covering, a thin piece of foam was originally used to add padding to the dash. Similar foam padding is available from medical supply companies or foam outlets in 0.25 in. thickness. Use closed-cell foam as it will not soak up and store water that may leak onto the dash and cause rust underneath. The foam is glued down using either a spray or brush-on vinyl glue. Then cut around the edges of the dash to fit; in the front, the foam is folded over the dash lip, so darts will have to be cut to make it lay flat. John Kremer

New-old-stock dash covers are virtually impossible to find for the 101 Series Giulias, but they can be fabricated. Here is the bare body of John Kremer's Giulia Spider being ready in preparation to have the interior restored. John Kremer

With the foam padding glued in place and cut to shape, lay out your piece of vinyl and trim it to fit. Holes will have to be cut for the heater vents and the rearview mirror that mounts on top of the dash; use a sharp razor for clean cuts. The metal plate that mounts the mirror is the same thickness as the foam, so cut the foam to go around the base rather than under it. John Kremer

restorer has learned, and has intentionally steered clear of a how-to on turning a rusted hulk into a 100 point jewel. I have suggested those areas in which skills must be learned in order to restore a car, and generally outlined how one goes about learning them—or avoiding them, if all that is wanted is to manage the restoration.

Restoration allows you to trace the hand of a master. I would not have designed it so, of course, but that is Alfa Romeo's genius and my ignorance: to understand the difference is truly the main point of restoration. For the enthusiast, restoration is a path of discovery.

To glue the vinyl in place, start at the defroster vents and work outward in all directions. Use either spray or brush-on vinyl glue and lay the prepped vinyl across the dash. Work with a heat gun to stretch the vinyl slightly as you spread it over the contours in the dash; when it cools, the vinyl will contract to fit the corners. If you flatten the vinyl with your hand as you work, the coolness of your skin will keep the vinyl from overheating and melting. To fit the vinyl around the larger humps, such as the dash pod, you will need to cut more darts in the fabric so the ends can butt up against each other. You can then use a vinyl repair kit to fill in the seams. John Kremer

Giulia Engine Component Interchange Chart

Legend: X stands for original equipment; O stands for optional equipment; R stands for race equipment.

Engine blocks	TI	TI Super	Super	GT & GTC	GTV	GTA	GT Junior	Duetto	TZ
10500.01.010.05	X		X	X	X	X		X	
10516.01.010.03	O	X	O	O	O	O		O	O
10506.01.010.05							X		
10511.01.010.00	O	O	O	O	O	O		O	X
10532.01.010.99						R			

Cylinder heads	TI	TI Super	Super	GT & GTC	GTV	GTA	GT Junior	Duetto	TZ
10500.01.053.00	X								
10121.01.053.01		X	X	X	O			O	O
10530.01.053.00							X		
10536.01.053.00	O	O	O	O	X			X	O
10532.01.053.00						X			
10532.01.053.99						R			
10511.01.053.02	O	O	O	O	O			O	X

Crankshafts	TI	TI Super	Super	GT & GTC	GTV	GTA	GT Junior	Duetto	TZ
10500.02.010.00	X	X	X	X	X			X	X
10128.02.010.00							X		
10532.02.010.00 steel	O	O	O	O	O	X		O	O
10532.02.010.99 special						R			R

Connecting rods	TI	TI Super	Super	GT & GTC	GTV	GTA	GT Junior	Duetto	TZ
10500.02.020.00	X		X	X	X			X	O
10512.02.020.00 heavy-duty	O	X	O	O	O	X		O	X
10111.02.020.00 heavy-duty							X		

Oil pumps	TI	TI Super	Super	GT & GTC	GTV	GTA	GT Junior	Duetto	TZ
10532.06.013.01						X			
10514.06.013.00 18 mm deep	X	X	X	X	X			X	
10514.06.013.01 28 mm deep	X	X	X	X	X		X	X	

Oil pans	TI	TI Super	Super	GT & GTC	GTV	GTA	GT Junior	Duetto	TZ
10511.01.039.01 drop spacer	O	O	O	O	O	O	O	O	R
10511.01.021.00 inclined	O	O	O	O	O	O	O	O	X
10500.01.021.05 aluminum	X	X	X	X	X	X		X	

	TI	TI Super	Super	GT & GTC	GTV	GTA	GT Junior	Duetto	TZ
Pistons									
10514.02.030.00	X	O	X	O	X			X	O
10502.02.030.08	O	O	O	X	O			O	O
10121.02.030.07	O	X	O	O	O			O	X
10100.02.030.04							X		
10511.02.031.07	R	R	R	R	R			R	R
10532.02.030.00						X			
10532.02.030.98						R			
10532.02.030.99						R			
Flywheels									
10500.02.040.01	X	X	X	X	X	O		X	O
10506.02.040.00							X		
10532.02.040.00 steel	O	O	O	O	O	X	O	O	O
10510.02.040.00 steel	O	O	O	O	O	O	O	O	X
Camshafts									
10502.03.200.00	X								
10502.03.200.01 sport	O		X	X	X	X	X	X	O
10121.03.200.00 sport	O	X	O	O	O	O	O	O	X
10121.03.200.01 race	R	R	R	R	R	R	R	R	R
Weber carburetors									
40 DCOE 24			X						
40 DCOE 28							X		
40 DCOE 27					X			X	
40 DCOE 4				X					
45 DCOE 14		X	O	O	O	X	O	O	X
Valve springs, outer									
10514.03.303.00	X	X	X	X	X		X	X	X
10511.03.303.03	O	O	O	O	O	O	O	O	O
10532.03.303.00						X			
Inlet manifolds									
10516.01.060.02	O	X	O	O	O	O	O	O	O
10502.01.060.02	O	O	X	X	X	X	O	X	O
10514.01.060.01	X								
10530.01.060.00							X		
10511.01.060.00	O	O	O	O	O	O	O	O	X
Exhaust manifolds									
10500.01.705.00 1-4							X		
10500.01.706.00 2-3							X		
10502.01.705.03 1-4	X	O	X	X	X	O	O	X	
10502.01.706.03 2-3	X	O	X	X	X	O	O	X	
10516.01.071.00 1-4	O	X	O	O	O	X	O	O	
10516.01.072.00 2-3	O	X	O	O	O	X	O	O	
Oil pans									
10500.01.211.03 18 mm	X	X	X	X	X			X	O
10514.01.211.00 28 mm	X	X	X	X	X		X	X	O
18 mm magnesium	O	O	O	O	O	X	O	O	O
28 mm magnesium	O	O	O	O	O	O	O	O	O
Oil radiator adapter									
10516.01.014.00	O	O	O	O	O	O	O	O	O

	TI	TI Super	Super	GT & GTC	GTV	GTA	GT Junior	Duetto	TZ
Oil radiators									
10532.31.045.00						O			
10516.31.045.00	O	O	O	O	O		O	O	
10121.31.045.00								O	O
10511.31.045.00									O
Distributors									
10500.05.011.02	X								
10121.05.011.00	O	X	X	X	X		X	X	X
10511.05.011.06	O	O	O	O	O		O	O	O
10532.05.011.00						X			
Alternator, Bosch									
10600.05.061.00	O	O	O	O	O	O	O	O	O
Generator									
10532.05.050.00	O	O	O	O	O	O	O	O	O

Parts Sources

Let me warn you up front that if you walk into an Alfa Romeo dealership and ask for a part for your Giulia, you're likely to be regarded as someone from another planet. The Giulia is some twenty-three years old at this writing and virtually anything for it falls under the definition of an obsolete part.

The precious few exceptions to this rule are listed here.

New Parts Sources

AFRA
Via F. Caracciolo, 24
Milan, Italy

AFRA bought all of Alfa Romeo's old stuff (NOS in the business) and still remains a primary source of new parts.

Automotive Systems Group
6644 San Fernando Rd. *818-956-7933*
Glendale, CA 91201

John Shankle and Brad Bunch's Alfa Ricambi have combined forces to offer the widest selection of parts available anywhere. If they don't have the part, it probably can't be found (and, unfortunately, there are a few of them). Knowledgeable help and real enthusiasm make this a favorite source.

International Auto Parts *804-973-0555*
Rte. 29 North
Charlottesville, VA 22906

Not just Alfa Romeo parts, the selection is still good and their catalog will tell you just what they have.

EuroParts
1425 Gardena Ave. Unit 7 *818-*
Glendale, CA 91204

Another generalized source of parts. Ask for the catalog.

gone

220

Valco Enterprises, Inc.
13551 Method St.
Dallas, TX 75243

Gary M. Valant's operation specializes in restoration and competition preparation for Alfa Romeo and other Italian marques.

Dealerships

Ereminias Imports
3000 S. Main St.
Torrington, CT 06790

John Ereminias is an enthusiast and active member of the Alfa Club.

Bobcor Motors
120 Passaic St.
Hackensack, NJ 07601

An old-line dealership under new and enthusiastic management.

DeFinizio Imports
Routes 291 & 420
Essington, PA 19029

Active supporters of the Alfa Club, you can be sure they at least speak the language.

DiFatta Brothers
5928 Belair Rd.
Baltimore, MD 21206

Another regular Alfa Club supporter.

Used Parts Sources

Alfa Parts Connection
3711 Byron Hwy.
Byron, CA 94514

Larry is the Social Chairman of the Alfa Romeo Association of California, knowledgeable and very helpful.

Tom Zat
Alfa Heaven
Zagato Ln.
Aniwa, WI 54408

Sure, Tom has one, and probably two or three. They may be a bit rusty, because basically he's got a junkyard. But what a yard! Also a source of new parts and information. Worth a trip within your lifetime.

Clubs

AROC
2468 Gum Tree Ln.
Fallbrook, CA 92028

The club. They have a monthly publication and a list of all the other clubs in the world. An AROC chapter is probably nearer than you think. You should join.

Alfa Romeo Association
546 W. McKinley Ave.
Sunnyvale, CA 94086

Not associated with AROC, and over 1,000 members strong from all over the United States.

Other Sources

Looking for Giulia parts is a pure treasure hunt. If you've tried all the sources listed, there are still plenty of places to look. One always hopes to find an Alfa Romeo owner who just happens to have a leftover piece from the spider he owned ten years ago. That's why I've listed the clubs. The problem with businesses is that they tend to come and go a bit faster than books go in and out of print. As a result, I'd rather tell you how to find the sources than list them here.

The primary source for any old car or part is *Hemmings Motor News*, a monthly publication. For a subscription, contact Box 100, Bennington, Vermont 05201. If you've never seen a copy, be prepared for a surprise. This is about 1,000 pages of irresistible advertising for everything from literature to Kaiser-Frazer parts and running Whizzers. Warning: *Hemmings* can be addictive and will lead to bankruptcy for those who can't resist a bargain.

AutoWeek is an occasional source of complete cars. You can order it from 965 E. Jefferson, Detroit, Michigan 48207. The other enthusiast magazines are virtually useless as a source of parts for the old cars.

I also want to list an English source simply because it's so engrossing. *Classic and Sport Car* magazine is, in my estimation, the perfect avocational reading. Literate but not too stuffily British, it will depress you with the prices Europeans are willing to ask for old cars, but elate you if you own one. Sign up with Eric Waiter, Box 188, Berkeley Heights, New Jersey 07922.

Index